Portuga_
The Scramble for Africa

Paul Southern

África
São muitas as riquezas que escondes
No fundo desta tua misteriosa alma
Cobiça de Reis, Nobres e Condes

Waldir Araújo

Many are the riches you conceal
Deep within your mysterious soul
Greed of Kings, Nobles and Counts

1

ISBN: 978-0-946995-63-9
Published by Galago Books - 42 Palace Grove, Bromley BR1 3HB England

Printed and bound in Great Britain by MPG Biddles Ltd, King's Lynn, Norfolk

Portugal and Portuguese Africa

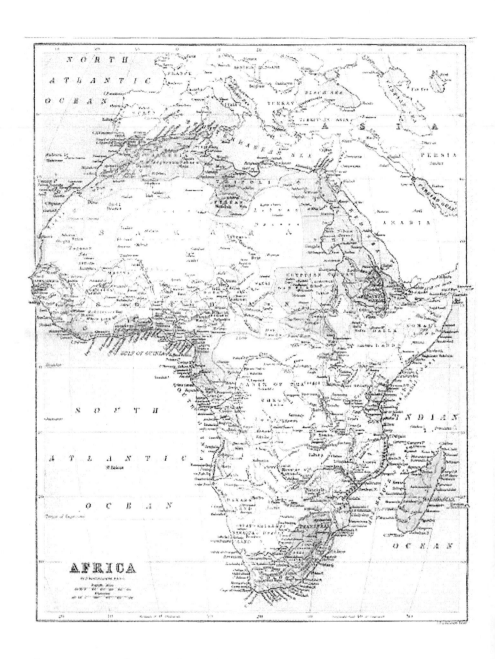

Africa 1914 (J. Bartholomew)

Contents

Chapters
List of maps and illustrations
Map and Illustrations Credits
Acknowledgements
Preface
Glossary
Bibliography
Index

Chapters

1   Colquhoun at the Cape
2   Paiva de Andrada Counters Colquhoun
3   The Lisbon Geography Society and the Rose-Coloured Map
4   The Royal Commissioner and the Scramble for Portuguese Africa
5   Rebellion in Gazaland
6   Portuguese Offensive Operations in Gazaland
7   Paiva Couceiro – Knight Errant
8   Operations in Lourenço Marques and Inyambane Districts
9   Mopping up in Gazaland
10 Angola – The Coming Storm
11 Artur de Paiva Confronts the Kwanyama Threat
12 Silva Porto – The Death of a Legend
13 Major Padrel and the Humbe Column
14 The Boers Exact Revenge
15 Slaughter at Jambacamufate
16 The Relief of *Forte Humbe*
17 British and German Designs on Portuguese Africa
18 Disaster at Pembe Drift
19 Roçadas in Southern Angola 1906-07
20 Kalibulala – An African Tragedy
21 João de Almeida and the Dembos Campaign in 1907
22 Regicide and Revolution in Lisbon
23 Clinging on in Portuguese Guinea
24 The Oyo War in Portuguese Guinea
25 The Cacheu Column
26 Taking the War to the Balanta

27   The Pepel and Grumete Campaign- Bissau Region

28   German Machinations - Angola 1913

29   Portugal Considers War in Africa and Europe

30   Blockade Breaking in Angola

31   Defending the Angolan Border

32   Major Franke - The Victor of Naulila

33   Trouble Brews in Portugal and Africa

34   Conflict in German South West Africa and in Angola

35   Paramount Chief Mandume

36   Major Pritchard, Chief Mandume and General Pereira de Eça

37   Germany Declares War on Portugal

38   Operations in Mozambique after Germany's Declaration of War

List of Maps and Illustrations

Cover illustration   Wagons Across Angola
Watercolour by Patsy Warwick

Back cover   Mousinho de Albuquerque during the Namarral
Campaign
Watercolour by Roque Gameiro, Museu Militar, Lisbon

Centre pages   João Teixeira Pinto at Dongoena in 1907
Agência Geral das Colónias
Chief Abdul Injai, commanding Auxiliary forces,
Portuguese Guinea 1914
Agência Geral das Colónias
Nkumbi Hunter, Angola, 1890
Struik
Kuvale Warriors, Angola 1896
Struik
Captain Roçadas at Aucongo in 1907
Imprensa Nacional
Kwanyama men and women, Angola 1896
Struik
Kalibulala at Naloeke in 1907 with nephew Samuel and
servant
Imprensa Nacional
Chief Mandume of the Kwanyama
Ilustração Portuguesa
Raising the colours at Bailundo Fort
Agência Geral das Colónias
Chief Gungunyana, 1895
Fundação Portugal-África
Crossing the Kakulovar River, Angola 1896
Struik
Crossing the Kunene River, Angola 1896
Struik

Maps/Sketches

Portugal and Portuguese Africa - P3

Africa 1914 – P4
J. Bartholomew

Rose-Coloured Map – P18
Biblioteca Nacional de Portugal

Mozambique 1900 – P42
Rodrigues

Battle of Marracuene, Mozambique 1895 – P56

Operational Map of Northern Column, Mozambique 1895
Edições Gama – P67

Operational Map of Southern Column, Mozambique 1895
Edições Gama – P68

Interior of Gambos Fort, Angola 1897 – P77
Império

Interior of Humbe Fort, Angola 1897 – P95
Império

Captain Möller's Map of Angola and Ovamboland – P128
Struik

Gunboat Flecha, Portuguese Guinea 1912 – P160
Fundação Portugal-África

German South West Africa – P184
Deutsche Kolonialgesellschaft

German route through Mozambique 1917-1918 – P226
Hurst & Blackett

8

Acknowledgements

First of all, I must thank my publisher, Tony Stiff of Galago Books, for his kind encouragement and also Amba Hall. The following institutions have greatly assisted me in England, the Brotherton Library – University of Leeds, The Brynmor Jones Library - University of Hull, The JB Morrell Library - University of York, The John Rylands Library - University of Manchester, The Maughan Library – King's College London, Scarborough Public Library; in Bermuda, the Bermuda National Library – Hamilton; in Canada, the RCMP Heritage Centre – Regina; in Germany, Bundesarchiv, Militärarchiv – Freiburg; in Malawi, the National Archives – Zomba; in Namibia, Government Archives – Windhoek; in Portugal, Arquivo Histórico Militar – Lisbon, Biblioteca Central da Marinha – Lisbon, Biblioteca Nacional de Portugal – Lisbon, Fundação Portugal-África - Oporto, Museu Militar – Lisbon, Museu Militar – Oporto, Sociedade de Geografia de Lisboa; in Sweden, Museum of Ethnography – Stockholm; in Tanzania, the National Archives – Dar Es Salaam; in South Africa, the former African Studies Institute - University of Witwatersrand – Johannesburg, the Cannon Association of South Africa – Cape Town, the Military Information Bureau – Pretoria, Museum and Library – Musina.

I am indebted to the following; in England, my father – George Southern, Patsy Warwick, Carol Williams; in Canada, Rhonda Lamb; in Mozambique, Professor Gerhard Liesegang; in Portugal, Vaughan and Dawn Birbeck, Professor Fernando Castelo-Branco, Rear-Admiral Victor Manuel Trigueiros Crespo, Lieutenant Colonel Carlos Alberto Borges da Fonseca, Colonel Nuno Bessa de Almeida Frazão, Jorge Miranda, Sofia Ferreira Durão, Luís França de Sá, José Manuel Gomes da Silva, Dr Carlos Sangreman Proença; in South Africa, Joan Marsh, Dr Patrick Pearson, Professor Charles van Onselin, Gerry de Vries, Dr André Wessels, and in the United States, my old, firm friend from Coimbra days – Dr Frank Serpa. Last but not least, I wish to thank Professor Harold Livermore, with whom I had a long and highly instructive conversation on the subject of what was then Portuguese Africa, in the Library of the Casa da Inglaterra in Coimbra – he may well have forgotten it – I have not.

The above people and organisations carry not the smallest responsibility for any errors or misinterpretations of which I may have been guilty.

Preface

The idea of writing about Portuguese Africa started when, as a student of Portuguese language and history, I had the privilege, thanks to a scholarship, from the Lisbon-based Fundação Calouste Gulbenkian, and the then, Instituto de Alta Cultura, to attend the Universidade de Coimbra in Portugal.

At that time, Portugal was involved in its protracted colonial wars in Angola, Mozambique and Portuguese Guinea. Apart from being the seat of one of the world's oldest universities, Coimbra was also a garrison town of soldiers. In fact, Portugal appeared to be one huge garrison, where newspapers, radio and television carried daily (censored) reports on the war and its consequences.

Portuguese books had plentiful information on the 'discoveries' – Vasco da Gama and Magellan's opening up of the sea-routes of the world, Luís de Camões, extolling the virtues of the Portuguese people in his epic 'Lusiads', it was dramatic reading, but there was little on the Portuguese of later centuries who had thinly populated its colonies and founded its settlements and cities.

I have, over almost half a century, studied the writings in Portuguese, of politicians, geographers, soldiers, empire builders, hunters, rogues and adventurers. Given that I knew a number of Portuguese and Portuguese Africans, and experienced a Portugal under threat; a place and society where the Salazar regime emphasized abnegation and sacrifice, I felt it would not require too great a backward leap of the imagination to find myself in another period, in which the stability and security of Portugal was equally under threat in both Europe and Africa.

The 'Scramble for Africa' found Portugal weak, vulnerable and completely unprepared to deal with the new realities foisted on it by the signatories of the Conference of Berlin. Portugal's initially shaky response is contained in journals of exploration, of dry, government reports and of dour or jingoistic diaries of military occupation. I do not seek to glorify or to justify Portugal's rôle in her former African colonies. What I wish to do, is present the reader with an historical picture of a certain kind of endeavour, and its consequences on Portugal and Portuguese speaking Africa from the middle of the 19th century up to the end of the First World War.

I have tried to lend colour to the lives and stories of those who by choice or circumstance, stepped on to African soil and created or attempted to create, a life of sorts from the harsh reality of the continent. I have also tried to give the reader some feeling for the native Africans, who found that the Portuguese, who until the Conference of Berlin, had lived almost exclusively in small coastal outposts, suddenly began to encroach upon their ancestral lands and change their way of life for ever. A victory of arms for the Portuguese represented a demoralising defeat, and the imposition of the colonial yoke, for the vanquished. For African leaders caught up in the maelstrom of the 'Scramble' it meant, if they were lucky, internal exile, or as in the case of Chief Gungunyana and his family, perpetual exile and eventual death on a volcanic Portuguese island in the middle of the Atlantic Ocean, far away in time and space from the Gazaland of 1895.

I tell the narrative of some victors and some vanquished, but not all – it would take more than one lifetime.

Paul Southern

Scarborough
England

Glossary

Askari	African soldier in German colonial army
A Portuguesa	National anthem (Portugal)
Baga-Baga	Termite hill (Guinea Bissau)
Bagaço	Colourless spirit/brandy (Portugal)
Balanta	Ethnic group (Guinea Bissau)
Banza	Kraal (Dembos - Angola)
Baster	European and indigenous Khoisan, term used with pride by Baster community (Namibia)
Bayete inkose	Traditional greeting 'The King Who Rules' (Gazaland)
Bergdama	Nama in mountainous area – hence Bergdama (Namibia)
Bolenha	Extensive paddy field (Guinea Bissau)
Boma	Village (Mozambique)
Bombolom	Drum – bush telegraph (Guinea Bissau)
Bushmen	Collectively, San peoples (north-eastern Namibia and Botswana)
Cacimba	Small reservoir containing water throughout dry season (Kwanyamaland)
Chana	Long, broad, shallow depression (Kwanyamaland)
Dacoit	Robber band (Burma)
Difaqane	Crushing and hammering/total war (South Africa)
Dongo	Inyambane canoe, hollowed out of a tree trunk (Mozambique)
Drift	Ford (South Africa)
Etanga	Tactical group - 100 warriors (Kwanyamaland)
Embala	Kraal (Kwanyamaland)
Fulani	Ethnic group (Guinea Bissau)
Grumete	Ethnic group (Guinea Bissau) Detribalised peoples often in the employ of the Portuguese – grumete – 'ship boy'
Guerra	Regiment – 6 etangas - (Kwanyamaland)
Herero	Ethnic group (Northern Namibia and southern Angola)
Hottentot	Ethnic group - Khoikhoi preferred to negative sounding Hottentot (Namibia/Angola)
Kimbanda	Spirit medium (Angola)
Knobkerrie	Weapon - short stick with knobbed end (South Africa)
Kubata	Large timber built, straw-roofed hut (Kwanyamaland)
Laager	Encamp, camp formed by circle of wagons (South Africa)
Lenga	Battle chief (Kwanyamaland)
Libata	Kraal (Kwamatoland)

Manga	Regiment (Kwanyamaland)
Maji	Water (Mozambique/Tanzania)
Milongo	Magical potions/magic (Angola)
Moçambique	Province of Mozambique and former capital
Mubango	War of succession between Mwawe and Muzila (Gazaland)
Muene Puto	King of Portugal (Angola/Mozambique)
Mukunda	Stockaded kraal (Kwanyamaland)
Muti	Medicine (South Africa)
N'anga	Spirit medium (Gazaland)
Nano	Ethnic group (Mbundu - west-central Angola)
Nsimba	Wild cat (Gazaland)
Ohita	Army (Kwanyamaland)
Olupale	Central Courtyard (Kwanyamaland)
Omalodu	Native beer (Kwanyamaland)
Omaramba	Shallow, grassy depression (Kwamatoland)
Omuya	Ox hide leather belt (Kwanyamaland)
Ondiai	Spirit medium (Kwanyamaland)
O Século	Daily newspaper (Lisbon – Portugal)
Pepel	Ethnic group (Guinea Bissau)
Posto	Military post (Portuguese)
Pour le Mérite	Military honour (Imperial Germany)
Sekulo	Induna/elder (Portuguese designation - Angola and Mozambique)
Shintlontlo	Ostrich feathered-skull cap (Gazaland)
Schutztruppe	Colonial forces (German)
Soba	Chief (Portuguese designation - Angola and Mozambique)
Tabanka	Village (Portuguese Guinea)
Thirstland Boers	Trekboers (Angola)
Timbava	Black seeded, earpod tree (Gazaland)
Tinkosho	Plaited, leather thong necklace (Gazaland)
Tlhari/Mathlari	Short stabbing spear/assegai (Gazaland)
Torre e Espada	Military order – Tower and Sword - (Portugal)
Vlei	Shallow, grassy depression (South Africa)

Chapter 1
Colquhoun at the Cape

On a glorious summer's day on 18 December 1889, the 4,668-tonne Union Line Mail Steamer *SS Mexican*, having sailed from Southampton in England via the Portuguese island of Madeira, disembarked its passengers at the Cape of Good Hope. Newly arrived Archibald Ross Colquhoun received a badly scrawled letter from no less a personage than Cecil Rhodes. He rushed up country to Kimberley where an appointment had been arranged with 'the great man.' On the verandah of the Kimberley Club, Rhodes offered him a post with a retaining salary of £800 per annum, as an administrator with the British South Africa Company. His salary would be increased to £1,500 immediately upon Rhodes obtaining the administration of the territory. Rhodes' plan was to put Colquhoun in charge of the whole of Mashonaland as soon as practicable.

Forty-one-year-old Archibald Colquhoun was a former Indian Government civil servant and British Deputy Commissioner for the Sagaing District south of Mandalay, on the Irrawaddy River in Upper Burma. However, Colquhoun had left Burma under a cloud; he had ruffled diplomatic feathers by publicly criticising certain senior administrators in *The Times* and was later libelled in the *Mandalay Herald* of 22 January 1889. The offending article blamed him for sanctioning an ill-timed, ill-planned attack against a stockaded Dacoit band, leading to the death in action of Lieutenant Nugent of the Hampshire Regiment. Colquhoun was suspended, pending an investigation and on 26 November 1889, was officially absolved from responsibility in the death of the young officer. He was gazetted to a post in Baluchistan in western British India, but while on leave in England, a chance meeting at his London club with Alfred Beit, Rhodes' business partner, changed all that.

Two hundred armed and mounted British and colonial volunteers, under command of the irascible beanpole of a man, Lieutenant-Colonel Edward Graham Pennefather of the 6th Inniskilling Dragoon Guards with legendary scout and big game hunter Frederick Courtney Selous, began to assemble at Mafeking. On 6 May 1890 after kitting out, and drilling under the keen eye of second-in-command, Sir John Willoughby of the Royal Horse Guards, the force moved north to Macloutsie. The plan envisaged the Bechuanaland Border Police patrolling the Matabeleland borders while the Pioneer column moved towards Mashonaland

Though Selous held the rank of captain in the Pioneer Corps, he was first and foremost an individualist and consequently, had little use for rank distinctions. He travelled with his own wagons, bearers and horses and did not deign to wear a uniform like the rest of the column; nevertheless, he was the eyes and ears of the Pioneers. Captain Maurice Heany a quiet, powerfully built, red-headed and bearded American from Virginia, commanded 'A' Troop while 'B' Troop was commanded by the youthful livewire, Lieutenant Borrow, and 'C' Troop by the rough and ready Irishman, Captain Jack Roach. The plan was simple; the Pioneer column would open the way to a given objective, and then the British South Africa Police would follow up, secure and fortify it and then use it as a firm base to patrol the area prior to moving on to the next leg. On 14 June the column laagered at Grobler's Drift and thirteen days later on 27 June the Pioneers, reinforced by 200 of Chief Khama's Mangwato acting as scouts and road cutters, struck out towards Mount Hampden in column formation over the roadless veld. In the far distance, hazy, blue-shaded mountains framed the horizon as Fred Selous and his scouts moved on ahead of the main body of the column and spread out on either side of it. The Pioneers kept close to the creaking, lurching wagons while the field guns escorted by scouts were brought up the rear. As they approached Matabeleland, the colonel and his men knew that in the increasingly broken and scrubby country, they could easily ride into a trap and be cut up and annihilated by Chief Lobengula's impis. Between four and five in the evening, Selous and his scouts would be busy looking for a good place to laager. Once a suitable spot was found, the draught oxen were grazed and then tied to the wagons while the horses were picketed inside the laager. Sentries were posted and after their evening meal, the Pioneers bedded down on tarpaulins under the wagons while a large, electric searchlight began to play its eerie beam across the veld. At night there were often false alarms. The Pioneers would reach for their weapons, and in groups of four take up their allotted positions in the wagons, behind a defensive wall of ammunition boxes, biscuit tins and sacks of mealie, to await a possible Matabele onslaught.

Ten weeks later on 12 September 1890, the Pioneers celebrated the accomplishment of their endeavour, and a Chartered Company camp was established, and given the name Fort Salisbury, in honour of the British prime-minister, and the Union flag was hoisted over it. With the Pioneers formed up before him, Dr Leander Starr Jameson, gravely read out a proclamation stating that the country was now under the control of the Chartered Company and that anyone found guilty of murder or rape would be shot. Colquhoun was then duly installed as the administrator of Mashonaland with the heavily moustachioed Harrison as his private secretary. *Blazer* Colquhoun, a nickname earned for his hotheaded behaviour in his Burma days, was now instructed by Cecil Rhodes to increase the Chartered Company's territory at the expense of its Portuguese neighbour.

Archie Colquhoun was dressed like the rest of the Pioneers in grey cord jodhpurs, khaki tunic, a large brown, broad-brimmed 'smasher' hat, looped up at one side by a silver badge, and was armed with a six-chambered Webley revolver, a hand-axe, and a Martini-Henry rifle carried in his saddle holster. The small detachment struck out east from Fort Salisbury into the highland vastness of Portuguese Manicaland to seek out the kraal of Chief Mutasa, also known as *Mafamba-Basuko* – the lion who walks by night. Colquhoun and Harrison reached the towering, weather-beaten, granite fastness at Umtali without mishap, to hold an *indaba* with the chief who strode up to the bemused Colquhoun preceded by a 'court jester' dancing and yelling his chief's praises. Mutasa was accompanied by three young women carrying native beer and by his aged *indunas*. The chief was quaintly dressed in threadbare trousers and a battered Portuguese military tunic, topped off with a naval cocked hat, to that odd assortment of clothing, had been added a leopard skin, which hung loosely from his shoulders. Mutasa held honorary rank bestowed upon him by the Portuguese crown, but that did not deter him from signing a treaty ceding Manicaland's mineral rights to the Chartered Company. From Mutasa Colquhoun learned that Portuguese traders with the Mozambique Company had established themselves at Massi-Kessi, and that the Mozambique Company claimed a large tract of land west of Massi-Kessi, that is, in land already claimed by the British South Africa Company. Colquhoun repeatedly asked the chief whether or not he had ceded his lands to the Portuguese. Chief Mutasa was firm in the conviction that he had not, however, he admitted that he had 'allowed' Baron de Resende to live at Massi-Kessi. He told Colquhoun that the Portuguese 'held an assegai at his heart' and that should he refuse to do as Baron de Resende asked, the hated and feared de Sousa would be called in to invade his lands. Colquhoun was satisfied with the chief's explanation. He believed that the importance of Manicaland lay not only in the fact that it brought the British South Africa Company's frontier nearer the coast, putting a definite stop to Portuguese expansion, but that great things were expected of the Manica goldfields, which had been worked from time immemorial.

The Portuguese hill station at Massi-Kessi was little more than a palisade of rough poles, yet its natural beauty had impressed Colquhoun. It was a well-chosen location, nestling deep between two 600-metre high, msasa-clad hills, with twin, gushing rivers flowing past banana groves, 280 kilometres north-west of the coastal port of Beira. It was a lush area made even wetter by the exceptionally heavy rains that had fallen that year. In fact, most of Portugal's territory towards the coast was under water as the swollen rivers had flooded their banks. At the conclusion of Mutasa's *indaba* Colquhoun and Harrison turned back to Fort Salisbury bearing the Chartered Company's signed and sealed treaty to be forwarded to Cecil Rhodes with all possible haste.

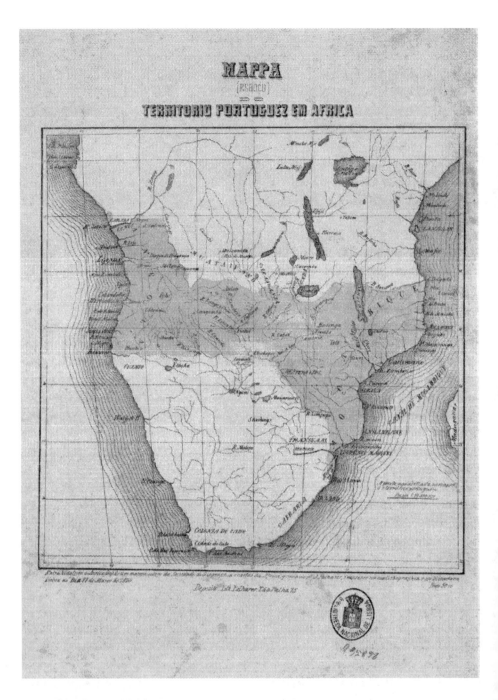

Rose-Coloured Map
Shaded portion indicates Portuguese ambition to unite Angola and Mozambique (BNP)

Chapter 2
Paiva de Andrada Counters Colquhoun

Forty-five-year-old Joaquim Carlos Paiva de Andrada was a slightly built yet handsome, bearded, Portuguese artillery officer, who had served as an observer during the Franco-Prussian War. In 1871 he was invited to the Belgian capital by that country's armaments ministry to assist in the design of the *Christophe* and *Montigny* machine guns. Later, while serving as military attaché in Paris, he made known his interest in the exploration of Portuguese East Africa and his need for financial backing. An elegant and witty man, fluent in both French and English, he was often spied enjoying champagne-filled Paris nights with socialite French bankers and their bejewelled wives. Upon his return to Portugal the war ministry offered him the dual governorship of the districts of Quelimane and Tete. He not only wanted responsibility, but also profit and turned down the offer, countering it by requesting Lisbon's permission to continue his exploration of the Zambézia region. His superiors acquiesced. He would soon be on his way to Portuguese East Africa.

During his first visit, that intrepid adventurer had gained extensive first-hand knowledge of the vast northern Zambézia District. In 1884 he had formed the Ophir Company and was granted the mining rights to Manica and Kiteve districts, but due to a singular lack of funds the company was forced into liquidation. Paiva de Andrada had trekked through Manicaland and had been impressed by its rich vegetation and by its limitless coal deposits; furthermore, he was driven by dreams of gold. The British constituted a major problem, but he was determined that Manicaland would remain Portuguese. Not unnaturally, Cecil Rhodes saw this as an attempt to block the British South Africa Company's expansion into Mozambique.

Paiva de Andrada was relieved to return once more to Manicaland. He had quickly tired of Lisbon and its ponderous and inefficient bureaucracy and immediately took ship for the colonies. Before the ageing packet steamer had even dropped anchor in the wide estuary of the Pungwe River at Beira, he had formulated an ambitious plan for the future of the area, which included the possibility of constructing a railway line through the Pungwe valley. He immediately set up his headquarters in a tin-roofed hut on the river's northern bank, and with a watchful eye open for the British, began a vigorous programme of building and consolidation. He organised the long needed fortification of the port of Beira and oversaw the clearing of sunken hulks, of mangroves and of the rotting carcasses which drifted down the Pungwe River to eddy and swirl in the tidal waters of the harbour. In order to assist the skippers of Portuguese gunboats and merchantmen, he personally charted the ever-shifting and treacherous sandbanks of the estuary.

Paiva de Andrada was a plucky man, impervious to personal danger. Using his considerable military and technical skills, he reconnoitred the tsetse fly infested Pungwe River in a *dongo* - an Inyambane canoe hollowed out of a solid tree trunk. His river journey took him past thick mangroves, where the banks of the river receded into the steamy distance as it deepened and widened to almost two kilometres. Hippopotami and crocodiles were ever-present obstacles to the canoeists. At night, they drew their heavy *dongos* up on to the spongy bank of the river under the yellow branches of the thickly entwined fever trees. Sometimes they slept aloft in African huts built high up in the trees against the threat of hungry crocodiles, and the unpredictable Mozambique Channel tidal water. Oftentimes he slept fitfully, chilled to the marrow in the dank bush, while his Inyambane bearers kept marauding hyenas at bay with lighted brands, which they tossed into the howling blackness. His neck, arms and legs had succumbed to burning rashes. The sun's glare was relentless, the heat was life sapping, and the attentions of the millions of riverine mosquitoes almost too much to bear. His face lost its healthy hue and turned yellow. His skin became taut as though the Pungwe were draining him of energy and vitality.

One morning his Inyambanes found him face down in the mud, an empty brandy bottle at his side. At first they thought he had given up and died; they had seen Europeans do that before. He was carried inside while the Inyambanes secured the *dongo* and his portmanteau of documents. For days on end he lay semi-conscious in a low, airless African hut, shivering and sweating, his head spinning and whirling; in his lucid moments he feared that he would die alone without a Christian blessing to ease him into eternity. But his Inyambane bearers tended him and forced crushed bananas and millet mixed with wild fruit down his swollen throat. Later they fed him strips of lightly cooked waterbuck flesh until his strength began to return. He was soon able to tell an indifferent Inyambane audience, that thanks to providence, he had decided to establish a river settlement there on the right bank of the river at Mapandas. Once recovered, he continued his journey by canoe and established a trading post close to Chief Guenjere's kraal, which he later renamed Sarmento. Finally, before heading back down the Pungwe, he established his most important settlement 175 kilometres from Beira. Chimoio was the home of the Chief of Ganda, who had sheltered him during his fever; the Portuguese settlement was named in his honour. Back at Beira, Paiva de Andrada painstakingly mapped the route of the river in his torn and muddied logbook; the Pungwe was navigable!

It was due to his hardheaded determination that on 20 December 1888 the Mozambique Company came into being. Paiva de Andrada's brainchild had started as a simple mining company. The company had grown to such an extent that in February 1891 it was given a 30-year Royal Charter. The company's lands covered a vast area of Mozambique; the ever-watchful Lisbon government had stipulated that one of its requirements would be to promote Portuguese colonisation of its concession. This was to be done by setting up within the first five years, in places chosen in concert with the colonial authority, 1,000 families of Portuguese origin. The government for its part, agreed to transport those families to their destinations within the concession and provide them with accommodation, agricultural land and tools on very advantageous terms.

Paiva de Andrada's eyes were now set on the 'fabulous' gold fields of Manicaland, but it troubled him that Chief Mutasa might not allow his Mozambique Company prospectors to reconnoitre the potentially gold-bearing hills without first getting permission from his sovereign, Chief Gungunyana – the king of Gazaland. Paiva de Andrada decided to visit Gungunyana and personally request the powerful chief to order Mutasa not to obstruct his prospectors.

His column set out from its base camp deep in the Gorongosa Mountains and slowly trekked towards Massurissi where Gungunyana had built his first royal kraal. After two weeks' march he halted the column within an hour's distance of Massurissi and sent one of his people as an emissary to request a royal *indaba*. Paiva de Andrada was in a jovial mood and whiled away his time noisily chasing guinea fowl through the bush. When Gungunyana's *indunas* arrived at his camp, he could hardly contain himself and ordered Manuel his interpreter, to fetch a large hemp bag that he had previously filled with trinkets and copper coins. He untied the bag and spread his wares out on the ground. The tallest *induna* slowly bent forward and picked up a light brown, leather case and unhooking the fastener, took out a pair of German-made binoculars. The *induna* was captivated by the feel of the solid, well-made object and twirled the eyepieces repeatedly. Paiva de Andrada was delighted with the tone of the meeting and taking the binoculars from the elderly man, held them to his eyes and focused on an ox grazing in a clearing some good distance from the camp. He then held the binoculars to the *induna*'s eyes. The *induna* stepped back in surprise clicking his tongue; the ox was suddenly standing right in front of him yet when the Portuguese removed them, the ox was again far away! Buoyed up by this reaction and with visions of limitless gold seams flashing through his mind, he inverted the binoculars and smilingly motioned to the bemused *induna* to look again. The effect on the *induna* was dramatic but not what the adventurer had expected. The old man was visibly shocked; the ox was now a tiny shape in the far distance – how could this be so? The *indunas* spoke rapidly to each other and though Paiva de Andrada did not understand a word, he could feel the tension mounting. The increasingly angry *indunas* accused him of magic, and throwing the binoculars down in horror, quickly made off without another word and without looking back at the perplexed Portuguese and his interpreter.

Chief Gungunyana was told of the stranger's magic and became visibly agitated – if the foreign wizard could turn a powerful ox into a distant midget, then how could he prevent the wizard from doing the same thing to him, Paramount Chief Gungunyana of Gazaland? Gungunyana's *indunas* were sent straight to Paiva de Andrada's camp and he was ordered to leave Gazaland immediately. A disconsolate Paiva de Andrada trekked all the way back up to the Gorongosa. The disastrous enterprise had taken almost five weeks and had succeeded in turning Gungunyana against the Portuguese adventurer. It was an inauspicious beginning for the company's founder.

Yet in spite of this early setback, Mozambique Company agents were soon sailing from Portugal round the Cape to the port of Beira. From Beira they began to push through pestilent, waterlogged lowlands to the interior to consolidate Portuguese control over its limitless concession. Baron João de Resende, an enthusiastic and indefatigable Company agent, had quickly established and maintained friendly relations with Chief Mutasa and his *indunas* and as soon as Resende received word of Colquhoun's *indaba* at Mutasa's kraal, he prepared a written complaint in English, which he dispatched to Colquhoun. He was disturbed to hear from one of his Mashona foremen that three armed horsemen had been seen slowly forcing their way through the dense bush toward his station. Fred Selous appeared with two Pioneers and cantered up to an unsmiling and fidgeting Resende; the Portuguese nobleman was fearful that the presence of Selous would cause him to lose face in front of his Mozambique Company workers. However, Resende politely offered the Englishmen food, and fodder for their horses, while he secretly sent a fleet-footed young courier into the bush to alert Major Jaime Ferreira, the governor of Manicaland and Inyambane Districts.

The news of the Chartered Company's incursion into Portuguese territory spurred Paiva de Andrada and Reserve Colonel Manuel António de Sousa to show the Portuguese flag in Manicaland. Manuel de Sousa also known, as Gouveia, was a Goanese born Portuguese trader, who by combining a menacing brutality with a charismatic character, had built up a large following from the peoples around Sena and the Zambézia region. He had been nominated captain of Manica and Kiteve after his spirited defence, against a 3,000-strong enemy horde, of the so-called Gouveia kraal at Inyango, renamed Vila Gouveia, in the

Gorongosa Mountains. Gouveia had served with the Portuguese army in a number of campaigns and after Chief Bonga's uprising was successfully quelled; he was invited to Lisbon where he was made honorary colonel of the Portuguese overseas army. In October the two men had independently set out for Mutasa's kraal that was to be occupied by Gouveia and 70 of his followers.

Near the end of October, Mutasa was told of the approach of the feared Gouveia and sent a runner to the British South Africa Company to ask for its protection. Having received the unwelcome news and Mutasa's request, Colquhoun ordered Major Forbes who was in charge in the absence of Colonel Pennefather, to lead a small detachment of mounted police to Mutasa's kraal. Major Pat Forbes learned that Paiva de Andrada and Gouveia were concentrating close to Massi-Kessi in force. The sixteen-strong 'B' Troop of British South Africa Company Police left Fort Salisbury and rode east towards Manicaland. Every one of the troopers carried a .45 single-shot, breech loading Martini-Henry carbine, a 6-chambered Webley revolver, with a 100 round, leather bandoleer slung over the shoulder and a leather-cased hand-axe. Once in Manicaland, 29-year-old Major Forbes joined Lieutenant James Graham and his troopers. Forbes was a gritty, blond-haired Rugby and Sandhurst educated, former Iniskilling Dragoon Guards' officer and crack shot. He was vastly experienced, having served in the Bechuanaland Expedition under General Sir Charles Warren in 1883 and in operations in Zululand in 1889. In 1891 he was seconded from his regiment for special service with the British South Africa Company Police.

The detachment reached Mutasa's kraal on Guy Fawkes Night and Gouveia appeared three days later followed by Paiva de Andrada on 11 November. On 14 November, Resende joined Paiva de Andrada and Gouveia with 200 well-armed followers. Major Forbes' sixteen troopers were now outnumbered by the Portuguese and their numerous African levies, and he was obliged to withdraw and set up camp out of sight of the chief's kraal, and await the arrival of reinforcements made up of 25 troopers under Lieutenant Eustace Fiennes. Fiennes was yet another adventurous soul who had served in the Canadian Militia under General Middleton during the Riel Rebellion, and was then attached to the 9 Sudanese Battalion in Egypt in 1888. A year later he found himself in South Africa. Forbes' second-in-command, Graham, was dispatched with a letter requesting the Portuguese officers and soldiers to leave Mutasa's kraal and keep out of British South Africa Company business. Colonel Paiva de Andrada was surprised and initially amused to find himself referred to as General Paiva de Andrada – in command of the Portuguese forces in East Africa - but after reading the note he became enraged and tearing it up, ground it into the glutinous red soil while cursing the British officer's effrontery. Forbes penned a message to Colquhoun from his position near Mutasa's kraal, saying that as soon as ever 'A' Troop detachment arrived from Mashonaland, he would arrest Gouveia and Paiva de Andrada, should they still be at the kraal. At the same time he would send a party to disarm their 'bearers', then Lieutenant Graham would be told off at once to occupy Massi-Kessi with twenty troopers.

Paiva de Andrada ignored Forbes' letter, and on 13 November after discussions with Gouveia, called Mutasa and his *indunas* together for an *indaba* to be held on the following day, however, it was abandoned due to the continuous heavy rain. The *indaba* was yet again postponed until 15 November.

Trooper Monty Bowden, a fine English amateur wicket keeper, who had captained England in two tests in South Africa, was on lookout duty armed with an admiralty pattern telescope. His keen eye for a boundary spotted an *indaba*, taking place between the chief and the Portuguese officers. He scrambled back down the smooth granite kopje and swiftly passed that intelligence to Major Forbes. Forbes wasted no time, his small detachment quickly invested Mutasa's kraal executing a daring flanking movement. Forbes, with Webley revolver at the ready, placed an arresting hand on Paiva de Andrada's shoulder accusing him of plotting against the Company's interests. The Portuguese officer protested vehemently in English and warned a somewhat surprised Forbes that he had British friends in high places and was an acquaintance of Gladstone. But Forbes was determined to make Mutasa understand who would rule Manicaland; it would certainly not be the Portuguese.

The captives mutely watched, as the Portuguese flag was unceremoniously hauled down by khaki-clad Company men and in its place the Union flag was raised over the forbidding thatches of Mutasa's stockaded kraal. Paiva de Andrada's patience snapped and he protested loudly to Major Forbes that he was there on a peaceable mission. He pointed out that he was on legitimate business, as both he and Gouveia were directors of the Mozambique Company and Baron de Resende was its local agent, and that they were discussing their Company's mining interests with Mutasa. Paiva de Andrada told the British major that he had arranged for an *indaba* on the following day when Mutasa would publicly declare that he had ceded his territory to Gouveia at least twenty years before. Major Forbes ignored Paiva de Andrada's protest and leaving a small, armed detachment to maintain the security of Mutasa's kraal, he marched westward towards Fort Salisbury with Colonel Paiva de Andrada and Gouveia riding in a Cape cart under armed guard while Baron de Resende – considered a superior person - was paroled. From Fort Salisbury, Colquhoun ordered the towering figure of Lieutenant Marmaduke Mundell, to escort the two men down the 'Selous Road' to Cape Town and into the custody of Sir Henry Loch. As Gouveia had threatened to turn the British out of Manicaland and Mashonaland by force with the help of Gungunyana and even of

Lobengula, it was not felt wise to set them free. They arrived at Cape Town on 28 December and three days later were put on a steamer bound for Lisbon.

As Colquhoun noted, the incident had caused a great stir in Portugal and had created a bitter feeling against England. On their return to Portugal the two officers lost no time in airing their grievances against the Britons' actions. Enraged Portuguese students at Coimbra had openly insulted English ladies in the streets of the ancient university town, before going on to Lisbon and taking ship from the capital en route to Beira, with the naïve intention of marching on Manicaland and turfing out the British.

Meanwhile, Lieutenant Graham had gone down to Massi-Kessi where he had been joined by Captain Melville Heyman and his troopers. In view of the grave political situation, Captain Heyman of 'A' Troop, formerly of the Cape Mounted Rifles and the Cape Field Artillery, and officer commanding the Company's detachment at Massi-Kessi, was reluctantly ordered to withdraw his force from the station. Thirty-two-year-old Captain Heyman was an impressively tall figure with a shock of black, wiry hair. At the age of eighteen he had left England for the Cape. On arrival, he joined the Cape Mounted Rifles seeing action in the Gaika and Galeka Wars in 1877 and the Basuto Wars in 1879, transferring to the Company's Police in 1890. Heyman was very popular with his rough and ready troopers and furthermore, was well versed in the ways of the bush and an excellent shot. He now pulled his men back from Massi-Kessi to a fortified position near Mutasa's kraal in the Chua Hills, some two to three kilometres distant and about one and a half hour's ride from the Portuguese hill station.

In Lourenço Marques' stifling Council Chamber, the town's elders unanimously voted to organise and equip a battalion of volunteers to be dispatched to Manicaland in order to halt British expansion into Portuguese territory, and at the same time punish Chief Mutasa's double dealing. Initially 157 volunteers signed up, they were mostly civilians employed by the Public Works Department of Lourenço Marques. The volunteers' trades ranged from gas pump operative, carpenter, stonemason, painter, locksmith, to a typographer and a foreman. The force was composed of seven officers with four companies of 122 men making a total of 495. Civil Engineer Miguel de Sousa was placed in command, and all the officers were given appointments based on their civilian occupations. The volunteers had the same rank badges as the regular Portuguese army, but they were worn on the arm instead of the collar or shoulder. After initial training, it was decided to mobilise just one company and volunteer Second Lieutenant Augusto César de Brito was given the job of training it. Overall command was invested in a regular army officer, 39-year-old Major Alfredo Augusto Caldas Xavier. The major knew Manicaland well, having first gone to Mozambique in 1877 with the express purpose of exploring and mapping the Limpopo River valley and the hostile Gazaland region north of Lourenço Marques. Caldas Xavier possessed a wry sense of humour and his easy manner endeared him to the volunteers.

The makeshift 170-strong expedition composed of a detachment of 4 Portuguese Light Infantry with Lourenço Marques Police elements, a civilian volunteer company and a company of African Irregulars, with second-in-command, Captain Augusto de Bettencourt, left Lourenço Marques on 11 January 1891, on the Portuguese Royal Mail steamer *Rovuma* bound for Beira. The *Rovuma* was a tiny craft and the volunteers were crowded on its deck and in its hold. The heavy weather caused most of the men to be violently seasick – a situation that did not change until the storm tossed *Rovuma* dropped anchor at Beira four days later, and the soldiers and volunteers thankfully disembarked the stinking ship. Caldas Xavier, who had been ill on embarkation at Lourenço Marques, was carried off the steamer and taken to the military commander's home in Beira to receive immediate medical attention. Initially the volunteers were billeted in two large warehouses but as the Mozambique Company needed the storage space, they were temporarily moved to a sandy spit on the left bank of the Shinavane River close to its mouth. The volunteers were more than glad to vacate the low-lying, mosquito-infested warehouses, but after a month of living under canvas and putting up with constant torrential rains they were relieved to be on the move. The month's delay had been caused by the difficulty in hiring porters and by the end of January only 80 men had been taken on. Governor of Manica, Colonel Joaquim José Machado had requested 400 porters but rumours of war between the Portuguese and the British had discouraged many. Eventually 300 men arrived from Inyambane – they had to be embarked at gun-point - and were incorporated into the volunteer column and used principally to transport the two Nordenfelt machine guns, and the two Hotchkiss light machine guns, which they were to take on when they reached Sarmento. Caldas Xavier had recovered sufficiently to resume command of his men and the volunteers set out for Neves Ferreira, the Mozambique Company station. The porters slogged up to their waists in water while the Portuguese were transported in 21 sailing launches. After six days of constant struggle and sleepless, mosquito-filled nights, the launches were finally moored to the muddy landing at Neves Ferreira. During the dry season the volunteers' six-day journey would have taken just 36 hours. On 28 February the volunteers left Neves Ferreira for Sarmento. Due to the incessant rains almost the whole area was flooded; it became enormously difficult to make any headway. The launch-borne force reached its objective on 6 March but it took the machine gun section and the Lourenço Marques Police detachment until 20 March to reach Sarmento; it was not looking rosy for the volunteers.

Those who had fallen ill during the journey were given basic medical treatment at Sarmento. The rest were housed in the relative comfort of Mozambique Company buildings, where they had their first opportunity to sleep with a roof over their heads since vacating the mosquito-ridden warehouses at Beira in January. After a few days' welcome rest, the volunteer officers organised musketry training and military instruction on a large patch of flattish, dry ground behind their sleeping quarters.

On 25 March the column set off towards Mandanjiva some 100 kilometres from Sarmento. The journey took five days due to the endless deep rivulets and the thick elephant grass, which whipped their faces and soaked them through to the skin. By this time the exhausted porters were struggling to carry the component parts of the machine guns on their backs. After leaving Sarmento, Captain Bettencourt and his staff had become increasingly concerned for Caldas Xavier's state of health and on arrival at Mandanjiva they had been prepared to administer the last rites to him. The rest and medical attention Caldas Xavier received at Mandanjiva enabled him to resume command of the force that set off towards Chimoio. Fortunately for the Portuguese, the rains had virtually stopped; however, they were fast running out of supplies and the volunteers' uniforms were in tatters; most of their footwear had rotted away. On 30 April the weary column staggered into Chimoio; they were now just thirteen hours from Massi-Kessi. After a short rest at Chimoio they set off with district governor Major Jaime Ferreira on 2 May, leaving many of the sick in the care of medical officer Fernando Soares Poças who himself was ill with a fever.

After four months of trekking along the stinking, slimy banks of the tsetse infested Pungwe River, the exhausted and depleted force finally emerged from the tangled bush to occupy Massi-Kessi on 5 May. The disease-ravaged column now composed of only 112 Portuguese officers and men; 47 African soldiers and 93 Inyambane porters, was drawn up in front of the hill station and to the bugle strains of the Portuguese national anthem a trembling Caldas Xavier pulled down the Union flag.

On 7 May pickets observed two riders approaching the Massi-Kessi position; Captain Heyman and Lieutenant Morier had come to parley with district governor Ferreira and Caldas Xavier under a flag of truce. Through interpreter Morier who, according to Caldas Xavier, spoke fluent Portuguese, Heyman requested the Portuguese to keep well away from the Chua River in order to forestall any possible incidents between the British South Africa Company men and the volunteers. Heyman wanted to know what the column's intentions were and if the *modus vivendi* was to be adhered to. Though irritated by Heyman's manner, Caldas Xavier produced a map of the area and patiently pointed out that he had orders to occupy Portuguese territory agreed by Britain and Portugal in the interim treaty of 20 August. Heyman countered the Portuguese, saying he was convinced that Umtali lay within Chartered territory – not wishing to exacerbate the situation further, Heyman and Morier withdrew.

Later that day Portuguese pickets reported semaphore messages coming from a high granite outcrop close to the Chua River. Three Mashonas came into the Portuguese position and informed Caldas Xavier that it was rumoured a cannon pulled by an ox-wagon, under a small escort, was expected at the British position before dark. Caldas Xavier requested permission to take out a patrol and capture the British cannon but was turned down by the district governor; instead another letter was written to Heyman ordering him to withdraw at once from Portuguese territory.

At his fortified position in the Chua Hills, Captain Heyman found himself in a quandary as he was in receipt of two sets of conflicting orders; the first was from the Portuguese governor of Inyambane, Major Ferreira, instructing him that unless he crossed back over the Sabi River, he would be driven out of Portuguese territory by Caldas Xavier and his volunteer column; the second was a furious letter from Rhodes which equally unambiguously informed Heyman to leave his defensive position and turn the Portuguese out of Massi-Kessi.

As Major Ferreira's demand had gone unanswered, Caldas Xavier was ordered to eject the British from the Chua Hills and then bring Mutasa securely back into the Portuguese fold. However, the Portuguese officers knew it would not be an easy task. Heyman was well dug in behind earth and granite entrenchments, holding a strong defensive position with 40 well-armed men, and a 7-pounder gun that had wisely been concealed from Portuguese eyes by Sergeant-Major Hickey. Now Major Caldas Xavier lay ill in his tent delirious with black water fever; he would play no further part in the hostilities, having handed over command to Captain Bettencourt. On 9 May Captain Santos e Silva and Police Second Lieutenant José Francisco were hard at work strengthening the stockaded fortifications and parados at Massi-Kessi while Captain Carlos Roma Machado and his men were busy setting up a rough tree trunk redoubt close to the Portuguese station

Captain Francisco Maria Correia de Brito and two corporals laboured up the hill towards Heyman's position under a white flag and requested him to withdraw his men from the fortified post at Chua. Heyman met them 200 metres from the entrenched position and after listening to the Portuguese demands, said he would consult a senior officer who was presently at Umtali but that the request would probably have to be passed on to higher authority. Just before nightfall on 10 May, Second Lieutenant Tomás Freire commanding the army detachment at Gorongosa arrived at Massi-Kessi staggering under an enormous valise – he explained that the porters had fled leaving all the volunteers' supplies to rot in the bush close to the Révuè River, and to make the situation even worse, at Chimoio, Doctor Poças was now too ill to treat his patients. Captain Bettencourt was faced with a stark reality; there would be no more food supplies, ammunition or medical aid available to the volunteers.

Early in the afternoon of 11 May 1891, four days before the *modus vivendi* was due to expire, the motley volunteer column slowly advanced towards Heyman's position in open order with little or no cover, and with Captain Bettencourt at its head. In an attempt to discourage the attack, Heyman fired a blank charge at the Portuguese, the attackers momentarily wavered then Bettencourt and de Brito were seen to rally their men by beating them with the flat of their swords as they attempted to lead them towards the higher ground to outflank the position. The British had no alternative other than to open up on the advancing men at a distance of 1600 metres with the 7-pounder gun, while raking the ground in front of the Portuguese attackers with Gatling gun and volley fire. The hapless Portuguese began to falter and the inexperienced irregulars broke ranks and fled into the bush carrying their wounded with them. The Portuguese officers had shown extreme bravery and sang-froid leading their volunteers in a foolhardy attack up steeply rising terrain against the British South Africa Company's well-defended position. Bettencourt was already bleeding – a bullet had entered his left wrist and grazed his neck, yet he and de Brito sauntered back after their fleeing men while bullets kicked up the ground around their feet. Just before they disappeared from view, the two men turned and doffed their hats to Heyman and his troopers. The badly trained, ill-equipped levies had been no match for the seasoned troopers; six African soldiers were killed and a public works official's arm was smashed by a bullet; the five wounded men were in an unenviable position as the volunteers did not even carry the most rudimentary medical kit. As the Portuguese fell back on Massi-Kessi the 7-pounder's last shot landed in the middle of the Portuguese hill station and believing that the British had got their range, they rapidly withdrew down the hill. The next day Heyman sent a trooper under a white flag to offer medical aid, but Massi-Kessi had already been abandoned, so Heyman ordered 'A' Troop to secure the deserted, straw- hutted fort. 'A' Troop liberated the two Hotchkiss machine guns recently brought from Sarmento, and the two Nordenfelts minus firing pins, 100,000 rounds of ammunition, eight armchairs, litres of red wine and a large stock of tinned food, which they triumphantly carried back to Umtali. The way was now open to Beira and the Indian Ocean. Captain Heyman and his men were fully prepared to make the long, arduous trek via foul smelling Chimoio to Sarmento through the 'fly' belt down to the port of Beira and claim it for the Company and for Britain. However, *Blazer* Colquhoun had a singularly contemplative moment and instead of encouraging

Captain Heyman to further acts of derring-do, ordered him to pull back from Massi-Kessi; even he was forced to acknowledge that the Portuguese had been established in the region for hundreds of years.

Meanwhile the ill-starred Portuguese force had withdrawn deep into the bush and after dark the officers gathered together to discuss a plan of action. Captain Correia de Brito counselled retiring on Chimoio as the volunteers had no rations – the few remaining porters on hearing the exchange of fire between the volunteers and the British South Africa Police had dropped their loads and fled into the bush. The Portuguese had very little ammunition – each man had carried 70 rounds which were almost expended and the spare ammunition was now lying somewhere in the dank bush along with their resupply of rations. Just before midnight Correia de Brito moved off towards Chimoio with the wounded, including Captain Augusto Bettencourt who was carried by stretcher, while the rest walked as best they could. At first light Correia de Brito halted the column, and made a fire and boiled up a handful of mealies, which the wounded and dispirited column mutely consumed. A sudden noise on the track behind had de Brito leaping up and cocking his rifle. Fortunately for the Portuguese captain it was the advance guard of 3 Light Infantry of Lourenço Marques under command of Second Lieutenant José Bettencourt, which had caught up with the slow moving wounded. Within the hour, de Brito's bedraggled men were overjoyed to see the rest of the volunteer column approaching through the bush.

The upshot of that undeclared war was the delivery of the *Ultimatum* and a consequent deep-seated hatred and mistrust of the British and of the Anglo-Portuguese Alliance. After a frenzy of heated diplomatic claims and counter claims between the Portuguese and British governments, a frontier treaty was concluded on 11 June 1891 and initialled by Lord Salisbury and Carlos Valbom. The Portuguese border was finally and irrevocably drawn between Massi-Kessi and Umtali, however, three years later, the Royal Colonial Institute held a meeting in the Whitehall Rooms of the Hotel Métropole in London. The speaker who was non-other than Archibald Colquhoun, declared that the extension of the British Empire in Africa was a national and social necessity.

Chapter 3
The Lisbon Geography Society and the Rose-Coloured Map

Portugal's position in Africa had long been a delicate one; her role earlier in the nineteenth century had been relegated by the Conference of Berlin in 1884-5 to that of a rank outsider in the Scramble for Africa stakes and the Portuguese government was only too aware of its lacklustre image and form. It was in the latter years of the century that Portugal felt the need to consolidate her position on the African continent.

Army captain and former commandant of the Lubango military district in Angola, and directory of Luanda Observatory, Francisco António Pinheiro Baião, held tightly on to his high crested, patent leather, peaked cap as the gusting October wind scudded townwards from the Tagus. Captain Pinheiro Baião's carriage laboured uphill over the uneven and broken cobblestones and turned into Alecrim Street. At a light tap on the shoulder from the officer's brass topped swagger stick, the driver reined in his horses outside a featureless, grey-stuccoed corner block. After paying off the cabby, he swiftly passed through the crumbling portals and climbed the dusty, cheerless, echoing stairs, which led him breathlessly to the rented second floor rooms. This very ordinary metropolitan façade described as No. 89, Alecrim Street, on the corner of Baron Quintela Square, was the new home of the Lisbon Geography Society. The date was 28 October 1876. Almost a year earlier on 10 November 1875, the Society had held its inaugural session in which it agreed to use its good offices to promote study and research into all aspects relating to Portugal and her colonies.

In the cramped surroundings of the Society's second floor chambers, thirty-two-year-old Luciano Cordeiro slowly rose to his feet. He presented an interesting figure framed against a large cloth map of Portuguese Africa. He had a large aquiline nose, a firm chin, strong mouth and a bristling moustache. Above his large, dark, quick eyes, his forehead gave way to unruly wavy black hair. Luciano Cordeiro had begun his literary career at the age of 21 and had written on a whole range of subjects covering literature, art, colonialism, politics, history and geography. At the time he was a lecturer at the Portuguese Royal Military College and with Rodrigo Afonso Pequito, was co-director of the *Portuguese and Brazilian Review*. In his capacity as the Lisbon Geography Society's first secretary, he confirmed to the membership that from the very beginning of its inauguration, he and others had recognised and emphasised that a Lisbon Geography Society would endeavour to firmly wed itself to a vital theme; the 'African Problem.' Warming to his subject, he declared that it was essential to increase public awareness regarding Portugal's overseas possessions. The shabby chambers at No 89 Alecrim Street rang to the lusty hurrahs and applause of its packed members.

Bandeira de Melo Madureiro asked for the floor and proposed that the Society should petition the government to organise an expedition through her African colonies. The motion was carried without abstentions, and entered in the minute book. Colonel Lopes de Oliveira, his heavily waxed moustache heaving, his reddened face, topped by a large glistening bald pate and looking for all the world like a pompous music hall brigadier, declared in a low voice cracking with emotion, that the government should do its utmost to vigorously maintain Portuguese honour and that the proposal of an African expedition should lead once and for all to a clarification of her colonial frontiers.

It was the Africanist, Captain Pinheiro Baião's moment to take the floor of the packed chamber. He quickly moved to the centre of the room and cramming his prepared notes into his deep uniform pocket, began to enlarge upon the previous speaker's theme. He proposed that in order to clarify the question of the effective occupation of Portugal's possessions to the north of Ambriz, bordering the south bank of the Congo River, any expedition dispatched to Africa should be tasked with linking the two coasts. Using for this purpose, the courses of the Kunene, Kubango and Zambezi rivers. Wild applause and backslapping congratulations erupted as the heavily perspiring army captain returned to his chair. In the heady atmosphere of excitement and exhilaration it was further agreed that the Society should direct an appeal to the Portuguese nation and hold an exhibition with the theme of 'Portugal in Africa.' To make the presentation easily available to all of Portugal's people, it was proposed that a map should be drawn up in which Portuguese Africa would be graphically depicted in rose-pink, stretching from Angola – fourteen times larger than Portugal - on the Atlantic, to Portuguese East Africa on the Indian Ocean. It would span the continent without touching the lands of any other colonial power. *O Mapa Cor-de-Rosa* – the Rose-Coloured Map - was about to trace its turbulent way into Anglo-Portuguese affairs.

The very first attempt to link Angola with Mozambique began in 1606, when Manuel Pereira Forjaz commissioned Baltasar Rebêlo de Aragão to make the arduous journey from coast to coast. However, he was unable to advance further than Lake Nyasa. Salvador Correia de Sá planned to link the two Portuguese possessions, but Dom Pedro II rejected the plan and consequently, it was shelved. Aires de Saldanha, who was governor of Angola in 1676, tasked Captain José da Rosa, to organise and lead an expedition to Mozambique but da Rosa was unable to complete his journey due to hostilities between warring chieftains in the Huíla Highlands of Angola. Over a century later in 1798, at the inaugural meeting of the Portuguese Royal Maritime, Military and Geography Society, the Secretary for the Navy and Overseas Dominions, Rodrigo Francisco Inocência de Sousa Coutinho, unveiled a long-held yet still unfulfilled project of linking up the two Portuguese possessions. Brazilian born doctor of mathematics, traveller and explorer, Dr Francisco José de Lacerda e Almeida, was appointed governor of Rios de Sena - the most westerly district of Mozambique, and charged with crossing the continent in a westward direction. By October of that year the expedition had trekked as far as Cazembe close to Lake Moero where an exhausted and fever-ridden Lacerda succumbed and died. It was not until March 1800 that news of Lacerda's death was received in Angola. In 1804, retired army officer, Francisco Honorato da Costa, was overseeing his vast farmlands when a messenger arrived with a letter bearing the seal of the governor of Angola, Fernando António de Noronha. Honorato da Costa, an experienced Africanist, had travelled extensively in the region, and the governor's letter requested him to study the possibility of crossing the continent from west to east. To aid him in that task, Colonel Honorato da Costa would be given the governorship of Cassinga district, Angola's most easterly province. The colonel accepted the commission and selected two experienced Angolan trackers and traders, Pedro João Baptista and Amaro José; the men would cross the hinterland and deliver a letter addressed to the governor of Rios de Sena district. The two men left Cassinga on November 11 1804, and crossed the numerous, treacherous tributaries of the Cassai River eventually reaching Mossumba do Muatianvua on 22 May 1806. After crossing the Garanganja, they entered the kingdom of Cazembe, but due to intense warfare between the Cazembe and Muiza clans, they were held up for almost four years. On 2 February 1811 the two men were at last able to deliver the letter into the hands of the governor of Rios de Sena. After a brief stay of three months, the two men set out again for São Paulo de Luanda carrying a letter from governor Constantino Pereira de Azevedo, arriving at the Angolan capital in 1815; it was the first successful two-way crossing. There was a further attempt in 1831, yet in 1852 the prospects for the commercial viability of cross-continent commerce looked even rosier, after the establishment of the port of Mossâmedes by Brazilian colonist from Pernambuco in 1849. However, it was to end in failure.

In May 1885, after expeditions by the explorers Alexandre Alberto da Rocha Serpa Pinto, Hermengildo Carlos de Brito Capelo and Roberto Ivens, the 52-year-old Madeiran naval and colonial minister, José Vicente Barbosa du Bocage, began serious discussions on the unification of Angola and Portuguese East Africa. During the course of his speech, he confirmed to his enthusiastic and receptive audience what they already knew, that the unification of the two colonies was a long held legitimate ambition. Portuguese pioneers had opened trade routes through Africa, India and Brazil, and Portugal, by virtue of history, claimed sovereignty over the entrance to the Congo, Kunene and Kwanza rivers of western Africa and the mouth of the Limpopo River, the Zambezi Delta and the Rovuma River of eastern Africa.

The British explorer Dr Daniel Rankin had discovered the Chinde estuary of the Zambezi River in April 1889. The discovery allowed steamers sailing to and from Nyasaland to leave or enter the Indian Ocean without touching Portuguese territory. Three years earlier, the Berlin Act had made navigation on Africa's rivers free to all the colonial powers, irrespective of whoever controlled one or both banks of the river. Trouble began to smoulder between the ancient allies when in 1888 a Portuguese mapping expedition led by António Maria Cardoso trekked into the Shire Highlands west of Lake Nyasa. A year later Cardoso was joined by Portugal's indefatigable explorer and imperialist Alexandre Serpa Pinto. The Makololo had attacked a British vessel in Niassa Province and the British consul requested the aid of Portuguese forces believed to be in the area. The Portuguese expedition under Serpa Pinto was in the province protecting an engineering project on the banks of the Shire, in an attempt to create access to Lake Nyasa. He was at that time on the left bank of the Zambezi when he received the consul's message. When the column reached Massingire between the Shire and Ruco rivers, he discovered that British agents from the African Lakes Company had been involved in the incident.

Serpa Pinto's men came under attack from both banks of the Shire and during the battle the Makololo were seen to raise the British flag over their riverine kraal. The Portuguese advanced on its defenders, briefly capturing the kraal and its British flag. The defeated Makololo fled towards their main settlement at Chilomo in Quelimane District. At that crucial moment, Serpa Pinto was laid low with dengue fever and command of the column was taken by Second Lieutenant João de Azevedo Coutinho, who chased them out of Chilomo, capturing and destroying the Makololo kraals at Mebeze, Maceia and Katunga.

In light of increased Portuguese 'flag waving expeditions' in what London interpreted as British territory, the Foreign Office re-examined the 'Rose Coloured Map,' which it began to perceive as a direct threat to London's empire building and Rhodes' dreams of 'Cape to Cairo.' Lord Salisbury, in one of his frequent irritable and melancholic moods, mumbled through his beard that Portugal's titles were purely archaeological, and on 6 January 1890 dispatched a strongly worded message to Lisbon through Sir George Petre, Britain's Envoy Extraordinary and Minister Plenipotentiary to Portugal:

Her Majesty's Government have not asked any apology for what has taken place, and they are quite willing to leave to the Portuguese Government the right which they claim - to judge the proceedings of the Portuguese officers after they have received a full account of the facts; but they must insist upon having a prompt and distinct assurance that there will be no attempt to settle the territorial question by acts of force or to establish Portuguese dominion over districts where British interests predominate. If Her Majesty's Government cannot obtain any such assurances from the Portuguese Government, it will be their duty to take measures, which they consider to be necessary and adequate for the protection of those interests. I am therefore instructed to report to your Excellency the categorical request for an immediate declaration that the forces of Portugal will not be permitted to interfere with the British settlements on the Shire and Nyassa, or with the country of Makololo, or the country under the government of Lobengula, or any other country declared under British protection; and further, that there will be no attempt to establish or exercise Portuguese jurisdiction over any portion of those countries without previous arrangement between the two Governments.

Salisbury gloomily sat back to await Portugal's apology, but as no satisfactory answer was forthcoming, an *Ultimatum* instructing the Portuguese governor at Lourenço Marques to order his forces to withdraw immediately into Portuguese territory, was handed to the Portuguese government on 11 January. Sir George Petre and the British legation were instructed to quit the Portuguese capital if a satisfactory reply was not received within 24 hours. The yacht *H.M.S. Enchantress* awaited them riding at anchor in the deep water harbour of the northern Spanish port of Vigo; the East Africa Squadron had been ordered to Portuguese waters; the Channel Squadron under sealed orders, was dispatched to the mouth of the Tagus River. The British *Ultimatum* shocked Portugal. Dom Carlos I returned his Order of the Bath bestowed upon him by Queen Victoria; the devil-may-care Duke of Palmela, who had served in the Royal Navy, returned his Baltic Medal. Students from Coimbra University solemnly shrouded in black crepe the revered statue of Luís Vaz de Camões, the author of the national epic *Os Lusíadas* celebrating the 1497 voyage of Vasco da Gama, and the founding of Portugal's Empire. The British Legation building was attacked and damaged by a stone throwing mob; its coat of arms was wrenched from its mounting and dragged through the streets of Lisbon by the outraged citizenry. A new national anthem *A Portuguesa* was written and performed in an upsurge of patriotic anti-British feeling while a national subscription was opened by the Royal Family to purchase warships and so strengthen Portugal's defences both at home and in the colonies.

On 20 August 1890, a treaty was signed in London, which it was hoped, would put an end to the ancient allies' squabbles. In its East African colony Portugal was granted a large area of hinterland to the north of the Zambezi River, but Britain refused to consider the unification of the two Portuguese colonies on the Atlantic and Indian Oceans, and retained the Shire region for itself. When the treaty was put to the Portuguese parliament, it was energetically rejected.

The Portuguese press considered it a deeper humiliation than the *Ultimatum* and it led to the fall of António de Serpa Pimental's government on 16 September 1890. The new government under João Crisóstomo reached an understanding with Britain; a *modus vivendi* was permitted to exist from 28 November 1890 for six months until the question of territorial claims could be settled amicably. Yet another cabinet crisis brought a change of leadership, thrusting octogenarian General de Abreu e Sousa into power. Carried along by popular anti-British feeling, he announced that the previously agreed *modus vivendi* would be dissolved.

As a direct result of the British *Ultimatum* a number of virulently anti-monarchist publications swiftly appeared on the streets of Lisbon and Oporto. The anti-monarchists were disgusted and angered by what they perceived as Portugal's weak response to the *Ultimatum* and of the monarch's lack of leadership. They were determined that the country should hear their voice. The lawyer, politician and poet, Guerra Junqueiro, penned *Finis Patriae* and the 'Song of Hate'; violently cruel satires on the ruling House of Braganza, and of Britain, appeared in the Portuguese press. In Oporto, the anti-monarchist, João Chagas, had edited the hard-hitting *República Portuguesa*, before being forced to flee to Paris. In the inaugural edition of another ephemeral publication *O Ultimato*, António José de Almeida wrote an inflammatory and provocative article entitled: 'The Last Braganza' in which he advocated putting Dom Carlos I behind bars in the Lisbon Zoo.

It did not take long before a pro-republican revolt broke out in Oporto on 31 January 1891. The instigators were army sergeants; only three junior officers: Captain Amaral Leitão, Lieutenant Manuel Maria Coelho and Cornet Rodolfo Malheiro were involved. Soldiers from 10 Infantry and 3 Light Infantry and elements of 6 Cavalry gathered at Campo Santo Ovidio where they attempted, without success, to enlist the soldiers of 19 Infantry Regiment. The insurgents, their ranks swollen by townsfolk, noisily marched to Dom Pedro IV Square singing *A Portuguesa*. The Oporto council chamber was invested and occupied. Dr Álves de Veiga raised the green and red flag and proclaimed the republic. The triumphant, cheering mass of soldiers and citizenry swept along Santo António Street shouting for more volunteers to join them; but at the end of the street their chaotic advance was checked; shots were fired, a stampede ensued and the revolution was postponed. On 27 February over 300 soldiers were court-martialled along with 21 civilians; the ringleaders were exiled. The British *Ultimatum* however, was not forgotten. It was to be the cause of continued bitterness and virulent anti-British sentiments for many years to come.

Chapter 4
The Royal Commissioner and the Scramble for Portuguese Africa

During the last decades of the nineteenth century and especially following the *Ultimatum*, Dom Carlos I and his ministers directed that military operations in Guinea, Angola and Portuguese East Africa be stepped up in order to combat what they perceived as foreign instigated rebellion and insurrection. This had to be carried out in order for Portugal to meet the requirements of 'effective occupation' that the Conference of Berlin had made the yardstick of sovereignty. In Portuguese East Africa, the northern part of the so-called Kionga Triangle, south of the Rovuma River, had been forcibly seized by the Germans on the strength of an agreement made with the Sultan of Zanzibar, who had claimed the coastal area between the Umba and Rovuma rivers. The British South Africa Company had established its control in Rhodesia, and the Boers were a force to be reckoned with to the south. Portuguese East Africa's new governor was determined to redress the balance.

Forty-two-year-old António Ennes an accomplished journalist, author and politician, had accepted the post of Naval and Overseas Minister in the government of General Crisóstomo. In 1891 he took ship from Portugal to Portuguese East Africa charged with studying the colony's economic and administrative conditions. Ennes was determined to see his vast fiefdom at first hand; too many colonial administrators had remained in the comparative safety of Lourenço Marques whiling away the interminable days and nights in the numbing solace of the brandy bottle. Some army officers, it was rumoured, who had been posted up country, had 'gone native' and disappeared forever in the endless steaming tropical labyrinths of the interior.

Lyons McLeod, Her Britannic Majesty's Consul at Mozambique in 1857, was most disappointed with the general aspect of Lourenço Marques. He was impressed by the magnificent natural harbour, but not by the town. The town was located at the foot of a high red cliff. There was a sand bank between it and the river, which by cutting off the sea breeze, made it unpleasantly hot and humid. Behind the town there was a foul-smelling swamp, but it prevented any attack from that direction. The town had a miserable looking square and furthermore, was filthy. As for its defences, the ramshackle fort possessed a large flagstaff and a few ancient guns, which could not be fired. The Portuguese settlement reminded Lyons McLeod of a slimy mud bank he had seen between Waterloo and Southwark Bridges on the Thames in London; the occupant of a hut built on such a mud bank would, in the height of an English summer, be nearly as liable to marsh or putrid fever as the inhabitants of Lourenço Marques.

But 24 years earlier, even before the building of the fortress was completed, the settlement's walls had been breached. In 1833 it was overrun and burned to the ground and its governor, Dionísio António Ribeiro, cruelly murdered. The Portuguese eventually fought back and in 1868, Governor José Augusto de Sá e Simas, commanding some 50 Europeans and auxiliaries, inflicted a defeat on Chief Amule and his warriors. In 1874 in an attempt to increase the vulnerable fortress town's security and trade, Andrade de Corvo ordered the construction of a rail line from Lourenço Marques to the Transvaal border. However, given Portugal's intrinsic financial weakness, the first train did not complete the journey until 1890.

But now in 1895, the European population of Lourenço Marques stood at 1,700 souls. Of this total, 700 were Portuguese nationals while the rest were mostly British traders. Yet within two kilometres of the fortress town lived an indigenous population of some 6,000 people. Down at Lourenço Marques' harbour side all was confusion; Governor Ennes had ordered the skipper of the Laird-built 549 tonne, 46-metre gunboat *Zaire* to chart a course 643 kilometres north along the shimmering Mozambique Channel to Beira. Beira was the key; the key to a vast African emporium, which Ennes was determined, would never fall into the eager hands of Cecil Rhodes, who saw Beira and the Pungwe River as the best route to Mashonaland. Ennes was impatient to get underway but there were problems with the *Zaire's* 500-horsepower engine; she was only able to make five knots instead of her normal ten. The *Zaire* was badly in need of an overhaul; seven years of steaming up and down Portuguese East Africa's coastal and inland waterways had taken their inevitable toll. A heavily perspiring rating remarked that it was only the cockroaches packed like glistening, treacly, brown ballast that kept her afloat.

Ennes was forced to wait another month until the *Zaire's* sister ship steamed up from Cape Town where she had undergone a refit after hitting a sandbank near the Chinde estuary. The *Liberal's* captain and crew looked well after their stay at the Cape; contrasting with Ennes' drawn and pallid face. At last the gunboat was underway cutting a wide bobbing arc north out of Delagoa Bay.

Though the *Liberal's* screws churned a constant white wake through the bucking cross currents of the Mozambique Channel, Ennes was feeling dispirited; from dawn until dusk there on the port bow was the never ending coastal monotony of his bailiwick. The *Liberal's* skipper had smiled laconically when asked by Ennes if the gunboat was actually making any headway, as the contours of the coast had not changed since leaving Lourenço Marques. The threat of ever shifting sand banks cause the *Liberal's* captain to head her out into mid channel forcing Ennes to squint against the glare as he attempted to separate the blue tones of the endless sky from the hues of the land. At the end of the first day, evening came tranquil, pitch black and full of stars, as Ennes, seated in his cramped cabin, began to ask himself if the occupation of so much land, so far away from Portugal was not just too much to ask of her people. Portugal, he reflected, could not even populate its provinces south of the Tagus River, as his countrymen had burned out much of their energies on their venture into the immense jungles and forests of Brazil. Of Portuguese East Africa's millions of hectares, how many came under the sway of warlike tribes who could only be vanquished by bloody, protracted wars, which would, in financial terms, cost more in one day than those lands could earn in one hundred years? Sleep was impossible. The day's images came back to haunt him. Kilometre after kilometre of barren brown coast, stinking swamps, impenetrable jungles, constantly shifting sand banks, lakes turned into searing cracked earth by the sun's vertical rays, vermin infested mountain ranges whose thick creeper and thorn clad granite cliffs would blunt the strongest axe. With its blight-stricken soil, it was a cursed land of rejection. He raised himself from his sweat stained bunk and stared out unseeing into the oceanic night, then, opening a blue leather bound diary wrote in pencil: 'Mozambique should only be opened up for exploration when no other unexplored area remains on the face of the earth.'

The day dawned bright and hot like every other day. The monotony of the muddy, mangrove-eaten coastline was broken by the captain's assurance that the port of Beira was only four hours' sailing time away. The screws had fouled almost within sight of Beira and the gunboat had drifted out of control, until a seaman sent overboard with a machete, was able to hack away the weeds imprisoning them. A blank shot was discharged from the *Liberal*'s gun. As the smoke whisped away, the gunboat gingerly negotiated sinister, half submerged boats and rotting hulks. The screws worked the mud from the harbour bottom into a frenzy of foul smelling stains. There was nothing to see, save for the dirty, green slime covered moorings. Ennes found it hard to believe that this was Beira; mangroves surrounded a thick liquid swamp into which slithered the fetid afterbirth of the Pungwe and Busi rivers. The reality of Mozambique was worse than any of Ennes' nightmares.

It was Ennes' job to prepare a detailed report on the colony; it would finally stretch to 666 pages. Though Ennes was manifestly not a military man, he was forced to give careful consideration to the use of the military and naval forces at his disposal for the defence of the Portuguese colony from within and without. Mozambique was divided into three administrative and military districts: Lourenço Marques in the south, containing the fortress of the same name, Moçambique in the centre and Zambézia in the north. The main settlements in the south were Inyambane and Sofala; in central Mozambique, Beira at the mouth of the Pungwe; in the north were Ibo Island, Moçambique

Island, the former capital, with Quelimane and Chinde at the entrances to the Zambezi.

The Governor-General was in command of all military forces with the district governors responsible for the troops under their command. In order to assist the governor-general, Lisbon had provided two adjutants selected from among the subalterns serving in the colony. The governor-general would be further assisted by an Inspector General of Military Forces in the rank of colonel, nominated by Lisbon, and not delegated from within the province.

Ennes intended to divide Portugal's military forces into two groups: Regular and Irregular troops. In time of war the Regular troops comprised four companies of light infantry, each with an artillery battery plus, the Police Corps of Lourenço Marques, and Police and Customs of Moçambique Province. Police and Customs of Inyambane comprised 1 Company stationed at São Sebastião in Moçambique Province with 2 Company at Ibo, 3 Company at Quelimane and 4 Company at Inyambane. Ennes envisaged that when the Inyambane and Niassa Chartered companies took over the supervision and running of the lands ceded to them by the Portuguese Crown, 2 Company stationed at Ibo, would transfer to Lourenço Marques District.

The light infantry companies were not to be involved in police work but were to be reserved exclusively for the defence of Mozambique and the suppression of rebellion. A captain would command each company with seven officers, 34 senior and junior NCOs and 100 men. Each light infantry company had an attached artillery battery commanded by a subaltern with one officer, four NCOs and sixteen soldiers. The battery was armed with two field guns and two machine guns.

The Irregular troops were divided into three groups that Ennes classified as Effective, Permanent and Reserve and would be spread out over the three military districts. The so-called, Effectives, were Native Police who were employed on lands run by the large stock companies; they received rudimentary military instruction. The Permanents were Native Police selected from the ranks of the Effectives, to serve alongside military and civil authorities. The Reserve was made up of all Native Police no longer in service. Each Native Police unit had one commander, one officer, four NCOs and 100 policemen. The role of the Native Police was to maintain public order in Mozambique, to guard the Chartered Company and Crown Lands, and at all times to be at the disposition of the authorities.

The Naval Forces of the East Africa Naval Division would be commanded by a naval officer in the rank of commander, designated by Lisbon as Chief of Naval

Forces Mozambique. The Naval command was divided into the three divisions: Northern, Central and Southern. The Northern Division encompassed the whole of Mozambique coastal waters. The Central Division was responsible for patrolling the coastal waters of Zambézia Province and the Southern Division, the coastal waters of Lourenço Marques.

The Portuguese gunboats on station were the *Neves Ferreira, Auxiliar, Marechal Mac-Mahon* and *Búfalo.* The vessels were tasked with transporting troops, and matériel around Mozambique and guarding the coastal waters against slavers and smugglers. Two steamers of between 200-300 tonnes, armed with two 75mm guns and two machine guns were to be used on loan when necessary. One sailing vessel of 200 tonnes was to be used as a training ship for Native Naval Forces. Three gunboats were to be used to police Mozambique's main rivers; six sailing boats were to be deployed by the Customs' Service within the colony's ports.

Police and Customs comprised four Divisions. Each Division had an establishment of one commanding officer with ten junior officers, twelve NCOs and 138 men.

Upon completion of his lengthy and detailed report on the state of the colony along with his proposals, Ennes returned to Portugal where it was published in Lisbon on 7 September 1893.

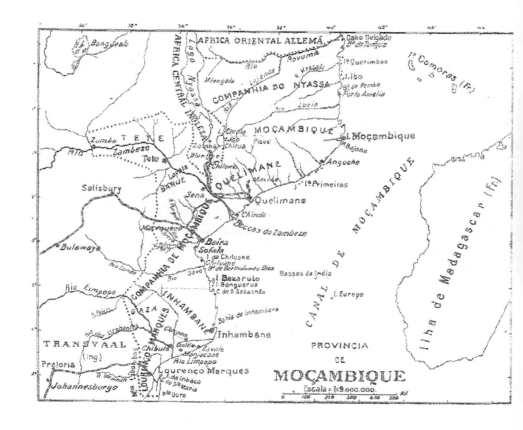

Map of Mozambique 1900 (Rodriguez)

Chapter 5
Rebellion in Gazaland

In August 1894 the harassed Portuguese authorities in Lourenço Marques called on Chief Matibejana of the Zishasha clan – a minor kingdom close to Lourenço Marques - to help them curb the depredations of Chief Mahazuli. Chief Amule, who rebelled against the Portuguese, dismissing them as 'hens', had previously ruled the kingdom, however, Chief Amule had been captured by the 'hens' and subjected to internal exile in Mozambique. On his return, he continued to rule his fiefdom, whilst instilling a hatred of the Portuguese in the young Matibejana. With his uncle now dead, the twenty-year-old ruled the kingdom of Zishasha. The young chief, who was known to his clan as both Matibejana and Zishasha, was seated on a small stool within his kraal when he received the Portuguese request. On hearing the news the *indunas* held an *indaba* and respectfully counselled the young chief to be cautious. Though the Portuguese as fighting men were of little concern, they feared the Europeans' weaponry. The young bloods were enraged and noisily called out for enemies to slaughter. Three months later on 6 November, Zishasha gave in to his hotheaded warriors and allowed a small raiding party to invest the outskirts of Lourenço Marques. The raiding party brought back cattle belonging to the Swiss missionary station and two prisoners, Tandane, a youngster who lived at the mission, and a man from the Maota clan who was kidnapped while walking along the track close to the outbuildings. As the young chief interrogated the cringing men, a warrior begged Zishasha to allow him to kill the prisoner he had taken. With a nod from Zishasha's head, the wailing captive was dragged into the bush and killed in cold blood by the excited young warrior while Tandane, much to his relief, was sent back to Lourenço Marques, bearing Zishasha's refusal to help the Portuguese. In view of Zishasha's hostile action, artillery colonel, António José de Aragão was tasked with strengthening the defensive lines at Lourenço Marques and given overall command of its meagre forces. Fortunately for the beleaguered defenders, two Portuguese naval ships, the corvette *Rainha de Portugal* and the gunboat, *Quanza*, were on station at Lourenço Marques. A naval contingent from the *Rainha de Portugal* commanded by Sub-Lieutenant Victor Leite de Sepúlvedra was sent ashore to bolster the defences. Before long the fortress town was attacked by impis from Zishasha and from Magaia under command of chief Mahazuli, but the Portuguese, thanks to Colonel de Aragão's careful planning, were able to repulse the attack in spite of being grossly outnumbered. However, the siege continued until early January.

In response to the continued unrest, and to the threat to Lourenço Marques, and the whole of southern Mozambique, António Ennes was again posted to the colony, leaving Lisbon on the *Sud-Express* bound for Marseilles on 8 December 1894. With him came his private secretary, Captain of Engineers Alfredo Augusto Freire de Andrade, aids-de-camp, artillery Lieutenants Henrique Mitchell de Paiva Couceiro, Madeiran born Aires de Ornelas de Vasconcelos and Naval Surgeon and Director of the Portuguese Red Cross, Dr António Rodrigues Braga. From the port of Marseilles they took ship on the French steamer *Iraouaddy*. The steamer was crowded with French troops bound for service in Madagascar. The Portuguese arrived in the colony on Monday 5 January 1895.

Ennes and his entourage had hardly transferred their sea chests and luggage from the *Iraouaddy* to the Thames-built, three-masted, armed sloop, *Afonso de Albuquerque*, when on 7 January an urgent telegram from the acting governor, Morais e Sousa arrived. According to a report brought into Lourenço Marques by a terrified and badly wounded survivor, approximately 3,000 Matola and Moamba warriors had appeared at a kraal near the railway line some three kilometres north of the capital and slaughtered 70 Gazaland women including a number of high ranking wives, and two Portuguese civil engineers. Earlier, African prisoners held in the gaol at Anguane had been set free by Chief Mahazuli's *indunas* and on 27 December, Lieutenant Felipe Nunes and a detachment of 3 Light Infantry Regiment of Angola had fallen to their assegais. The reason given for the uprising was a steep increase in the annual hut tax paid to the Portuguese authorities. Nevertheless, Ennes was requested to take immediate action against the rebel stronghold at Marracuene on the right bank of the Nkomati River.

The *Difaqane* – a period of constant warfare and waste had begun with the emergence of the Zulu people north of the Tugela River. Shaka had first come to prominence after being made a captain of one of Chief Dingiswayo's impis, and after his death in 1818, became king. His Zulu impis ravaged the countryside in devastating wars of conquest but not everyone was willing to follow Shaka's lead. Mzilikazi had been one of Shaka's most trusted captains but lusted after power, and one day his disaffection was brought to a head when he refused to hand over captured cattle to his king. To Shaka's anger, Mzilikazi's impis defeated a small force sent out against him; from now on Mzilikazi knew that to remain in Shaka's lands would mean certain death. He began to move north unleashing his hordes and overrunning neighbouring peoples and lands as far as the Limpopo River, where he eventually settled, in what was to become Matabeleland. Other malcontents had taken a north-easterly route into Portuguese territory. Soshangane, who had served as one of Chief Zwide's lieutenants in the 1818 war against Shaka, had fled Natal with his Shangani people, and after many vicissitudes settled in the south of Mozambique around Bilene in Gazaland. Soshangane, now called Manikuse, established his royal kraal at Chaimite in the highlands of the middle Sabi. Chief Manikuse controlled an 'empire' which stretched from the Nkomati River almost to the banks of the Zambezi, and from the Indian Ocean to the headwaters of the Sabi. It was a vast kingdom of half a million people.

After ruling for more than twenty years, Chief Manikuse died at Bilene in 1856, leaving two of his sons, Mwawe and Muzila to dispute the kingship. What followed was a bloody war of succession, which came to be known as *mubango*. In 1861 Muzila requested Portuguese military assistance from the governor of Lourenço Marques, Onofre de Andrade, saying that in return he would be willing to submit to Portuguese authority. The first bloody battle between the rival siblings took place in Matola. Mwawe left some 6,000 dead on the Matola battlefield, whereas the Portuguese assisted Muzila, lost only 400. Muzila and Onofre de Andrade's force determined to follow up their initial victory, and hotly pursued Mwawe's depleted warriors. Mwawe made a desperate stand, but after six hours of heated battle he lay dead with many thousands of his followers. Onofre de Andrade records that the Portuguese weaponry caused such terror that even Muzila's war chiefs begged him to cease the slaughter or Muzila would have no-one left to govern! After Muzila's victory, Onofre de Andrade declared that Muzila's lands were now under Portuguese sovereignty. However, Muzila soon forgot his promises to the Portuguese, and guided by the need to find food for his people and fodder for his animals, extended his lands by conquest from Lourenço Marques as far as Sofala and beyond the banks of the Zambezi.

Upon Muzila's death in 1884, Mondugaz, later known as Gungunyana, saw his opportunity to claim the throne of Gazaland, but first he had to eliminate possible pretenders to that throne, among those was his brother, Mafamama whom he had murdered. Having triumphed over his rivals, Gungunyana - the Lion - established his royal kraal at Manhlagazi. From 1890 Gungunyana began to forcibly reclaim lands formerly ceded to Portugal, having belonged to his father Muzila, though continuing to declare that he was a child of the Portuguese king and that his lands belonged to the king of Portugal. Yet the Portuguese commander of a military post on the Chicomo River complained to the colonial governor that when he had wanted to build a stone wall to better protect his post, it was opposed by Gungunyana, who threatened that he would not allow the Portuguese officer to take stones from his own river.

In order to appease the Portuguese government, Gungunyana sent two emissaries to Lisbon, and upon their return, agreed to the establishment of a permanent Portuguese resident in Gazaland. In recompense he was awarded the honorary rank of colonel, but he continued to refuse the Portuguese permission to survey the mines in Manicaland. In the following year

Gungunyana broke his promise to Lisbon and invaded the lands of the Massinga and Zunguze clans close to Inyambane. In order to justify his actions, Gungunyana sent a further embassy to the royal court, where Dom Luís I and his consort received Gungunyana's gift of seven elephants' tusks as a peace offering to the crown. Dom Luís informed Gunguyana's representatives of his pardon, but warned them that should it reoccur the King of Gazaland would feel the full weight of Portuguese arms. The Portuguese felt the need to impress the Gazans and took them under armed escort to visit an army barracks, fortresses, arsenals and naval men-of-war. One night, for their entertainment, the two ambassadors were taken to the Lisbon Coliseum where they watched in awe as an immaculately dressed lion tamer entered a cage armed only with a whip and a pistol. On their return to Gazaland the two men informed their king that not only did the Portuguese possess a powerful army, but also they were 'white witches', and was not Gungunyana the 'lion'?

From Gungunyana's viewpoint his embassy to Lisbon had been a great success. It had removed the threat of war with the Portuguese and, more importantly, Gungunyana following the warlike traditions of his uncle and father, Manikuse and Muzila, still ruled supreme over his Gazaland Empire with a potential army of 50,000 warriors composed of *mangas* - regiments.

In time of war Gungunyana could call on practically the whole of the male population, save for the very young and very old. From Muzila he had inherited five regiments:

Magwaga	Old Workers
Zebangwa	Brave Veterans
Inyati	Buffalos
Zingwenya	Crocodiles
Zimpafumane	Giants

The five original regiments could readily be combined with his eleven regiments to make a formidable and fearful fighting force.

Zinyone M'Shope	White Birds
Mazati	Bold Ones
Mangonde	Silent Ones
Zeyamba Inkwiyo	Brave Lords
Zeyamba Nyana	Brave Noblemen
Manyakabuko	Dangerous Ones
Mabanga	Pillagers
Mahalamba	Fearless Ones
Mangava-Angava	Courageous Youths
Mapepa	Crafty Youths

Henri Junod, of the Swiss Reformed Church, was seated in the shade under a tree at his mission school at Rikatla, 25 kilometres north of Lourenço Marques. The school children were playing in the dusty square with their mothers when he became aware of a gargantuan figure running swiftly towards him. The children's heads turned in response to the heavy, thumping rhythm, and becoming alarmed, fled screaming towards their mothers, who snatched them up and carried them into the schoolroom and bolted the doors. The monstrous figure halted in front of a startled Junod and greeted him warmly, only then did he recognise Shardi the school's cattleman; along with thousands more he had been summoned to attend Chief Mahazuli's military parade. Junod was struck by his grotesque and frightening appearance and could well understand how such a battle dress would strike terror into Mahazuli's enemies. Shardi's head was decorated with three, long straight plumes; one plume was placed at the front with the others at the sides of a small ostrich feather cap *shintlontlo,* which in turn was affixed to another skin cap, which was fastened by a chinstrap. It made the warrior's head appear twice as large, and with the addition of porcupine spines, created a heart-stopping appearance. Around his neck was a *tinkosho*, a black, calf-leather-laced thong. Shardi's arms were ornamented with white ox hide, as were his stomach and legs. Around his midriff, were the fine, red-striped skins of the wildcat *nsimba*, with antelope skin hanging down to his thighs. Finally, to complete the terrifying appearance, the thickness of his legs was exaggerated, as his calves and ankles were decorated with bracelets fashioned from large black seeds called *timbava*, each seed was the size of a large cherry. As he ran towards them, the rattling bracelets sounded like the tread of an elephant, and it was this ominous, heavy thud, which had so frightened the children and their mothers. When Junod asked him why he carried a sharpened ox rib, he explained that it was used to scrape the sweat from his face and body when in battle. Junod was fascinated and intrigued and wanted to know how Shardi had come about his fighting dress and was told that he kept it, as was the custom, in a straw covered construction close to his hut.

Whereas, the missionary Junod, a consummate linguist and ethnographer, wrote from intimate experience of and empathy for the African peoples, the same cannot be said of Ennes who firmly believed that Gungunyana's subjects had to be treated as irreconcilable enemies. Ennes opined that the warriors were men who blighted the ground they walked on, savagery was their trade whereas work was disdained; murder was glory, and rape their right. But Ennes' view was heavily coloured by the perilous situation he found himself in; he had not sought the post and had only accepted it at great personal cost.

Chapter 6
Portuguese Offensive Operations in Gazaland

Royal-Commissioner Ennes desperately needed to relieve the immediate pressure on the beleaguered and weakly defended port of Lourenço Marques, which was under daily threat of annihilation by rebel attack. After a brief situational report given to him by Caldas Xavier, he was strongly advised to send out a reconnaissance patrol. The patrol, consisting of 1 Company, 2 Light Infantry Regiment; 60 riflemen from 3 Light Infantry Regiment with two field pieces and thirteen mounted police, was hastily put together. The small ill-equipped patrol led by Major Caldas Xavier with Paiva Couceiro as second-in-command set off northward towards the Nkomati River before first light on 21 January. Paiva Couceiro's patrol was ordered to scout ahead but was to avoid engaging the enemy. The scouts were riding through a steep-sided ravine, towards a deserted kraal, when to their surprise, heavily armed warriors rushed towards them, from the wooded slopes. Paiva Couceiro reined in his mount and ordered his men to halt and fire on the enemy from horseback. A number of warriors were hit, while the rest dived into the long grass, enabling the troopers to make good their escape.

Ennes greatly valued his young officers' advice, and held many discussions far into the night with Paiva Couceiro, at Government House on the imposing, red sandstone, Reuben Point, lit only by large flickering candles, and by Caldas Xavier's self deprecating humour. Royal-Commissioner Ennes ordered an armed force under overall command of Major José Ribeiro Júnior to take the initiative away from the rebels, and move north to the swiftly running Nkomati River, where they were to establish a military post and a defensive line on Marracuene. The occupation of Marracuene would form the basis for further operations in the northern region. Lourenço Marques was to be defended by ratings from the *Rainha de Portugal* and *Afonso de Albuquerque*. Ennes was aware that the column lacked even the most basic of supplies; munitions, transport, tentage, ground sheets, medical equipment, and even slouch hats.

Early on the morning of Monday 28 January, while the day was still bearably cool, Major Caldas Xavier prepared to lead a flying column made up of cavalry and elements of 2 and 3 Battalions Light Infantry; 3 Battalion was composed of badly trained native Angolans confusingly named East African Light Infantry, Lourenço Marques Mounted Police and infantry contingents with four artillery limbers and two Nordenfelt machine guns. The column totalling 28 officers and 784 men, set off into Gazaland. Captain Paiva Couceiro tasked to scout ahead of the main column, dug in his heels and led his ten-man cavalry detachment forward in a wary canter. The first seventeen kilometres passed without incident, and after ten hours of foot slogging in the terrific summer heat, the weary column reached Angoane. Just as the men began to cook much needed rations and dig latrines, the skies opened up and the unfortunate men found themselves searching for any shelter they could find. After a soaking night, the sodden troops set off towards Guavá at 7:00 in the morning of 29 January. Ennes had had little alternative other than to mount the military operation in January even though December to March is the period of heaviest rain in Lourenço Marques district. Caldas Xavier ordered 50 soldiers of 3 Infantry Battalion to dig in at Angoane. The column halted early in the afternoon and ate their cold and soggy rations. Shortly after, scouts were fired on by a large group of warriors near Guavá kraal, and were pinned down and in danger of being cut up by the enemy. Major Caldas Xavier ordered his artillery limbers up, and the column doubled towards the sound of rifle fire; the field guns were rapidly unlimbered and Guavá kraal was bombarded. Soon the huts were burning fiercely, ammunition was exploding high into the air and warriors were seen running into the thorn veld carrying their weapons and their wounded.

At 4:00 in the afternoon, in pouring rain and gusting winds, the Portuguese reached Marracuene. They set up a defensive position on Massinga Heights close to the riverbank some twenty metres above the waters. The position was poorly sited facing thick bush, which would enable the enemy to advance towards the Portuguese defenders almost undetected. Paiva Couceiro reported to Caldas Xavier that he had located a better defensive position but as the troops were tired, wet and hungry, Caldas Xavier gave the order to dig in, mount guards and then take turns to eat and rest. At 6:00 that evening, *Neves Ferreira*, *Bacamarte* and *Xefina* steamed up river in support of the column. The incessant rain continued all night and the troops remained entrenched on Massinga Heights on the following day, 30 January. Caldas Xavier realised that the Portuguese position was vulnerable to a frontal attack and a defensive-square was formed. The right, left and rear faces were protected by field guns, while the fourth gun was placed facing north, and was covered by two machine guns. Eight, two-man advanced posts were sited 200 metres forward of the square and manned by the Angolans. During the night the Angolans made probing forays in the direction of the bush in order to seek out the enemy but none was found and the night passed without incident. However, the rain was incessant and the square soon turned into a quagmire, the soaking and dejected troops were unable to light fires to cook their rations; only the police contingent, who were used to living in the bush, were able to cook themselves something to eat.

On 31 January Caldas Xavier though cold, tired and hungry, was buoyed up by the expectation of seeing the planned arrival at his position of friendly African auxiliaries. While Caldas Xavier waited, the *Neves Ferreira*, under command of

Sub-Lieutenant Raul Bettencourt Furtado, steamed up river and fired on hostile villages; the bombardment met with little resistance. The sailors were able to capture three European type supply launches that the riverine villagers had abandoned in their haste to escape the Portuguese naval guns.

The massed Zishasha and Nondwene impis had gathered in the pouring rain close to Marracuene and the Nkomati River. They now stood in ominous silence, deployed in buffalo-horn formation with their *mathlari* - stabbing spears - held head high, looking on while an intoning *n'anga* – spirit medium - with the aid of young female handmaidens, began to prepare a magic potion by dramatically pounding leaves and roots into a bubbling frothy liquid. The watching warriors keenly followed the *n'anga*'s every move, knowing that very soon they would come face to face with the Portuguese and their powerful weapons of war. While invoking the warriors' ancestors the *n'anga* placed the heavy bowl on the ground, and then ordered his helpers to cut down two long, sinewy branches from the thorny, hallucinogenic dogbane, and drag them to a muddy open area in front of the impis. After they were in place, he called on the warriors to advance and leap over the spiky branches, before taking a mouthful of the magic, milky concoction, spitting it out and repeating the sacramental oath to their forebears; they were now infused with the spirit medium's potion and its mystical strength. By this impressive process the warriors had rendered themselves totally invulnerable to Portuguese rifle and artillery fire. Bullets would flatten against their bodies and the magic would only be broken if they turned their backs to the enemy. The dancing, jigging warriors listened excitedly as the aged *n'anga's* screeching voice ordered them to go and kill the enemy. On a signal from the battle chiefs, the impis regrouped and jogged off through the sheeting rain towards the Portuguese trenches at Marracuene.

With the arrival of the *Xefina*, Caldas Xavier received orders from António Ennes to withdraw to Angoane some fourteen kilometres distant, and then to Lourenço Marques, leaving a defended post at Marracuene. The *Neves Ferreira* was ordered to remain on station to provide protective fire and guard the Marracuene position. By 2 February, the weary column already laid low by black water fever and dysentery, was still encamped at Marracuene on the slippery banks of the flooding Nkomati River, having been unable to withdraw to Angoane. Rain soaked pickets reported sighting shadowy figures advancing towards their position through the blinding rain. In the darkness of the early morning the Portuguese were stood to. Using the torrential rain to their advantage, Matibejana's impis had skilfully begun to infiltrate the Portuguese positions from the direction of the Nkomati riverbank, stabbing the Angolan sentries as they crept forward. With the dawn came clear weather and some relief from the night's tension. However, the warriors who had stealthily crept towards the Portuguese during the night, suddenly rose up in front of the startled troops, and rushed towards the right face of the square guarded by 3 Battalion Light Infantry. The marauding warriors called out to its defenders in Portuguese, not to open fire. The ploy was uncovered by African Corporal Domingos of 3 Battalion, but not before the full weight of the attack fell on the Angolans and 2 Company, 2 Light Infantry.

With the *n'anga's* words still ringing in their ears, the massed impis, having spent the long night hiding in thick bush close to the riverbank, began a frenzied attack against the right face of the square. The Angolans who had had little formal infantry training began to waver and then broke in panic towards the centre. It was a critical moment; hand to hand fighting ensued within the square; Second Lieutenant António Manuel of police Cavalry was wounded in the shoulder and about to be finished off by a *tlhari* wielding warrior after his pistol had jammed, but somehow managed to grab hold of a discarded bayonet and dispatched his adversary. A tall and heavily armed warrior dashed through the square and was tackled by artillery Captain Carlos Machado's batman, who wrested the *tlhari* from his grip, and killed him with his own weapon. Fever-stricken Major Alberto Ribeiro, hearing the sound of rifle fire, had groggily staggered up from his cot when the tent was ripped open by a group of warriors who were immediately shot down by the major's men. After the battle, the corpse of a black soldier of 3 Battalion East African Light Infantry was found to have more than twenty stab wounds in its body. Above the din, Police Captain Francisco Roque de Aguiar called on his men to cover the right face; the policemen carried the attacking warriors with the bayonet. Caldas Xavier and Second Lieutenant Pinto of the East African Light Infantry rallied the Angolans in their own tongue. The Angolans' resistance stiffened and they were able to regain their position in the square.

Ennes had later been informed that although the Portuguese square had been breached – signalling almost certain doom - it had amazingly managed to reform. In a later debriefing, Ennes was told by Caldas Xavier, that Zishasha's warriors who attacked the Portuguese forward positions, were too far in front of their impis, and had become confused in the early light and entangled in the thick bush, giving the Portuguese the chance to open fire before the warriors had time to exploit the Angolan battalion's flight. Faced with accurate and sustained fire, Zishasha's impis hesitated; the *n'anga's* spell had been broken. Now they threw themselves down to escape the hail of bullets with only the most determined warriors pressing the assault. The last of the impis who emerged from the bush were cut down; had they been able to keep up with the rest of their regiments, the Portuguese would have been routed and massacred.

However, the remainder of the well-armed enemy continued to fire on the Portuguese square from the cover of the thick bush close to the river, but most of the riflemen committed the all too common error of aiming too high. By 6:00 that morning the enemy's rifles fell silent. The Portuguese square had held and carried the day. The Angolans had borne the brunt of the attack and their dead were lying out in the overrun, advanced position or grouped together where they had fallen close to the square. The exhausted Portuguese medical officers were struggling to deal with the twenty seriously wounded Angolans and the nine wounded Portuguese troops. Incredibly, only three Portuguese soldiers had been killed in the attack on the square. The impis were estimated at between 2,500 and 3,000; eight dead warriors were found within the square with another 50 lying bunched up just outside. Many of the attacking Zishasha and Nondwene warriors had been hit by rifle and artillery fire; smashed heads, legs and arms were strewn over the battleground. Some of the wounded were dragged away; others, less fortunate, had managed to crawl into the bush where they would die unattended and in agony. The expenditure of ammunition was relatively small for such an action; the artillery had fired four shrapnel and sixteen high explosive shells with the infantry having loosed off 4,500 rounds from their 8 mm black powder Kropatschek rifles.

The Portuguese sent out scouts to reconnoitre the bush. When they returned and reported the riverbank clear, they piled up the enemy dead and set fire to them, filling the air with acrid grey smoke. The Portuguese troops; black and white together, were buried close to the banks of the Nkomati, while the wounded were taken onboard the *Bacamarte* under command of twenty-year-old Sub-Lieutenant Filipe Trajano Vieira da Rocha. From there, the makeshift gunboat, originally bought second-hand for the use of the harbour-master at Lourenço Marques, steamed slowly on to Lourenço Marques. Only sustained and accurate fire from a small group of soldiers led by Major Caldas Xavier and Captain Paiva Couceiro had turned defeat into victory on that searingly hot summer's morning in Gazaland.

Meanwhile, at Government House, António Ennes was unaware of the events of the 2 February and when on 3 February the rains recommenced, Ennes and the population of Lourenço Marques anxiously awaited news of the Marracuene Column. The people of Lourenço Marques spent that night in a state of panic, with rumours of sightings along the railway line and close to Government House, where groups of frightened civilians had sought shelter. Every possible rating from the Portuguese ships anchored in Delagoa Bay was disembarked in order to patrol the streets of Lourenço Marques. To make matters worse, it was a pitch black, stormy night; people were constantly reporting the sound of 'firing' and the deep 'chanting' of advancing impis. And still Ennes awaited news from Marracuene; cables from Cape Town and

Pretoria spoke predictably of the massacre of Portuguese soldiers – some 500 dead and the rest hopelessly surrounded. Such news only added to the governor's sense of impending disaster. Finally, intelligence of the Portuguese victory on 2 February was brought to the jittery and beleaguered city by the gunboat *Bacamarte* along with 27 seriously wounded soldiers.

The late evening of the 2 February had seen the Portuguese frantically reducing the size of their square; defensive positions and ditches had been dug, and the bush close to the Portuguese position had been cleared of vegetation to provide an unrestricted field of fire and inhibit the enemy from getting too close to the square unobserved. Large bonfires were lit around the square, and throughout the night a detachment of troops was put on sentry duty to be relieved every two hours. At 1:00 in the morning of 3 February fire broke out against the Portuguese square; though the enemy could not be seen, flashes from their rifles were visible in the bush 80 metres away. The Portuguese answered with accurate fire and continued to engage the enemy sporadically until 6:00 in the morning. By first light, the enemy had melted away. By this time the Portuguese were too exhausted to pursue them and were not even able to reconnoitre the area to the north of their position; the makeshift cavalry had lost seven horses and others were injured. In spite of the break in the weather, the position was virtually waterlogged. Suddenly the heavy rain turned into a torrential, blinding, tropical thunderstorm of truly African proportions. Major Alberto Ribeiro, who had been shaking with high fever, and had played no part in the defence of the Massinga Heights, was carried aboard the *Neves Ferreira* to receive much needed medical treatment. A black night of heavy rain followed. The Portuguese now had difficulty in lighting their protective bonfires due to the soaked foliage. Desultory enemy fire kept the defenders awake all night. The following day, 4 February, the Portuguese received some relief when Lieutenant Emilio de Lemos embarked from the *Neves Ferreira* with a small force of East African Light Infantry, and mounted a vigorous attack against the left bank of the Nkomati destroying a number of hostile villages.

The Matola and Moamba clans – the column's long awaited 'auxiliaries' – had agreed to meet at Mukapane kraal, but the Moamba failed to appear. As the Moamba clan had sided with Zishasha at the beginning of the revolt, the Matolans had no confidence in them, and deliberately waited and watched to see which way the battle would go, rather than join the Portuguese Marracuene Column. Chief Mugundwana of the Moamba was already in the area and in a gesture of friendship and peace toward Chief Matibejana of the Zishasha, offered to protect the women and the cattle while Zishasha took on the Portuguese at Marracuene. On the morning of 2 February, Portugal's allies warily watched as Zishasha's impis launched themselves against the Portuguese square. When the dispirited warriors finally retreated in disorder and began the long trek to their kraals, their erstwhile friends the Matola and Moamba clans, fell on them. After attacking and killing many of Zishasha's shattered impis, Chief Mugundwana ordered his people to slaughter the womenfolk he had generously offered to protect. Chief Mugundwana's deceit had the effect of diverting the rebels' attention from the Portuguese. From then on, the main objective of the Zishasha peoples was to avenge Mugundwana's treachery.

Caldas Xavier received written orders from António Ennes to withdraw his troops from Marracuene, and at dawn on 5 February the Portuguese abandoned their fortified position. Though the victorious Portuguese had been ordered to torch the deserted rebel villages and fields as they withdrew, the continued heavy rain made it a difficult task. In a mood of generosity born of sheer relief, the Portuguese Royal Commissioner described it as: 'a sad and hateful necessity of war.'

In the late afternoon, after seven hours of forced march in blinding rain, the exhausted and hungry troops finally halted, and throwing off their kit bags and ammunition pouches, slept soundly under Angoane's corrugated iron roofs. A detachment of 2 Battalion East African Light Infantry was left to defend Angoane, and on 6 February the weary column resumed its march to Lourenço Marques.

Though the battle at Marracuene was a Portuguese victory, the troops were unable to exploit their success as Caldas Xavier had been ordered to withdraw due to the appalling weather and problems related to ammunition and food supplies. The Portuguese had hardly pulled back from their hard-won positions before the enemy swiftly reoccupied them. Many of the battle chiefs refused to believe they had been beaten, rather they had fled the scene of the battle, seeing it as a strategic move and not in itself suggestive of defeat. The African strategists had drawn an important conclusion from the conflict; in order to succeed they needed to attack the Portuguese at night in the bush. They had no intention of halting the struggle against their oppressors and happily returned to their villages and to the fields that Caldas Xavier's soldiers had failed to burn.

The Battle of Marracuene
2nd February 1895

Chapter 7
Paiva Couceiro – Knight Errant

A major actor and aid of António Ennes was Henrique Mitchell de Paiva Couceiro. He was born in Lisbon in 1861, to a Portuguese father and an English mother. Young Henrique was brought up speaking both Portuguese and English and at the age of eleven was given a copy of Sir Walter Scott's *Ivanhoe* by his literature-loving mother, which he avidly devoured. Six years later, a tall, slim, young man with an oval face, high forehead, deep set eyes, long nose and strongly pointed chin, presented himself for enlistment as a recruit at the Lisbon Cavalry Barracks. In 1879, he applied for and was accepted on an artillery course, and four years later was commissioned into 1 Artillery Regiment as a second lieutenant. Young Henrique longed for adventure and like Ivanhoe, the knight-errant of his childhood dreams, determined to vanquish his foes. On 31 August 1889 the steamer *São Tomé* dropped anchor in wide Luanda Bay. Once ashore, Paiva Couceiro made straight for Government House to receive his official instructions. He was posted to command the Irregular Cavalry Squadron at *Forte Humpata*, east of the southern port of Mossâmedes, relieving his future friend and comrade in arms, Light Infantry Captain Artur de Paiva, who had been commissioned to survey the Chela Highlands. Later that year, he was ordered to organise an expedition to establish Portuguese suzerainty over the Barotseland region in Upper Zambézia. In May 1890 accompanied by Justino Teixeira da Silva, he had struck out in a north-easterly direction from Catumbela Falls toward the hinterland and Bié district. Bié would soon become a transit centre for trading caravans passing between it and the future British colony of Northern Rhodesia and the Belgian Congo. At Belmonte in Bié district, he was dismayed to receive orders to abandon the Barotseland expedition due to the British *Ultimatum*. In that same year, as a consequence of the *Ultimatum*, he was appointed to command a Portuguese cavalry squadron, tasked to reconnoitre the Kubango River in southern Angola as far as its extreme easterly point, where it marched with German South West Africa. His mounted reconnaissance was successfully accomplished without loss and provided headquarters at Luanda with hitherto unknown information on the area and detailed mapping of the Kubango River.

In 1894, Paiva de Couceiro had been named as António Ennes' aid-de-camp in Portuguese East Africa. He had many excellent qualities and was a great patriot and ardent monarchist, but possessed of a fiery temper. As a bilingual Portuguese officer, he was uniquely able to evaluate the effectiveness of the Portuguese administration of the colony, and at the same time contrast it with the inflammatory and libellous reports dispatched daily to Durban and the Cape by English speaking journalists.

On 13 February 1895, the packet boat from Durban had brought up to Lourenço Marques the latest issues of the *Cape Town Mail* and the *Natal Mercury*, which Paiva Couceiro, recently returned from campaigning in Gazaland, read with ill-disguised anger. As usual, the resident English-speaking journalists had catalogued alleged cases of Portuguese military and civil ineptitude; Portugal's name was once again mud. Paiva Couceiro ate a hurried breakfast, and dressed in a light coloured linen civilian suit and straw boater, sought out the three foreign journalists responsible for those libellous reports. He confronted Eddie Brown, an American national and sometime newspaper scribe, over breakfast in the hotel restaurant. Paiva Couceiro thanked Brown for his journalistic treatment of Portugal and the Portuguese, and with one solid thump sent him crashing through the table, followed closely by his breakfast and coffee. Next Paiva Couceiro stalked off to the nearby 'Hotel Criterion', to find Joe Clarke. He entered the cigar-smoke filled billiard room, snatched the cue from the offending journalist's hand and proceeded to belabour the Briton's arms and flanks with it. Throwing the cue on to the green, baize-topped billiard table, he stormed out in search of the third offender. Ivory trader Albert Gould admitted writing reports for Natal and Cape newspapers but swore his articles were inoffensive pen pictures of life in Lourenço Marques. Paiva Couceiro checked himself, and after giving Gould a ticking off, left his store. However, the more Paiva Couceiro thought about it the less truthful Gould's explanation seemed. Sitting down at a nearby café table he ordered a coffee and *bagaço*, and in English penned out a declaration for Gould to sign, to the effect that he never had and never would write anything insulting to the Portuguese nation. Gould was lounging on his stoep drinking a beer, a Zulu knobkerrie rested against his chair. Gould eyed Paiva Couceiro suspiciously and winced when the Portuguese officer flung the declaration on to the table. Gould swore and shouted at him to go away, angrily leaping out of his chair. Paiva Couceiro punched him squarely on the jaw; Gould staggered back then launched himself at the Portuguese. Both men rolled from the stoep down on to the footpath and into the open doorway of an Indian tailor's shop, where the surprised owner was busily ironing a pair of trousers. Paiva Couceiro grabbed the ironing board and broke it over Gould's head, thereafter, quickly composed himself, paid for the damaged ironing board and returned to his bungalow well satisfied with his morning's work.

Chapter 8
Operations in Lourenço Marques and Inyambane Districts

Two months later, on 3 April, António Ennes was hard at work in the monastic isolation at Reuben Point. He was painstakingly engaged in the drawing up of a blueprint for future Portuguese conduct in the colony with his vigorous 'Plan of Operations in the Districts of Lourenço Marques and Inyambane.' The preamble stated:

The military operations which will take place in the Lourenço Marques and Inyambane districts will have the following effect: provide an overwhelming demonstration of force which will serve to impress upon the populace throughout the colony - presently intolerably rebellious - and foreigners who consider us incapable of governing Mozambique, that we have the means and the firm will to maintain our sovereignty over this colony and punish those who would rise up against us.

Due to continued unrest in Mozambique, and Portugal's desire to be seen to be 'governing' the colony 'effectively', Rodrigues Galhardo was placed in command of the Portuguese Expeditionary Force to Mozambique. It sailed from Lisbon on 15 October 1894 and after steaming 13,000 kilometres, arrived at Delagoa Bay almost one month later. The Expeditionary Force was made up of 2 Battalion Light Infantry, a battery of 2 Artillery plus cavalry with service and support - in total 24 officers and 603 men.

Forty-nine-year-old Eduardo Augusto Rodrigues Galhardo, had previously served with the infantry, artillery and engineers, and after a spell lecturing at the War College, had been posted to Macao as Portuguese governor of the tiny China Sea island. In order to bring his plan to fruition, Ennes decided on the deployment of three columns. The strongest was the Northern or Inyambane Column, under command of Colonel Galhardo. The colonel was to march from Inyambane to Kumbana and from there to Chicomo, to occupy and strengthen Portuguese control of the Nkomati area. The Limpopo Column, under command of Sanches de Miranda was to build posts on the right bank of the Limpopo River in the Shangane Estuary with gunboat protection; the third column, the Southern Column, was to march from Inyambane to Chicomo to within easy striking distance of Gungunyana's kraal, while Caldas Xavier would remain as commanding officer of the Lourenço Marques defences. Colonel Galhardo was a resolute if somewhat unimaginative officer who was intimidated by the responsibility of colonial campaigning. Ennes became exasperated by his interminable preparations but Galhardo followed the book page by page.

The Southern Column was formed in May 1895. It was tasked to form a line of military posts from Lourenço Marques north to the Nkomati River. The column would march on two different routes: easterly from Passene to the Sabi and from there over sandy ground to Stokolo and Magude; north-westerly from Manyissa military post – the proposed limit of the Marracuene campaign – on the Nkomati River, to Shinavane and Magude military post. In May, prior to the column's departure, Major Caldas Xavier had begun the building of the 92-kilometre long road from Passene to Stokolo. Although the task was completed without the Portuguese sappers being attacked, the officers and men felt very uneasy as the local clans were sullen and angry. They feared – not without justification - that allowing a road to be built through their lands would cause swift and bloody retaliation against them from Gungunyana's impis.

In late June, the Northern Column started out by land and river, to complete the occupation of the right bank of the Nkomati, in order to control Cossine and pursue the rebellious chiefs who had built temporary kraals close to Magul. The larger part of the column would advance and occupy Stokolo.

Colonel Galhardo had chosen Major Eduardo Ferreira da Costa, as second-in-command of the Northern Column, with Lieutenant Aires de Ornelas, commanding the cavalry squadron. The infantry contingent was comprised of 3 Battalion Light Infantry; 4 Company 2 Battalion East African Light Infantry; 1, 2 and 3 troops of 1 Cavalry; 1, 2 batteries 4 Artillery with service and support. The Northern Column totalled 1,300 officers and men.

The Southern or Lourenço Marques Column was commanded by Major Gomes Pereira, with Captain of Engineers António Freire de Andrade and Captain Paiva Couceiro. By 1890 Freire de Andrade was already an experienced colonial army officer who had first been posted to Mozambique as Commissioner of Mines and Precious Metals. He had then been given the task of mapping the frontier between Lourenço Marques and the Transvaal border. He was a good man to have in a crisis. The Southern Column was comprised of 1, 2 and 3 Companies of 2 Infantry Battalion; elements of 3 Battalion East African Light Infantry; 4 Squadron 1 Cavalry; Lourenço Marques Native Police, plus engineers, a field gun battery from 4 Artillery Regiment and service and support. The Southern Column totalled 800 officers and men.

On 1 June the advance party of the column composed of infantry and supplies set out north for Inyambane on the steamer *Ambaca*, escorted by the gunboat *Neves Ferreira* and followed four days later by the second detachment, composed entirely of 2 Infantry. Later in June, 1 Cavalry Squadron under the enigmatic 39-year-old Captain Joaquim Augusto Mousinho de Albuquerque, arrived on board the *Vega* at Lourenço Marques. Due to the chronic lack of transport the cavalry was forced to remain in Lourenço Marques and await the *Ambaca*'s return. Meanwhile Ennes had ordered three officers, including Aires de Ornelas from the Northern Column, to Durban to purchase remounts. On 15 June Mousinho de Albuquerque finally departed on the German steamship *General* with artillery and infantry. The small cavalry force totalled some 270 officers and men.

On 21 June, Ennes, with a view to averting a potentially disastrous and bloody conflict, ordered counsellor José de Almeida to seek out Gungunyana, and discuss the peaceable handing over of the rebel chiefs, Matibejana of Zishasha and Moazul of Magaia. José de Almeida's unsuccessful peace mission in Gazaland lasted until 12 August. Gungunyana simply did not believe that the Portuguese would mobilise so many troops in order to apprehend two rebellious chieftains. On the final day of peace talks at Manhlagazi, at 8:45 in the morning, the awaiting Portuguese observed warriors appearing from out of the bush from the direction of Gungunyana's kraal; they formed a dense black line blotting out the horizon. As they slowly moved forwards through clouds of dust the Portuguese were able to make out the *Zimpafumane* - tall men - and *Zinyome M'Shope* - white bird - regiments. Each regiment boasted some 3,000 warriors. When the advancing impis were approximately 500 metres from the Portuguese residency, the sweating *n'anga*, covered from head to foot in lion skins, with an immense black-feathered headdress, suddenly leapt out in front of the warriors, wildly barking and crowing. The impis halted and Gungunyana, a tall, heavily built, wide-faced man with intelligent eyes and air of superiority, appeared to deafening cries of *bayete*! At the termination of the inconclusive *indaba* the Portuguese were invited to watch a display by the disciplined and superbly organised troops; the chanting of 6,000 voices was an awesome and intimidating experience for José de Almeida and his officers.

Yet in spite of the unsuccessful *indabas*, António Ennes was still trying to avert war as late as 28 August when Almeida again attempted to parley with Gungunyana's *indunas* in Gazaland.

By 6 July, the Southern Column, having trekked through cloying sandy terrain, had deployed at Stokolo. Paiva Couceiro's mounted patrol uneasily bedded down in a wooden barrack protected by flimsy strands of barbed wire. Couceiro reconnoitred the area and then re-located from the indefensible Stokolo post to a position on high ground at Cossine. Within the space of twelve days a road of felled trees was rapidly constructed between Stokolo and Manyissa and a new post; *Posto X* was established. As previously planned, on 25 June, Freire de Andrade with 120 men of 2 Infantry Battalion and 4 Artillery was transported from Marracuene to Manyissa where they disembarked from the gunboats *Sabre*, *Carabina* and *Bacamarte*. Shinavane located at a fork of the Nkomati River was occupied on 13 July by a force of over 100 troops transported there by gunboats; it provided an ideal berth for the Portuguese vessels. Two hundred infantrymen, twenty gunners, twelve sappers and 28 cavalrymen occupied *Posto X* at Magude. Freire de Andrade built his headquarters at Manyissa; Lieutenant Krusse Gomes of 2 Infantry set to and constructed a road through swampland to Magude. Paiva Couceiro, writing to António Ennes from the Stokolo position, described Krusse Gomes' incredible feat, as being made even more difficult due to the depth of the mud and water. *Posto X* became the pivotal point in the Southern Column's advance and the focus of Portugal's renewed presence among the wavering clans. With the completion of two pontoon bridges over the Nkomati at Shinavane by Lieutenant Delfim Monteiro, the Portuguese were ready to begin the march into hostile Cossine territory on the opposite bank of the Nkomati.

On 28 June 1895, Paiva Couceiro, a consummate diarist, found time to pen a scribbled letter to his mother in Portugal. He wrote that he believed his mission to Gungunyana was to gain time while Portuguese troops took up positions on the borders of Gazaland, but as a soldier he regretted that Ennes was earnestly attempting to avert war with Gungunyana. However, Paiva Couceiro's hands were tied; he had been given explicit orders from Ennes that under no circumstances should he attempt to cross the Nkomati River into Gungunyana's lands, while José de Almeida was still negotiating with the Paramount Chief.

Yet on 17 July, in contravention of Ennes' instructions, Paiva Couceiro had ordered his troops over the Nkomati into Gazaland. The Portuguese force crossed the snaking pontoon bridge in front of *Posto X* and secured Cossine, fanning out into the adjacent area. Paiva Couceiro then placed Lieutenant Leitão in charge of the post at Cossine and sent an emissary to the nearby kraals calling for an *indaba* on 20 July. The *indaba* was well attended by some 300 *indunas*. Paiva Couceiro informed them of Lieutenant Leitão's role which, according to him, was readily accepted. Paiva Couceiro then held an 'installation' ceremony which included the consumption of generous amounts of beer and *bagaço* brought from Manyissa.

The house of the former resident in Cossine district at Magude was converted into a defensive redoubt. It boasted a high earthwork parapet surrounded by a four-metre wide ditch that had become overgrown and partially filled with vegetation; the ditch was cleared out and redug to a depth of three metres. Earth was piled up behind the ditch to form a high and thick parapet that was protected by three lines of barbed wire. A bridge over the ditch led to the entrance to the redoubt, which was surrounded by a high, thick wooden palisade. Within the stockaded post there was a substantial tin-roofed wooden building. Sleeping quarters were constructed and even an oven to bake bread was installed. Later, a more solid building of stone was built under the supervision of Lieutenant Tavares Leote. The post was defended by two machine guns with some 6,000 rounds of ammunition; 200 soldiers were tasked to garrison it. Once it was completed, all the troops manning *Posto X* were transferred to the new post at Cossine, and the old one abandoned on 22 August. In Paiva Couceiro's opinion, the well-defended post was almost impregnable as the devil himself let alone Gungunyana would not be able to take it!

In a letter to Ennes, written on 28 July in Chicomo, a furious Almeida referred to Ennes' guarantee that Portuguese forces would not cross the Nkomati until negotiations were completed, and requested the Royal-Commissioner to order the troops' withdrawal. The news of the Portuguese advance had been reported to Gungunyana and from then on Almeida's negotiations became ever more fraught.

On 15 August negotiations with Gungunyana finally broke down. On 16 August Ennes sent a message to Galhardo telling him that Gungunyana's conditions were unacceptable and that Galhardo was at liberty to begin offensive operations against Gungunyana. At the same time, Ennes ordered the Southern Column to continue its advance towards Magul. On 13 September a rider appeared at Reuben Point with a sealed letter from Major Gomes Pereira of the Southern Column; it had just arrived by British steamer. He nervously ripped it open and read that a battle had taken place at Magul; 275 Portuguese troops had faced some 6,000 warriors from the Magaia, Zishasha, Cossine, and Bilene clans. The Portuguese victory had cost five dead with 27 wounded.

On 8 September on Magul Plain, a powerful impi confronted the Southern Column led by Major Gomes Pereira. The Southern Column had crossed the Inkoluwane and slowly advanced in square order. The six cavalrymen under command of Paiva Couceiro were reconnoitring the flanks ahead of the square while the African auxiliaries covered its front with 50 to 100 metres distance between them. The Portuguese were met by a truly disheartening panorama: the ground to the left was monotonously flat and reed covered with foul smelling swamplands stretching out into the shimmering distance. The column followed a narrow sandy track where twisted trees gave occasional shade; there were no kraals, not even any scattered huts and absolutely no sign of life. The sweating Portuguese and their auxiliaries trekked on by tall, rock-hard ant heaps covered in wispy green growth – it was a hostile and unhealthy place. As the Portuguese advanced, a long, partially wooded, sloping hill came into view whereupon Major Gomes Pereira and his officers dismounted in order to consult their maps. It was decided that the best plan would be to keep the wooded hill to the right of the line-of-march as figures had been fleetingly observed on the hill moving about in the dense bush. Meanwhile Paiva Couceiro had recklessly ridden ahead of his scouting party, after being told by Sergeant Pita, that he recognised Chief Pazmane, the brother of the chief of Cossine district. Paiva Couceiro called out to the battle chiefs and slowly cantered up the sloping hill towards them. Chief Pazmane was surprised by the sheer pluckiness of his actions and allowed him a hearing. Paiva Couceiro spoke briefly, informing the battle chiefs that they had three days to hand over the rebellious chiefs. He then turned his horse's head and slowly cantered back to Major Gomes Pereira and the main force.

The Portuguese immediately began to withdraw across the Inkoluwane and bivouacked at Shinavane to wait the agreed three days. No answer was forthcoming. On 7 September, the soldiers were roused well before dawn to eat their cold rations before crossing Krusse Gomes' 197-metre long, pontoon bridge. Bluejackets from the *Lacerda* were tasked to transport the force over the river. The crossing took six hours to complete and the troops were safely on the opposite bank by early afternoon. The Portuguese halted three kilometres beyond the riverbank among high reeds by swampy ground. Muddy trenches were dug and earthworks quickly thrown up before darkness descended on the bivouacked column. Sentries were posted and rations – cold beans – were distributed. As there was no moon that night the troops bedded down in square formation. Next morning the column advanced in the same formation with the machine guns at the corners, bearers in the centre and Angolan troops on the flanks, while the six cavalrymen reconnoitred the track ahead.

The heat became almost unbearable as the soldiers laboured under their heavy packs and ammunition. After three hours, the flat, sandy terrain gradually gave way to dense bush. The ground again became boggy, with stagnant pools making the going extremely arduous. At 10:30 in the morning impis were seen some one and a half kilometres away moving in skirmishing order through the greeny-brown bush. The Portuguese column, which had become ragged and disjointed, swiftly moved back into formation as the Angolan infantrymen hurriedly ran barbed wire out in front of the square. The Angolans were ordered forward to draw enemy fire but the impis appeared reluctant to join battle and kept well out of range, moving into the swaying elephant grass. The Angolans advanced and fired on the enemy some 1500 metres away. It was a great relief to be engaged at last with the powerful impis; even though the Angolans' volley did little damage, it had the effect of steadying the Portuguese troops. As the smoke began to clear the Angolans withdrew into the relative safety of the square. The officers searched the elephant grass with their binoculars and counted thirteen impis that they estimated to number 6,000 warriors. The enemy was seen moving to the left flank of the Portuguese square in familiar 'horn' formation cutting off any possible retreat to the Inkoluwane River. The massed impis then immediately sat down. Meanwhile, deep in the rear, Gungunyana's regiments also silently watched and waited. Early in the afternoon Zishasha's warriors began to crawl forward over the broken ground. Before opening up on the attackers with his machine gun section, Lieutenant Eduardo Miranda looked at his timepiece – it was 1:20. The steady hammering of the machine gun was followed by ragged rifle fire from the square. The chanting regiments leapt up and repeatedly hurled themselves against the wavering Portuguese square, advancing to within 60 metres of it. Shells whistled over the Portuguese to explode among the packed, attacking impis. Sergeant Craveiro, who had climbed on top of an ammunition box to better his aim, fell dead, shot through the neck. A number of riflemen threw themselves down and began to fire, only to be dragged to their feet by Miranda and Paiva Couceiro. At that moment, Paiva Couceiro felt a stinging blow close to his left eye. Some soldiers distributing ammunition saw him stagger and clutch at his face and the cry went up 'the captain's done for!' Paiva Couceiro's large moustache was dripping with blood from the gash below his eye, but his vision was not impaired, and he continued to rally his men. The air was so thick with smoke from the field guns and rifles that the cornet was ordered to sound the ceasefire; it was impossible to make out the enemy. When the smoke had cleared sufficiently, the Portuguese repeated their deadly volley fire. The cornet sounded the ceasefire for a second time, and at that critical moment, Lieutenant Miranda reported two of the machine guns out of action. The lieutenant then tried unsuccessfully to clear one of the jammed guns. A soldier, who had been waiting to hand him ammunition, was hit and fell on to the machine gun, sending it crashing to the ground. Images of dark shapes and cries of pain came through the swirling smoke of the battlefield. After half an hour of renewed, fierce fighting and with the sun high and white hot, the battle Chief T'hope, loudly and impressively rallied his warriors for one last frenzied onslaught. The chief was hurled on to his back in a hail of machine gun fire and lay with his arms outstretched in a pool of blood close to the Portuguese square. An hour later the battle was over. The incredibly brave but severely dispirited impis turned and fled the battlefield leaving over 300 dead behind them.

Finally, on 4 November, Colonel Galhardo's Northern Column was ready to go on to the offensive. It comprised 577 Portuguese infantry and artillery with Angolan infantry; a field ambulance brigade of 38 wagons, commanded by naval surgeon Rodrigues Braga, assisted by a civilian, doctor Monterroso. The column's total strength was 785 officers and men. The column had rafted the Chicomo River and advanced towards Manhlagazi, the battle kraal of Chief Gungunyana. Even at this late stage, Galhardo carried orders from Ennes to negotiate with Gungunyana's *indunas*, which he tried to do, without success.

On the morning of 7 November, Galhardo was told by Dr Monterroso, that two officers and nineteen men were already too sick to walk; they had collapsed from heat exhaustion during the previous day's hellish trek through sandy scrubland under a broiling sun.

In the malarial waste of Coolela Flats, some twelve kilometres from Gungunyana's kraal, scouts reported sighting hordes of warriors moving in their direction. Colonel Galhardo tuned his mount and cantered into the centre of the rapidly forming Portuguese square to calmly await the attack. Eight regiments, with the king's lieutenant, M'shamene, at their head advanced towards the Portuguese at a swinging trot, oxhide shields and *mathlari* at the ready. Though the corners of the square were covered by artillery fire, the flanks were thinly defended by soldiers sheltering behind Boer wagons, and took the full force of the initial attack. The field guns recoiled in clouds of smoke, while the infantry held their fire and nervously awaited their officers' word of command. The tall, mounted figure of Major Machado, of 3 Light Infantry, was one of the first to be toppled as a bullet shattered his left arm. Captain Raul da Costa was hit in the right thigh as he bent down to assist a wounded infantryman, and though bleeding heavily, was able to drag himself to the ambulance wagon, where the doctor was busy patching up Second Lieutenant Costa e Silva's right shoulder. It was a difficult moment for the young and largely untested troops. Above the din of the impi war chants, the colonel calmly issued commands to his officers, as a fusillade of ragged fire erupted from the Portuguese square. Officers and senior ranks quickly calmed their men and the Portuguese rate of fire increased and steadied; the square held firm. The attackers fled the bloodied battlefield leaving the Portuguese in control.

As evening painted the sky, acrid smoke floated over the fetid waters of Coolela Flats. Startled flamingos rose and swiftly winged away to their evening nesting places through vast swarms of mosquitoes. Portuguese artillery and rifle fire ceased. The impis had fought ferociously and had doggedly advanced to within 30 metres of the square, but were no match for the 75mm French artillery pieces, British made Snider and Austro-Hungarian Kropatschek rifles. Five soldiers were killed, and three officers and 33 soldiers were wounded. More than 100 warriors were buried in a hastily dug mass grave, and many more bodies were later found in the bush decomposing and jackal ravished under the harsh, unforgiving African sun. The wounded, many suffering from the hideous effects of artillery fire, were dragged away to the brief safety of nearby villages. For Ennes, the victory was marred by Galhardo's unwillingness to move on Mahnlagazi before ensuring the safety of his wounded officers and soldiers. As the column was only seven kilometres from Manhlagazi, Ennes was critical of Galhardo's lack of foresight. He felt that the column commander should have had contingency plans in place for dealing with the question of the treatment and transport of the wounded. On 11 November Galhardo began his advance on Manhlagazi from his position close to the Mangwanyana River. The column met limited resistance from the *Zinyone M'Shope* impi, which had been sent into battle in order to give Gungunyana time to escape towards Makosi, between the Shangane and Limpopo rivers. After dispersing the enemy, the deserted royal kraal was bombarded and burned to the ground by the column. The Portuguese now controlled all of Gazaland between the Limpopo, the Shangane and Sabi rivers. After the battle, in recognition of his battalion's actions at Coolela, General Galhardo presented the wounded Major António Júlio de Sousa Machado, commanding officer of 3 Expeditionary Battalion, Light Infantry, with a captured British-made Martini-Henry rifle and a bandoleer containing two rounds. The block-action, breech-loading Martini-Henry was a robust and easy weapon to use, it had often been issued to the colony's local troops and auxiliaries but many had been bought by Gungunyana from the unscrupulous and aptly named 'smoke traders.'

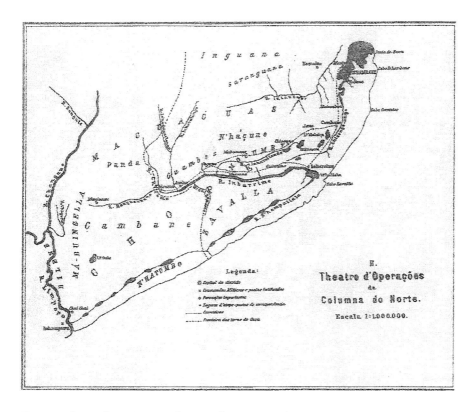

Operational Map of Nothern Column Mozambique 1895 (Edições Gama)

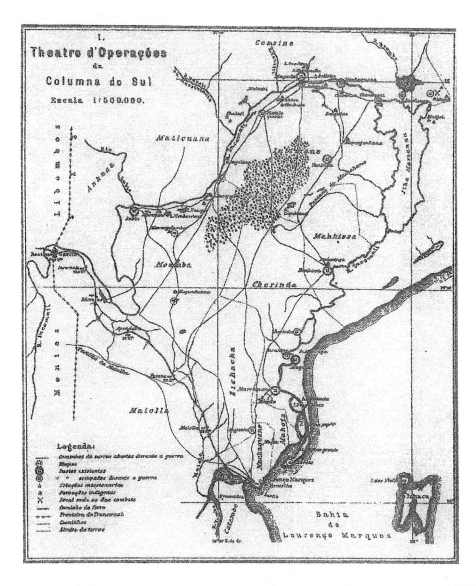

Operational Map of Southern Column Mozambique 1895
(Edições Gama)

Chapter 9
Mopping up in Gazaland

King Gungunyana was no longer unconquerable in the eyes of his people. His power to resist the Portuguese was in decline and a month later on 27 December 1895, in the teeth of a violent thunderstorm, he was captured with his *indunas* Manyune and Keto, at his royal kraal in the imperial city of Chaimite. A flying column of 48 men under command of Captain Mousinho de Albuquerque, with artillery Lieutenant Aníbal Augusto Sanches de Sousa Miranda, Lieutenant José da Costa Couto and medical officer Francisco Maria do Amaral, had boldly set out to invest his kraal. Mousinho de Albuquerque entered Gungunyana's enclosure and loudly called out the chief's name. After what seemed an eternity, the chief appeared from inside his hut and faced the Portuguese officer. Mousinho de Albuquerque ordered two of his men to tie the chief's hands behind his back, and then force him to sit down on the ground as a sign of submission. The 300 warriors who watched the scene began to cheer at the sight of the beaten war chief. Manyune and Keto, two implacable but fiercely proud enemies were immediately shot.

Gungunyana's capture, and subsequent lifelong exile and imprisonment, in Angra Castle in the Azores, ended the first large-scale insurrection against Portuguese authority in Gazaland. On 24 January 1896, Ennes received a letter of appreciation for his work in Mozambique from Dom Carlos I, who awarded him the Grand Cross of the Order of the Torre Espada. In that same year, António Ennes was named Portuguese minister at Rio de Janeiro – he would never return to Mozambique.

Mousinho de Albuquerque was made governor-general of Mozambique in March after António Ennes' return to Portugal. But Mousinho was given little time to rest on his laurels. It had come to the notice of the authorities in Lourenço Marques, that the chief of the Namarral region in Moçambique District, between the Ligonya River and the Lurio River, would only permit Portuguese traders to journey through his lands upon the payment of a heavy toll, and close to Infusse, the local chief of Kivolane, was heavily involved in the slave trade, in spite of Lourenço Marques' attempts to suppress that inhuman practice. Eight years earlier in 1888, Portuguese forces had been sent against the war-like Namarral clan. The region was occupied and the chief's kraal razed to the ground. However, the Portuguese were once more unable to capitalise on their success and were obliged to withdraw, allowing the Namarral to reoccupy their lands. The governor-general needed firm bases to operate from if he intended to achieve lasting success against the Namarral. After careful planning, he divided the region into three military districts. In the Northern District a military post under command of an officer in the rank of captain was to be set up at Fernão Veloso, with a post at Mossuril in the Central District, and at Angoche in the Southern District. He concentrated his force at Natule, and on 19 October, with Lieutenant Aires de Ornelas as second in command, began the advance towards Naguema. A great problem for Mousinho de Albuquerque was the complete lack of accurate maps of the region. In spite of the Portuguese having been in Mozambique since 1505, little of the colony had been accurately charted.

The Portuguese command had to resort to the use of African guides who led the exhausted force into a trap at Mujenga. The enemy had set an ambush for the Portuguese column, which hardly had time to form a square. The Mujenga battle, over two days on 19 and 20 October, was fierce and continued for almost twenty hours. The Portuguese began to run short of ammunition and were almost out of water. It was then that the desperate Mousinho de Albuquerque noted that the Namarral had hacked down all the drooping, succulent, pale yellow cashew nut pods from the thick trees close to the track, in order to deny them to the thirsty soldiers. Mousinho de Albuquerque was forced to make a fighting withdrawal with the warriors harrying the Portuguese all the way back to Natule. A number of Portuguese soldiers were so exhausted that they begged to be left to die in the jungle, but their pleas were ignored and their comrades carried them back to safety. The Portuguese had been frustrated by the Namarral's refusal to take them on in the open. Instead, the Namarral repeatedly sniped at them from the cover of thick bush, a tactic that had caused the column heavy casualties. The campaign in the Namarral region was seriously affected by the Portuguese setback and it became necessary to regroup and organise fresh troops, and to make matters worse, both Mousinho and Aires de Ornelas had been wounded during the withdrawal.

In order to deal with the worsening situation, the governor-general, while recovering from his wounds in the military hospital at Lourenço Marques, requested reinforcements from Lisbon. Captain Eduardo Costa, was given command of the expeditionary force plus a company of Mozambican troops, and a naval detachment, under command of Lieutenant João de Azevedo Coutinho. During the field force's initial advance inland, Costa's soldiers had been surprised not to meet with any resistance. The column pushed on to Naguema kraal close to Mossuril, but they found it eerily deserted yet Portuguese scouts had reported seeing many Namarral warriors in the area. The Portuguese dug in close to the abandoned village at Naguema and sent out further scouting parties who reported seeing Namarral activity. Next morning, a large group of warriors advanced on the Portuguese entrenchments but retreated into the bush in the face of accurate rifle fire. The Portuguese followed up their initial success and routed Chief Matulo's warriors at Ibraimo, not far from the port of Moçambique, and then at Calaputi. The victory was marred by Costa's withdrawal due to wounds he received while at the head of his column.

Meanwhile, the recently recovered Mousinho de Albuquerque defeated Chief Marave, in a bloody battle which effectively preventing him going to the aid of the Namarral. During the Namarral campaign, the key operation was the defence of *Forte Muchelia* on the north bank of Mocambo Bay. An estimated 3,000 warriors repeatedly attacked the fort but were repulsed by a strong Portuguese column. Yet again the victorious Portuguese were forced to withdraw; the column retired on Lourenço Marques due to international tensions between Britain and the Transvaal Republic.

A year later in 1897 trouble was again brewing for Mousinho de Albuquerque. Mugundwana of the Moamba clan, had been one of Gungunyana's chiefs at the battle of Magul, and had survived the 1895 campaign, escaping capture by the Portuguese. As the leader of the renewed rebellion, he was determined to avenge that defeat. Mugundwana had ravaged the Bilene region and his followers had ambushed and murdered Second Lieutenant Chamusca and eight soldiers as they left their military post at Palule. The chief's aggressive actions provoked a rapid response from Mousinho de Albuquerque. He ordered Captain Gomes da Costa, at that time governor of Gaza District, with Aires de Ornelas as second-in-command, to suppress the revolt. Gomes da Costa left Shibuto on the Limpopo River, 193 kilometres north of the capital, and led a fighting column composed of 52 horsemen, and 93 soldiers of West African Light Infantry. At Macontene, between 5,000 and 7,000 warriors armed with *mathlari* and Martini-Henry rifles launched an attack against Gomes da Costa's force. The column formed a defensive square, and held fire until the impis were 400 metres from it, before opening up on the attackers. As Mugundwana's impis wavered, the Portuguese square suddenly broke, and Mousinho de Albuquerque, sabre at the port, thundered out from its centre at the head of his cavalry troop. The unexpected counter-attack caught the warriors by surprise; many fell under the flying hooves or were dispatched by cavalry sabres. Mugundwana's resistance was broken. The chief escaped on horseback towards Palule, surrounded by his bodyguards and then, as the Portuguese flying column neared, leapt from his mount and was swallowed up in the heavily thorned Mapulangwene bush. Mugundwana was spotted and followed into the bush, where he was fleetingly seen by interpreter João Massablano, who loosed off a number of rounds in his direction. The chief collapsed, wounded in both legs. Pedro, a Native Policeman, had quickly dismounted and worked his way through the bush towards the sound of firing. Suddenly, he came upon Mugundwana from behind, and quickly plunged his lance into the chief's back. Mousinho de Albuquerque ordered the dead chief's head to be cut off and taken to Mangude where it was temporarily preserved in alcohol. Mousinho de Albuquerque then ordered Mugundwana's former allies to gather at Canja, where they were to be shown the severed head as irrefutable proof of Mugundwana's death. With that gruesome act, Mousinho de Albuquerque had finally secured Gazaland for the Portuguese crown.

In 1899, the Portuguese began to plan for military operations in the neglected, far northern Niassa District of Mozambique. In that same year, Lieutenant Eduardo Prieto Valadim with Second Lieutenant Manuel Tomás de Almeida was passing through heavily wooded-country in the fiefdom of the Sultan of Mataka, leading a small expedition of 50 auxiliaries towards the banks of Lake Nyasa, when the column was ambushed. During the fighting, the Portuguese-led force was quickly overwhelmed - the two Portuguese officers were killed and the African auxiliaries captured. The Sultan of Mataka's triumphant warriors dragged the bodies of Valadim and Almeida, back to their sultan's *boma*. The sultan was delighted with his warriors' work and after examining the bodies, ordered the officers' heads to be cut off. Then, Valadim's skull was boiled, cleaned, and used from that time on, as a vessel for drinking *pombe* – beer. The feet and hands of de Almeida were severed and cooked, and then eaten by the sultan himself. The captured African auxiliaries, in the service of the Portuguese, were not killed but sold into slavery.

The Sultan of Mataka's writ ran across almost the whole of an enormous region stretching south from the Rovuma River border with German East Africa, covering Lugenda, Luchilingo and east to the Luamba Luambeze River. Ten years after the deaths of Valadim and de Almeida, the sultan's iron grip was eventually broken. A column commanded by Major Manuel de Sousa Machado moving through the Shire to Chilomo, entered Mataka's lands. The sultan was warned of the Portuguese column's presence and fled his *boma* rather than stand and fight. The few settlements in Niassa District, that refused to submit to Portuguese control, were burned to the ground. Portuguese army engineers, with infantry protection, were ordered to build a fort on Lake Amaramba, close to the border with British Nyasaland. In the northern region, military campaigns against those clans who refused to accept Lisbon's rule, continued during the early years of the new century and it was not until 1903 that military anti-slavery operations were successfully carried out against Sultan Karropo-Memo at Matadama and Saleie.

Chapter 10
Angola – The Coming Storm

Until the last decade of the nineteenth century, much of southern Angola remained unexplored by the Portuguese. The region encompassed an area running east of the Kunene River, limited in the west by the Kubango River. In the south was German South West Africa and to the north the Chitanda River, a confluent of the Kunene. The occupation of the Gambos region and Humbe between 1856 and 1859 brought Portuguese settlers and missionaries to the borders of Kwanyamaland. It coincided with the time when the Kwanyama clans had begun to appear as far north as southern Benguela; warlike impis commanded by mounted battle chiefs, were to leave terror, death and destruction in their bloody wake.

In this vast region of Angola, an area covering some 563,000 square kilometres, at the very limit of Portuguese control, lived the Ova-kua-nyama: the meat-gorgers. Wejulu new paramount chief of Kwanyamaland sensed his dog's excitement; the smell of water impregnated the air. With a wave of his arm Wejulu ordered his bodyguards to stand firm. The silent Kwanyamas placed their tan and grey ox hide shields on the sun baked earth and stood motionless to await further commands. With a yell born of youthful exuberance Wejulu rushed forward, his feet inured to pain, hammered against the rock-strewn path. He began to sweat. Spittle flecked his lips as he took the final incline. His tendons ached as he breasted the crest. There before him in all its terrifying magic ran the moaning waters of the swirling Kunene River; its banks lined with lush shade-giving vegetation, smelling richly of fertility and life. For Wejulu it was the lion of experiences.

His first memories were those when his uncle, paramount chief Namhadi, had taken him hand in hand down to the banks of the Kunene, to silently watch the rippling waters. Some evil glance, some squirming, slithering thing of the night, had caused Namhadi to topple from his sheepskin covered, iron stool, in a swoon like some young kraal maiden. They had waited, the men in silence, the women wailing and beating themselves, until finally, Namhadi's death was confirmed. There was much blood letting among the Kwanyama people. A huge grave was fashioned deep in the red earth of the dung-covered royal cattle kraal and the steaming hide of a freshly slaughtered black ox was laid within it. A handsome, female slave was then forcibly seated on the still warm hide, and Namhadi's withered corpse was placed in the young woman's lap; the king and the slave girl were swiftly wrapped in the hide and the grave was quickly filled in. Namhadi's wives and trusted *sekulos* were strangled, to give him company and service in the afterlife; the slaughter was fearful. But now the wailing and the ceremonial breaking of necks were only memories carried away by the winds, which sprang up on the thickly-reeded banks of the Kunene. Now Wejulu was paramount chief and lord and master of Kwanyamaland. His instinct was to run on down through that thick vegetation, to feel the sand, turn first damp, then to mud beneath his feet, then leap headlong into the snaking waters; yet he dared not. Wejulu feared no man but greatly feared the spirits of his ancestors. Dire warnings, passed from generation to generation, prevented him from entering those moaning waters. There was something malignant, something too frightening, even for the imagination to contemplate, that lurked deep beneath the Kunene's shining surface. To enter the river would be to surrender body and soul, to become a grinning hyena or jackal of the night. Wejulu recoiled at the thought. He stepped back, lost his footing and rolled down the crest to where his bodyguards swiftly helped him to his feet. Twenty-two-year-old Wejulu possessed a massive frame and powerful, muscular arms and legs. He was a handsome man with sharp eyes and a quizzically mobile mouth. He was ambitious too and had schemed of leading his mounted impis over the lands of neighbouring Kwamato and Evale. His warriors would be an unstoppable force sweeping all before them, including the unwelcome Europeans.

In late May of 1885, the South African trader and hunter, William Worthington Jordan, the son of an English father and a Cape Coloured mother, outspanned his ox wagon close to the wooden stockaded royal kraal of Chief Namhadi. He had come to seek trading rights from the Kwanyama ruler, and his ability to speak to them in their own language, made him a not unwelcome guest at the king's *olupale*. Having enjoyed the king's hospitality, drinking freshly brewed *omalodu* from beer gourds, carried to him by young girls, wearing their familiar, wide, red-stained ox-leather belts – *omuya* - Jordan concluded his negotiations and set off south towards the Kunene River. It was shortly after Jordan's departure that Namhadi became seriously ill. Inevitably, his mysterious death was blamed on the absent Jordan, who had now forded the Kunene River and was heading towards Grootfontein in German South West Africa, far out of harm's way.

In the absence of Jordan, Chief Wejulu's attention now focused on the European missionaries who, it was said, had held Namhadi under their evil spell and had contrived in his death by poisoning. The Europeans were soon to grieve as Wejulu and his people had grieved for Namhadi.

The new king spoke to his youngest battle-hardened warriors, and on 6 June 1885, sent them to destroy the European witches at the *São Miguel* mission station at Kauva. The warriors had fallen on the missionaries and exacted Wejulu's blood price; twenty Africans and Europeans were murdered in cold blood. Among them was 30-year-old Father Isidore Delpuech who was repeatedly stabbed, and 27-year-old Lucius Rothan, who was shot to death.

The trader, William Leball, was at work in his store checking over his supply of storm lanterns with his daughter, while the two younger children played outside with their dog close to the stoep. He heard shouting and then the sound of running feet coming from the nearby mission building. Looking out into the bright light from the semi-darkness of the store counter, he heard an ear-splitting shriek, and watched in horror as his two children fell under the swift, frenzied stabbing motions of the Kwanyamas' spears. His momentary paralysis over, he covered his daughter's mouth with his hand to stop her screams and dragged her away from the counter, and through the store to the back door. Father and daughter ran and stumbled into a grove of massive kiaat trees where they hid until nightfall, shaking from fear, their arms and faces bloodied by thorns. Trader Leball's only weapon was a Webley revolver which he had had the presence of mind to pick up before dragging his daughter out of the store, but there were only the six rounds in the chamber. Smoke from the burning mission and the trader's store drifted into the thorn bush; Leball realised his only hope of survival, was to make for the safety of the Portuguese fort at Humbe, under the cover of darkness. That night, tightly holding his daughter's hand, he struck out north for *Forte Humbe*. When the pair staggered exhausted and terrified into the Humbe settlement, Leball had just two rounds left in the chamber of his revolver; one for his daughter and the last bullet for himself. The haggard face and bloodshot eyes of the father and the sallow expressionless stare of his fear-stricken daughter were enough to throw the small Portuguese settlement into uncontrollable panic.

Twenty-eight years earlier, in 1857 during the Nano War, the chief of the Nano clan in southern Bié had surrounded the Portuguese settlement at Huíla with close to 8,000 warriors. The small fort, defended by a mixed force of Portuguese soldiers and settlers, commanded by Captain Godinho de Melo, held out against the attackers and after a four-day stand off, Chief Nano withdrew his warriors. As a consequence of Chief Nano's actions, the Portuguese occupied the Gambos region in the following year. After this small success, the Humbe region was occupied in August 1859 and a military post was built close to the chieftain's kraal. In 1860 the fort at Huíla was again surrounded. The warriors first drove out the African and European settlers, and then set up their camp facing the beleaguered Portuguese fort, from where they taunted and insulted its defenders. The fort's commander, Major Tomás Silveira, led a doomed sortie against Nano's warriors but all were cut down, and even though the remaining defenders put up a stout resistance, they quickly ran out of ammunition; the two metre high walls were easily scaled, and the remaining soldiers massacred. Major Silveira had been gravely wounded leading the sortie, and was now dragged from under one of his dead soldiers and roughly manhandled by four of his captors, who stretched him out over the fort's one and only cannon and beheaded him. The entire Humpata region was sacked and Nano's warriors rapidly descended the Chela Highlands towards Mossâmedes. Such was the unpreparedness and state of panic in Mossâmedes that Portuguese colonists had to seek refuge on ships standing out in its wide bay.

In 1882 the mission and seminary of *Nossa Senhora do Humbe* was established under Father Carl Wurnenburger. Now, three years later, the newly arrived district commissioner, Lieutenant João Rogado de Oliveira Leitão, had assumed command of Humbe's small fort and its garrison of 50 soldiers. However, he had spent much of his time office-bound or out hunting the region's abundant game and had failed to maintain order in his district. Portuguese traders and colonists believed, that in their somewhat dubious dealings with their African customers and workers, they could do as they pleased, and as a last resort turn to the Portuguese military and legal presence, in the shape of Lieutenant Rogado Leitão. Manpower was always a weakness in Portuguese Africa; there were no more than 200 Portuguese in the entire region and most of those were in Mossâmedes. District Commissioner Rogado Leitão, simply did not have a sufficiently large garrison to give him the authority to deal with the exaggerated claims piled on his desk, by the apparently, morally outraged, Portuguese colonists. The arrival of Leball and his daughter now made his situation untenable. He ordered immediate preparations for withdrawal from Humbe and telegraphed a message for help to the governor-general at Luanda, 965 kilometres distant.

Francisco Joaquim Ferreira do Amaral's overseas career had begun as military governor of Mossâmedes in 1882. His administrative talents came to the fore, however, his combative style was not to everyone's liking, and he was eventually removed from his post. Upon his return to Portugal, he put up a spirited defence of his actions and as a consequence, at the age of 38 was named governor-general of Angola. Ferreira do Amaral immediately ordered a column to prepare to relieve Humbe and ordered the *Forte Humbe* garrison to remain and await the column. There were inumerable delays but the force finally set out for Humbe on 31 October 1885, led by Captain Pedro Augusto Chaves. The column was composed of 100 troops from 4 Portuguese Light Infantry Regiment, under command of José da Costa Alemão Coimbra, six gunners, 200 irregulars and supply and ammunition wagons. The Gambos chief, known to the Portuguese as *Cabeça Grande*, and his warriors, now threatened the settlement. Such was the dearth of troops available, that the district governor of Mossâmedes, Guilherme Gomes Coelho, was obliged to order the skipper and crew of the gunboat *Zaire*, to assume responsibility for the policing of Mossâmedes, in the absence of the Humbe bound troops. The European townspeople of Mossâmedes, once again began to fear for their security, in the coastal outpost at the very edge of the desert. Peter Möller, the Swedish big game hunter and explorer, who was to visit Mossâmedes eleven years later in 1896, described it as a small port with some hundred or so European inhabitants and roughly the same number of Africans. It functioned as the sole entry point for vital shipments to the Portuguese settlements on the Huíla Highlands.

Meanwhile, *Cabeça Grande*'s warriors launched an attack against *Forte Humbe* and its garrison of 50 troops, but the Portuguese defenders were able to hold out, and when the chief's spies warned him of Captain Chaves' approaching column, he withdrew back to the Gambos.

Fortaleza dos Gambos (interior) — 1897

Gambos Fort (Império)

Chapter 11
Artur de Paiva Confronts the Kwanyama Threat

After Namhadi's death in 1885 the threat of a bloody, northward advance by Wejulu and his mounted Kwanyamas became a reality; it would have to be checked, otherwise the Portuguese would lose control of the region. Portuguese military headquarters, in far off Luanda, tasked Artur de Paiva with that mission. De Paiva was born in Leiria on the Liz River in Portugal, yet he had a deep knowledge of soldiering in Angola. His father, a former army officer, had wanted his son to follow a career in business, but his seventeenth birthday in 1874, found him already in Angola, serving as a private with 3 Light Infantry Regiment. Within a year he had been under fire in a number of border skirmishes and at the age of 25 was commissioned as a second lieutenant into 4 Light Infantry Regiment. Two years later, he was appointed district commissioner for the Boer settlement at São Januário de Humpata, on the 2,350 metre high plain, 128 kilometres west of Mossâmedes. The vast, high plain, which became de Paiva's home, stretches south and east towards the Kunene River, and in the west, runs towards the Chela Mountain range. In the southern Humbe region, there were sparse European settlements, clinging to the fertile banks of the Kunene River. However, the central area was the most favoured by the Portuguese, who had built forts and trading posts at Chibia, Humpata, and Lubango. At Huíla Father José Maria Antunes e Duparquet had founded the Spiritan mission in 1882.

The first 'Thirstland' Boer column, under Commandant Jakobus Frederick Botha with Gert Alberts and P. J. van der Merve, transported 270 men, women and children across Swartboois Drift on the Kunene River into Portuguese territory. With the oxen straining at their yokes and the leaders swerving away from the sjamboks, the exhausted yet exultant Boers fired an impromptu and joyful rifle salute outside the Portuguese military post at Chitado. The ox wagon column then trekked on up into Humpata arriving there on 4 January 1881. The Portuguese authorities in Angola had promised the Boers two hectares of land per family plus freedom of religion and tax exemption for the first ten years, as an inducement to populate and stabilise the settlement. The Portuguese authorities saw the Boers as a useful barrier against the African peoples, and as a cheap way of colonising the region. The Boers set to, building small, thatched-roofed houses, with stone or mud walls and had soon created a viable settlement. In January 1883 District Commissioner de Paiva, with a handful of soldiers, and a Boer commando under Willem Venter, relieved *Forte Huíla*, which was again under threat. After a welcome lull in the fighting, he found time to marry a young and attractive Boer woman, Jaquemina Botha, the eldest daughter of the trek Boer Commandant, Jakobus Botha, now a local magistrate.

The wedding ceremony took place at the Spiritan mission at Huíla. There was to be little time to enjoy married life as Artur de Paiva was suddenly recalled to Mossâmedes. Disgruntled Portuguese colonists and traders had complained to the Portuguese authorities that de Paiva had been favouring the newcomers over his own people. Fortunately for the Portuguese and the Boers, the accusations were found to be baseless and he was quickly re-instated. On 5 April 1884, 42 newly arrived Madeiran colonists from Funchal were sent to Humpata, under the care of the French missionary, Father Ernest Lecomte, in order to swell the settlement's Portuguese inhabitants.

One of the most important campaigns of the period in Angola was to take place in the eastern Kubango region. When the Conference of Berlin was convened, Lisbon had prepared a military expedition to the Kubango, with the aim of establishing a line of military posts, in order to limit the depredations of the warring Kwanyama. On 15 February 1886 the district governor, Colonel Sebastião Nunes da Mata, gave de Paiva overall command of a small expedition tasked to occupy the Nganguelas region, and establish a post on the right bank of the Kubango River. Jaquemina, de Paiva's strong-willed Boer wife, who had been born and brought up on the veld, flatly refused to be left at home with their three-year-old son, so in spite of his entreaties and dire warnings about expeditionary life, Artur was forced to give in.

The Kubango Column was composed of three Portuguese officers; de Paiva; Captain Augusto de Sousa and Lieutenant Miguel Duarte de Almeida, with 82 African soldiers, and a fifteen strong Boer commando from Humpata. The eleven-wagon column left Huíla to a thirteen-gun salute on Easter Saturday 24 April 1886. Artur de Paiva was at the head of the column with his wife and child, in a two-wheeled cart pulled by a donkey. Within sight of the settlement, one of the wagons strayed off the track and hit a large rock breaking its wheel. Shortly after, one of the Humpata bearers slipped and fell under the wheels of a bouncing wagon and was very gravely injured. After a third wagon had careered towards a precipice and luckily lodged in the thick, drooping branches of an ancient fig tree, de Paiva decided it was time to halt and laager his wagons, treat his seriously injured bearer and repair the damaged wheels. Early the following morning, after burying the African bearer, the column trekked in a south-easterly direction towards the Kakulovar River, which they forded on 4 May. Although the river was low at that time of the year, it proved difficult to get the heavy wagons across its sandy bed. As gemsbok and kudu were plentiful, de Paiva decided to stock up on meat and hunted there until 11 May. Soon, the expedition was to be down to half its strength due to malarial fevers and the ever-present danger of dysentery. The wives of de Paiva and Duarte de Almeida, although ill themselves, ministered to the sick as best they could, but were powerless to save the life of a young child who perished from dysentery.

The fever-wracked column rumbled across the veld, and on 27 May scouts sent out to forage for food and water reported that the Kalungo River was less than an hour away. After fording the river and replenishing their water supplies as best they could, de Paiva's scouts warned the wagoners to beware; the ground ahead was pockmarked with deep holes that had been dug to capture the region's abundant game. In one of the holes, de Paiva came across an enormous, starving, writhing crocodile. He dispatched it with a shot to the head; neither African nor European cared to linger. Later that day disaster struck the column; one of the Boer wagons, whose fever-stricken driver had fainted, toppled over into a hole followed by one of the oxen; it took precious hours to extricate the wagon. The land ahead now began to slope sharply, giving the column the hope that fresh water might not be far off. And sure enough, away in the distance, in a southerly direction, the column could make out the silver, snaking, Kunene River. De Paiva's guides told him that further north was the Luceke post, commanded by Captain Matias Rodrigues da Costa. Acting upon that intelligence, de Paiva sent a rider with a message inviting the captain to join his column on their eastward trek. Captain da Costa was not only a firm friend of de Paiva's but was a gifted linguist, with an excellent knowledge of the clans living between the Kubango and Kunene; his presence would be an asset to the expedition.

The riverbanks were covered in thick wait-a-bit thorn bush, and de Paiva's soldiers were given the unenviable task of cutting a path through them; it was nightfall before the column finally forded the Kunene. The wagons were laagered and sentries posted. The exhausted column was soon fast asleep, in spite of the roaring of lions in the bush close to the river. The following day they set off keeping close to the riverbank searching for signs of its confluence with the Kubangui. Sharp eyes were needed due to the presence of wallowing hippopotami, and the even more dangerous, mud caked crocodiles, basking on the riverbank. The column came upon a section of the bank, which was almost free of thorn bush and where a multitude of spoors denoted a favoured watering place. De Paiva told off a party of his men to replenish the column's water supplies while he and his fellow officers, carbines at the ready, kept a sharp lookout for crocodiles. From then on the march became a nightmare; the thick, tangled umbrella thorn bush had to be hacked down branch by branch in order for the column to make any headway. The Kubangui was finally reached, and forded on 18 June, and then the wagons turned in a north-easterly direction, following the right bank of the river. On 28 June, the exhausted column came up with the chief of the Nganguelas' kraal at Dongo. Chief Kitokulo had already been warned of the Portuguese column's arrival in his lands, and fearing an armed confrontation, would have flown with his wives and *indunas*, had he not recognised Captain Rodrigues da Costa. An *indaba* followed under a marula tree and de Paiva was asked by the chief's son to build a fort on his lands, which he readily agreed to do. As was customary, de Paiva presented the old chief with a blue and white Portuguese flag, which was soon hoisted on a pole over the entrance to his kraal. The column's sick took full advantage of the rest, and the cooler air appeared to have a positive effect on the entire expedition. While at Kitokulo's kraal, de Paiva was visited by Father Lecomte, who had ridden from Cassinga in order to meet the Portuguese column. The two men were delighted to see each other and talked long into the night about de Paiva's dream of building a railway from Mossâmedes or Benguela to the Kubango region; it would open it up for development and stall any attempts by Britain or Germany to annex the region.

At the kraal, de Paiva's guides reported that rumours had begun to circulate of a possible attack against the column. Many of the chiefs in the Kubango region were resentful of the Europeans and simply wished to be left alone to live as they had done for centuries. The rumours were not baseless; de Paiva received intelligence that Second Lieutenant Simpliciano de Almeida, who had set off for the column had lost most of his Angolan troops, who had deserted rather than cross the Kunene River. De Paiva gave orders for the expedition to advance in column with the wagons ready to be laagered at any moment, in case of attack. The column forded the Chitanda River and came up with the kraal of *Soba* Chikarapira, who told a relieved and delighted de Paiva that he wished to become a subject of the Portuguese crown. The impressive, stockaded kraal was built on top of a small kopje and measured 400 metres in diameter; at its foot, the Bua River flowed away towards the Chitanda. The column was now passing through a healthier, elevated region, rich in cotton plants, cane and peanut plantations. On 14 July the column crossed the Kwanza River and laagered within sight of a tributary of the Kubango. On the following day it reached the Kubango itself, and in the distance, on the opposite bank, saw the massive kraal of Luís Shinako, one of Kitokulo's sons. The Kubango River, some 120 metres wide at this point, was crossed on 16 July, and as the column warily approached the heavily stockaded kraal, de Paiva was met by the sight of a large number of warriors who were making towards him, carrying a small, leather-seated chair and a large straw hat. Moments later, on a word of command, the warriors stepped back and Shinako dramatically appeared, slowly walking towards de Paiva and his translator. De Paiva was confronted by a tall, slim, middle-aged man, wearing a greasy straw hat and a blue jacket with white buttons, which de Paiva felt, might have long ago belonged to a London bobby.

Shinako's kraal was sited in the middle of a wide, fertile valley, surrounded by mountains with extensively cultivated slopes. Before partaking of the chief's hospitality, de Paiva ordered his wagoners to laager the transport, and his men to be vigilant, before he headed through the narrow opening into the chief's kraal. Before his friendly *indaba* with the chief, de Paiva presented him with a flagon of Portuguese *bagaço* and in return received a calabash of beer. The chief then explained that he wanted the Portuguese to build the fort on his lands. At the end of the *indaba* the Portuguese flag was raised over Chief Luís Shinako's kraal. After surveying the area, de Paiva decided on a point above the river, six kilometres from *Muene* Dilunga's kraal at Kotoko, overlooking the drift used by the thousands of bearers who regularly carried wild rubber over to Benguela. De Paiva saw the fort as the key to controlling the vast region between the Kubango and the Zambezi, and should be located in the centre of the lands of the Nganguelas, whose numbers de Paiva estimated to be 200,000 in all. *Forte Princesa Amélia*, named in honour of the Portuguese Royal Prince's French born consort, would establish Portugal's military and administrative control over the region, once and for all. The column set to digging trenches, and earth and palisade defences. The fort gradually began to take shape and was constructed in the manner of all Portuguese forts: a square with two circular bulwarks. It was completed on 9 August. Duarte de Almeida was left in command of *Forte Princesa Amélia*, with a field gun, 14 artillery rounds, a supply of Snider ball-ammunition and sufficient provisions for its garrison of 30 men. De Paiva then built a second post, *Forte Maria Pia* named after Maria Pia of Savoy, the wife of Dom Luís I and the daughter of the Italian monarch, Victor Emmanuel, at Dongo, 300 kilometres east of Humpata. The Portuguese now had a line of interconnecting forts from *Luceke* on the Kunene, *Maria Pia* on the Kubangui and *Princesa Amélia* on the Kubango.

De Paiva's column had forded the Kunene River and in doing so had caused panic and anger among Wejulu's superstitious people. The building of the forts, though apparently with the blessing of the local *sobas*, created strong suspicions among the indigenous clans that they were being hemmed in by the Europeans, prior to being expelled from their lands. This was further exacerbated by the building of a mission station close to Katoko by Father Lecomte. De Paiva was concerned to learn that a group of seventeen Kwanyama warriors had visited Chief Kitokulo's kraal. Early in the morning of 26 August, sounds of a disturbance came from the kraal and de Paiva was informed that the Kwanyama, now totalling 200 warriors, armed with Enfield rifles, had begun to attack adjacent kraals in the area. De Paiva and 22 men mounted up and went off to search for the Kwanyama. Smoking kraals greeted the small Portuguese force.

Chief Shinako of Kubango, had earlier greeted the column, flown the Portuguese flag, and proclaimed himself to be a friend of the Europeans, and not inimical to the building of a mission station. Not long after its construction, he was to lead an uprising of Kubango peoples against Portuguese authority. Father Lecomte and his workers were captured at their mission station, where the priest was severely beaten and lashed to a tree. Lecomte would have died had Chief Lhambeze not risked his own life to free him. During a surprise attack on *Forte Princesa Amélia* by Chief Shinako, its commandant, Captain Andrade, and the 50 soldiers guarding it, had been slaughtered and the fort burned to the ground.

Shortly after returning to the comparative safety of Huíla with his wife and son, and oblivious to the fact that *Forte Princesa Amélia* had been reduced to rubble, de Paiva took ship to Portugal, where as the guest speaker of the Lisbon Geography Society, he read his account of the peoples of the Kubango region and of the building of *Forte Princesa Amélia.* His theme was a popular one with the Society's members; the Portuguese fort on the Kubango would be the key to the small European nation's eastern expansion in Angola.

Three years later in 1889, in the limitless scrub lands of southern Angola, Captain de Paiva, commanding 5 Light Infantry, again led a much stronger column to the Kubango region composed of 100 Portuguese infantrymen and cavalry; 64 Boer volunteers, 112 Bushman and Damara auxiliaries, with two 8cm cannon. His task was twofold: to secure and supervise the rebuilding of the now derelict mission station at Katoko, and rebuild the nearby ruined *Forte Princesa Amélia* close to Cassinga, 80 kilometres south of Dongo.

The column reached Kipungo on 31 August where scouts from *Forte Maria Pia* told him that both the fort and the mission station at Cassinga were under threat from Chief Shinako and his 15,000 warriors. De Paiva ordered his column to move forward with all possible speed. At one point, while heading towards the Kunene, the column laagered in thick bush, while de Paiva's spies were sent off to observe a large caravan, which could clearly be seen in the far distance. They returned with the information that the caravan was made up of over 200 bearers who were carrying gunpowder to Chief Shinako. On 6 September de Paiva's column crossed the Kunene River and after an exhausting trek, reached the walls of *Forte Maria Pia* eight days later. Lieutenant Simpliciano de Almeida, who had come to reinforce the beleaguered fort, met up with de Paiva who ordered him to make a strong mounted reconnaissance of the area. De Almeida learned that Chief Shinako was busy fortifying his own kraal and those of his people and was preparing for war. On 27 September the column laagered in Chief Chikarapira's lands. The next day the Portuguese column came up with what appeared to be a deserted kraal. Scouts were sent forward and immediately a large group of warriors, armed with rifles and stabbing spears began to jog towards the startled men, yet the warriors told de Paiva's interpreter that they bore the Portuguese no ill will. The column redoubled its vigilance and continued to march towards Chief Shinako's fiefdom.

On 22 September, Axel Eriksson, the Swedish elephant hunter and explorer, joined the column, bringing with him two Boer wagons and sixteen horses. It was on 2 October that the column first made out the ruins of *Forte Princesa Amélia* in the far distance. The column laagered, while de Paiva and his officers stared across the Kubango River, towards the enormous and now threatening royal kraal of Chief Shinako. They observed a mass of warriors moving rapidly towards the riverbank where they took up positions on a sandy island; it formed the drift, which de Paiva had previously used to cross into Shinako's lands. The Portuguese were now able to observe that the chief's warriors, who began to shout insults at them, were occupying all the drifts. Artur de Paiva knew that he would need to cross the Kunene on the following day, in spite of the large number of warriors, though any approach toward the river would put the column within easy reach of the enemies' rifles. At first light, the column was ordered to advance towards the river; three platoons commanded by Lieutenant De Almeida, Second Lieutenant Amado and Sergeant Morais, made for the southern end of the island, in order to provide covering fire for the horsemen crossing the drift. The Damara levies bravely rode across and into the massed impis. Behind them followed Second Lieutenant Pereira with the artillery limber, while two platoons remained on the Portuguese side of the river to guard the wagons, the women and children.

The Damara riders had successfully beaten back Shinako's impis at the drift and began to gallop towards the royal kraal, while Pereira's men had rapidly unlimbered and opened fire on the enemy with the column's one surviving field gun. By 2:00 in the afternoon the battle was over. In order to show that he held no personal grudge against the local clans, de Paiva ordered the women and children taken prisoner by the Portuguese, to be freed. Shinako's kraal was now a smouldering, blackened ruin; however, there was no sign of the chief among the dead. De Paiva desperately needed to know of Shinako's whereabouts, if he could not capture the chief, then his mission could well end in failure, and in the annihilation of his entire column. Earlier, de Paiva had been told that Father Lecomte had been saved from certain death by the timely intervention of Chief Lhambeze, who was certainly no friend of Chief Shinako. During an *indaba* with Lhambeze and his father, Dilungo, the Portuguese commander had criticised the elderly chief for allowing himself to be led astray by Shinako, and gave him three days to find and bring the rebel leader to the Portuguese camp outside the ruins of *Forte Princesa Amélia*. Should the old chief fail de Paiva would put his villages to the sword. Three days had passed without any sign of Lhambeze, Dilungo or Shinako and de Paiva was reluctantly forced to carry out his dire threats against the elderly chief's villages. While the punitive operations were taking place, and perhaps in order to ease his conscience, de Paiva rode out to the ruined mission station at Katoko with a small escort. The mission had been completely destroyed and he was dismayed to note that even the fruit trees on the mission's small, enclosed plantation, had been hacked and burned in the frenzy of destruction.

The Portuguese had taken longer than planned in the lands bordering the Kubango. The rainy season had already begun to set in, and if the soldiers were not to fall prey to sickness, then accommodation needed to be built, or the column would have to make its way as best it could back through potentially hostile country, to its point of departure. But de Paiva was still hunting for Shinako, and in a desperate attempt to speed his capture, had begun to take hostages from the kraals devastated by his soldiers. The rains were proving a trial, as there was nowhere to securely house their hostages, yet the search went on. Day after day soaked to the skin and covered almost from head to toe in mud, riders and foot soldiers alike scoured the countryside without success. Until one day, just as de Paiva had ordered a detachment to mount up in preparation for yet another punitive raid, two figures approached through the blinding rain and in broken Portuguese brought the message that Shinako had been taken prisoner. The starving and disease-ridden hostages were set free and Chief Shinako held under armed guard. The captured chief was taken back to Huíla with the column and then down through the Chela Highlands to Mossâmedes, and like so many others, he soon found himself aboard an alien craft steaming into exile and despair.

Chapter 12
Silva Porto – The Death of a Legend

Lieutenant Paiva Couceiro had arrived in Angola in August 1889. A year later he was given special orders by the governor-general of Angola, to organise and lead an expedition to Barotseland to establish Portuguese suzerainty over the region, and build a small military post close to the kraal of the king of Barotseland at Libonta. The Lisbon government wanted to forestall any possible British claims to the region, and district-commissioner Justino Teixeira da Silva, who was stationed at Belmonte, was chosen to accompany the expedition as Portuguese ambassador to the Barotseland king – both men were sworn to secrecy.

Paiva Couceiro was immediately confronted with a problem, the Portuguese had been refused permission to pass through Chief Dunduma's lands – he claimed that he had made an agreement with the authorities that troops would never be stationed in the region. In order to clarify the situation and await the arrival of supplies and ammunition, Paiva Couceiro had gone to Belmonte, the home of the legendary Silva Porto, in the Bié region, accompanied by the Bailundo district commissioner, Teixeira da Silva.

António Francisco Ferreira da Silva was born to impoverished parents in the northern Portuguese city of Oporto in 1817. As a youngster, he had crossed the Atlantic to Brazil, where he had learned first hand about the slave trade on the colony's many coffee plantations. After ten years in Brazil, he took ship for Angola arriving at the port of Luanda, from where he trekked into the interior. It was then that the young man decided to take the name of his native city and became known as Silva Porto. After a number of years building up a farming business he turned to elephant hunting and ivory trading. By 1890 Silva Porto had more than 50 years' experience of the Angolan bush, having ridden and hunted over much of its harsh terrain. Years earlier, he had taken up residence as a trader close to the royal kraal at Ekovongo and had built a house and store within a wooden stockade, which he named Belmonte. Although the Portuguese flag flew over Belmonte, and in spite of being made an honorary assistant district-commissioner of Bié in March 1885, by Francisco Joaquim Ferreira do Amaral, his writ did not run to Chief Dunduma's imposing kraal at Ekovongo. In order to integrate with the Bién clans, he had married a chieftain's daughter. His prolonged trading contacts with the Bién had given him fluency in a number of regional languages.

Now getting on in years, he would spend most of his time seated on the stoep of his stockaded trading post talking to passing townsfolk. He was shocked to hear from an ivory hunter visiting his store to buy food-stuffs and ammunition, that his one time friend, chief Dunduma of Bié, had warned the Portuguese that he was about to expel all missionaries and traders from his lands. The chief believed the Portuguese were about to encircle the region with forts. Silva Porto decided to visit the chief's kraal in an attempt to dissuade him from what he believed would be a disastrous course of action. Silva Porto suspected that foreigners in the region, who had been actively intriguing against Portuguese authority, had influenced the chief. Though Silva Porto held honorary rank, he had not been told of Paiva Couceiro's imminent presence in Bié or of Lisbon's plans, and when questioned by Chief Dunduma, denied that the Portuguese were mounting an expedition, and returned to Belmonte in a mood of exasperation. Within a matter of days, on 21 January 1890, Dunduma's warriors reported the approach of a small column of Portuguese-led African soldiers. The angry chief gathered his warrior clans together and began to take defensive measures while threatening to deal severely with Silva Porto and any other Portuguese who might dare to cross his path.

To Silva Porto's horror and consternation, a dust caked expedition under Paiva Couceiro, marched into Belmonte with two Portuguese army sergeants and 40 African troops. After a briefing from Teixeira da Silva, and fearing an attack on Belmonte, Paiva Couceiro gathered together what forces he could. The Portuguese captain invited the trader Resquete, and Chief Jamba and his clan who had fallen foul of Dunduma, to help defend the stockade.

Word arrived at Belmonte that the expedition to Barotseland had been cancelled due to the British *Ultimatum*, and Silva Porto begged Paiva Couceiro to withdraw from Belmonte. He feared the expedition's presence would inflame the already delicate situation. Paiva Couceiro was now in receipt of a fresh set of orders; he was to march south following the route of the Kunene to establish Portuguese control over the Kubango River region, and study its navigability. In late March Silva Porto made another visit to Dunduma's kraal, where after a long *indaba*, the chief became impatient with the old man, and warned him that if he did not cease his arguing, he would grab him by his long, white beard, and even went so far as to show Silva Porto a panga, with which he threatened to chop off his head. The disconsolate, Portuguese trader and sometime slaver climbed into his wagon and wearily headed back over the rutted track to his residence at Belmonte.

Silva Porto was greatly concerned by Dunduma's attitude and feared for the safety of the two Portuguese officers and their men. He again counselled caution, and during a heated argument, the old man attempted to persuade Paiva Couceiro and Teixeira da Silva not to carry on with their mission and instead, retire on Bailundo. But the two officers had their orders to organise the Kubango expedition and haughtily refused the old man's advice. Silva Porto was distraught as he could visualise the mission ending in the deaths of the two young officers and the slaughter of their column.

Whatever was going through the old trailblazers mind can only be guessed at, but shortly after his fruitless conversation, and without speaking to anyone; he entered his storeroom where he opened two powder kegs, then wrapped himself in the blue and white Portuguese flag, lit a match and threw it into the keg; it fizzled out. He lit another match and the gunpowder ignited. The explosion blew off the roof but the stone and mud walls remained standing. After the smoke and dust cleared away, Paiva Couceiro found him lying unconscious among the charred ruins. Miraculously, he had only a few minor injuries, but the weakened old man died from the effects of shock on the following day in the presence of the Scotsman, Frederick Arnot and Dr Fisher, the Protestant missionaries from the English Brethren Mission at Kwanjululu. Almost immediately after the explosion, Chief Jamba with his warriors and the expedition's African troops fled, leaving the two officers and two sergeants on their own at Belmonte. After overseeing the old man's burial, the four men quietly rode out towards Cutáto some two days' march away.

So once again in 1890, Artur de Paiva was called on to lead a punitive expedition, this time to Bié in order to avenge the death of the colony's hunter-trader, Silva Porto.

De Paiva's 'avenging' makeshift force was composed of nine Portuguese officers, 365 NCOs and men of mixed cavalry, light infantry and artillery, with Portuguese, Humpata Boers and Damara auxiliaries. Lieutenant Evaristo Simpliciano de Almeida, was officer commanding the infantry, while Second Lieutenant Quintino Rogado and Cornet Paulo Amado de Melo Ramalho, were in charge of the artillery and cavalry respectively. *Vita* Tom commanded the Damara auxiliaries; the expedition totalled 882 men. In order to keep down costs, the governor-general of Angola required the Humpata Boers to provide their own wagons and supplies, and also transport government stores, for which they were paid a daily sum by the Portuguese authorities.

The leader of the Damara auxiliaries, *Vita* Tom, was born at Otjimbingwe Mission station on the Swakop River in 1863. It was on a day of ferocious slaughter and the boy was given the name, *Vita* – war. His mother was an Herero and his father a Tswana, known as 'Old Tom Bechuana.' He had spent his formative years at the mission and when he was old enough to hunt, had joined his father and the hunter explorer Fred Green, on shooting expeditions to the Okavango and Ovamboland. There he had met and hunted with the Swedish explorer and elephant hunter Axel Eriksson; known to the peoples of the region by the name *Karuvapa*. *Vita* Tom and his father then moved further north to the Boer settlement at Humpata where they worked under Artur de Paiva. The Boers translated his name into Afrikaans and he became known as Oorlog. Standing over two metres tall, the young Oorlog was an imposing figure and an influential member of de Paiva's column

The column departed in a straggling file headed by a Boer commando and a platoon of light infantry. The column was followed up the rear by some 50 Boer wagons pulling two Krupp field guns, two Nordenfelt machine guns and two light mountain guns. The column reached Banda, where they came across a heavily bearded, German gold prospector, who was able to give them useful information on the state of the rebellion. When the column reached the Luceke region on the banks of the Kunene River, they were faced with almost impenetrable bush, and de Paiva ordered a detachment forward to cut a road through the forest; it was escorted by a small mounted troop. The field force slowly trekked towards Kakonda to link up with the Benguela district commissioner, Francisco de Paula Cid. The district commissioner handed over a number of 'salted' horses, mules and military supplies and was also able to give de Paiva the latest intelligence on the situation in the Bié, Bailundo and Sambo regions, as was the indefatigable missionary Lecomte, who had turned up to see de Paiva and pray for the column's success and for its safe and speedy return.

The going was arduous as the region was a criss-cross of rivers. Large trees lined the level above the banks. The land then tilted towards a mass of thorn bush interspersed with lalla palm and fern, giving way to unending tall reed beds which had to be cleared by hand; then trees had to be felled and pushed into the shallow drift, to gradually create a semi-firm base, for the draught animals and wagons to cross. And there were always more obstacles just around the bend; enormous rocks which barred the way; lambi trees, which when felled were impossible to remove due to their gigantic roots. If they were lucky, they might come across a hippo or buffalo path beaten through to the water; all the while this painstaking work was going on, the column was at a standstill and vulnerable to attack.

The ponderous wagons crossed the Lindobe River, and while the officers and NCOs oversaw the laagering and the posting of sentries, Artur de Paiva took the opportunity of visiting the site of a former mission station, which he had been told was some 500 metres within a large forest, half a kilometre away. As the Portuguese camp was in an open, park-like area, de Paiva could easily make out the worn and rutted track, which led off into the forest. He took an escort of just two Damara horsemen and entered, riding on until he reached a small clearing where a creeper covered wall, the remains of a stone water tank and three silent burial mounds, indicated all that remained of some long forgotten missionary endeavour. Many times during his African career he had been struck by the way the continent absorbed all into itself and wondered if his efforts would count for nothing in the end.

On 7 October the sappers were busy completing the last section of a 22 metre span bridge across the Kunyangama, when local herdsmen told them that they had seen a large band of warriors at the column's previous laager, close to a group of kraals. A small reconnaissance patrol was sent back but the kraals were deserted except for an emaciated elder who told them he had heard that warriors were gathering at Huambo. De Paiva was troubled by the news and consequently ordered his officers to double the lookouts. During the night the wind began to rise and rapidly increased in strength. Tarpaulins started to rip and part from their wagons leaving clothing and food supplies open to the torrential rain. A terrific thunderclap, followed by a flash of lightning so brilliant that it momentarily lit up the entire laager, had children crying in terror while harassed mothers did their best to comfort them. The draught animals had also been unsettled, and the wagoners tumbled out of their makeshift beds into the driving rain to deal with the nervously flinching animals. The thunder quickly passed and the tarpaulins were eventually retrieved and lashed back on to the wagons. The laager then settled down for the remainder of the night when a number of shots rang out from the direction of the forest. The laager was stood to and de Paiva ordered a scouting party out. After almost fifteen minutes of tension, the scouts returned with a prisoner. The warrior was interrogated and sent back with a message for his Huambo chief, that once Dunduma had been dealt with, he would be next in line. First light revealed the extent of the storm damage; even large trees had been felled by the hurricane-like storm. While running repairs were being carried out, the soaked supplies and clothing were hung out to dry. The column inspanned and the wagons slowly began to creak their way along the riverbank towards Sambo. Once at Sambo, Artur de Paiva called all the European traders, hunters and missionaries together, and informed them that should they decline to seek sanctuary within the column, he would not be able to guarantee their safety as the situation in Bié was critical.

Scouts informed Cornet Paulo Amado that a group of men was approaching; some were on horseback others on foot. Cornet Amado followed the scouts to a vantage point, and standing up in his stirrups focused his binoculars on the distant group. To his great relief he saw the blue and white Portuguese flag being carried aloft by mounted men in Portuguese army uniforms. But what was a Portuguese column doing in the Bié region? De Paiva was greatly troubled by the news and ordered his officers to issue extra ammunition and double the sentries. A series of trumpet blast finally convinced the column of the incomers' identity. Paiva Couceiro led his mud-spattered troops into the laager among shouts of approval and loud applause from the tired and dejected column.

After a welcome late breakfast of coffee and biltong, Paiva Couceiro explained that he had originally been tasked with a mission to Barotseland, but because of ongoing diplomatic discussions with Britain over border issues, it had been cancelled and he had been ordered to the Lower Kubango region. He had completed his reconnaissance and on 14 October was at *Forte Princesa Amélia* with his men, when he learned that Artur de Paiva's column was on the march, the detachment set off in a north-easterly direction to meet up with him. After a long, circuitous journey through the Kubango, Paiva Couceiro and his men finally arrived at de Paiva's laager on 28 October.

On 30 October the reinforced column struggled its way across the Kutato River and in the hazy distance made out the silhouette of Dunduna's imposing hilltop kraal at Ekovongo. The kraal, the biggest in the whole of the Bié region, held some 700 men, women and children, and covered an area of over three kilometres; it was a formidable sight and it caused a ripple of uncertainty to run through the weary, ragged column. The column spent a sleepless night laagered close to the river with the disturbing vision of Dunduma's distant yet forbidding kraal in their mind's eye. The column was up well before first light to breakfast on mealies and coffee before inspanning and rumbling through open country close to the Kukema River. The vedettes reported seeing a large group of warriors moving about at the edge of the forest that bordered the open scrubland. The column was laagered and the Boer commando was sent out ahead of the main column to draw the warriors' fire. The Boer horsemen were suddenly faced by a large group of assegai carrying Biéns who leapt out from their hiding places in the elephant grass. The men dismounted and began to open fire on the advancing warriors. As the Boers fought their way back, the laagered wagons came under attack from other Bién warriors who had been waiting for their moment at the edge of the dense forest. The attack was repelled without heavy loss on either side but the column's unease was greatly increased. Later that morning, five of Dunduma's *indunas* appeared carrying two magnificent ivory tusks as a gift for de Paiva. The Portuguese officer was not impressed and refused the gift telling the *indunas* that he would only be satisfied with Dunduma's surrender.

Now only one river stood between de Paiva's column and Dunduma's kraal. The chief's spirit mediums loaded their rifles with a charge containing *muti* – a powerful magic powder of crushed bone, which when mixed with water, would instantly kill anyone who attempted to ford it; the spirit mediums then discharged their weapons into the river. On hearing the echoing crack of rifle fire, the Boer auxiliaries thought it heralded the signal for an attack against the column, and rushed up to the riverbank. After rapidly dismounting, the Boers took careful aim at the defiant medicine men and their bodyguards. When the smoke had finally cleared from the barrels of their rifles, they saw the bodies of two of the spirit mediums floating in the water while others lay on the riverbank.

On 4 November, the Kukema River was crossed, allowing the Portuguese to laager just two kilometres from Ekovongo. As it was late in the day, de Paiva decided to postpone the attack on Dunduma's kraal until the next morning, but Damara scouts under command of their charismatic leader *Vita* Oorlog, reported that large numbers of Dunduma's warriors had been observed issuing out of the kraal. A Boer scouting party was sent forward and fired on from within the kraal, suffering a number of casualties. On hearing the rifle fire, the column deployed in square formation with the machine guns covering the flanks and awaited the attack. Oorlog suggested to de Paiva, that as darkness would soon be upon them, they should immediately mount an attack on the kraal or they could find themselves enveloped by the impis' 'buffalo horns.' De Paiva reluctantly agreed, ordering his soldiers to fix bayonets, and under cover of artillery fire, advance towards the stockaded kraal. The soldiers moved towards the kraal in skirmishing order and on reaching it, a group was detached from the main force and set to pulling at the rough wooden palisade with ropes. Having made a breach, they streamed into the labyrinth-like kraal. Desperate hand-to-hand fighting ensued, and it was not long before smoke began belching from the straw roofed huts before bursting into crackling flames. As de Paiva and Oorlog surveyed the scene of carnage that had been Ekovongo, the prisoners, mostly women and children were led away. The men were ordered to make a careful search among the dead and bring them Dunduma's unmutilated body. But the chief had flown; only his scorched, wooden chair remained among the smoke filled ruins of the royal kraal at Ekovongo. In spite of the lateness of the day, de Paiva and a strongly armed scouting party rode over to Chief Utulumba's kraal, where the angry captain told the chief that he had four days to bury the dead and bring Dunduma in, as he was absolutely certain the chief knew of his whereabouts.

Again it was frustration for de Paiva. He had defeated his enemy but the chief had escaped, and until his capture, the column would have to stay in the field. The Portuguese then reoccupied the devastated Belmonte settlement. Dunduma's warriors had attacked the military post and taken the small Portuguese garrison captive. After beating the soldiers and taking their weapons, the warriors had gone on the rampage destroying every vestige of European influence, including Captain Teixeira da Silva's family quarters, and the banana and fruit trees in his kitchen garden. Except for his grave, all traces of Silva Porto's existence in Belmonte had been erased.

In response to the destruction of Belmonte, a 150-strong mounted detachment and a half battery of artillery under command of Cornet Amado, was ordered to make for Chikala in the Nganguelas region to search out Chief Dunduma. The flying column successfully invested the kraal at Kunyama, the capital of Nganguelas but Dunduma again escaped capture. De Paiva extended the truce, giving the Nganguela clans nine days to surrender him to the Portuguese forces, or all the kraals in the region would be destroyed. Reverend Sanders from the American Protestant mission at Komondongo, and Minister Frederick Arnot, had previously befriended Dunduma, and now fearing slaughter in the Nganguelas, had sent messages to all the kraals commanding the exit roads from the region, requesting them to stop Dunduma's escape. They then held an *indaba* with the chiefs and explained the seriousness of the situation; Artur de Paiva's threat to lay waste to the region was not an empty one.

On the final day of the truce, Dunduma was cornered in a hut within a kraal but his subjects were too afraid to lay a hand on their *soba* and instead begged Arnot to speak to him. It took a few moments for Arnot's eyes to accustom themselves to the darkness within the hut, but eventually he was able to make out the seated figure of Dunduma who was nursing a Martini-Henry rifle on his knee. The chief seemed relieved to see the missionary and offering no resistance, mutely handed the weapon over to Arnot. The chief so feared retribution from de Paiva that he begged Arnot and Sanders to accompany him to Belmonte. Dunduma arrived at Belmonte with a large entourage including five *sekulos*, two of his many wives and Sanders. Through Sanders, he asked de Paiva to be allowed to retain three human skulls; one of which still had flesh clinging to it, they were fastened to a leather thong around his waist. De Paiva refused the request and placed the chief under arrest. At night Dunduma was shackled, however during daylight hours he was locked in a hut, which the officers used as their mess. On the evening of 16 December, the officers dined rather later and longer than usual, sharing a goodly number of bottles of red wine, forgetting that their captive had not been shackled. It was a very dark night and the candles on the wooden table had begun to grow dim. In the gloom, Dunduma manage to crawl to the door, and while the Portuguese officers were toasting their success, crept out of the hut and made his way into the bush. The officers, who had been in a jolly mood, were astounded and not a little amused by Dunduma's daring escape. The alarm was sounded and the hunt was on. De Paiva was not amused; it represented a potentially enormous setback for him, as he would be in great danger of losing face among the Biéns. Fortunately for the Portuguese, Dunduma ran straight into an army picket and was knocked down and very severely beaten, in spite of putting up a brave struggle. From then on, the unfortunate Dunduma was guarded by Cornet Amado and made to wear a heavy iron collar around his neck and chains on his ankles, both day and night.

As far as de Paiva was concerned, the expedition had fulfilled its task. Dunduma was duly replaced by Portugal's choice, the pliant Chief Kaoko. Silva Porto's body was exhumed and placed in a wooden coffin; it would be taken to Mossâmedes prior to transport to Portugal. Lieutenant Simpliciano de Almeida, was made district commissioner of Bié region and put in command of an infantry platoon that was to remain as a temporary garrison and guarantee of Portuguese authority at the newly constructed *Forte Artur de Paiva*. The Portuguese column finally turned westward and the marching men and creaking wagons headed back to Huíla. Although the campaign was an undoubted success, the Boer and African auxiliaries had been forced to remain in the field with the Portuguese regular forces, and it was some six months before they were to see their wives and families again.

Two small columns slowly made their way down the tortuous, wagon rutted tracks from the Chela Highlands, through the windswept desert to Mossâmedes; one column carried the coffin of Silva Porto, draped in a Portuguese flag that the old man had made himself, and had flown over his home at Belmonte; the other column carried a heavily chained Dunduma to a waiting steamer, to be shipped to Cape Verde and exile.

Fortaleza do Humbe (interior)

Humbe Fort (Império)

Chapter 13
Major Padrel and the Humbe Column

Warlike clans again threatened the fort at Humbe a year after Artur de Paiva's successful yet brutal campaign against Chief Dunduma in 1890. Portugal's attempt to replace the charismatic Dunduma with a chief more sympathetic to Portuguese control was having little real effect. A number of Portuguese colonists and traders who had built homes and trading stations on the banks of the Kunene and Kakulovar rivers, had been forced to quit their properties, and after loading up the waiting wagons with their worldly goods, had made for the relative safety of *Forte Humbe*. Now 45-year-old Major Lourenço Justiniano Padrel was given command of a fighting column tasked with the relief of the threatened fort at Humbe.

Justiniano Padrel was born to colonist parents at sea between Praia de Cabo Verde and Bissau in Portuguese Guinea. He was a larger-than-life character who had led a colourful military career. He had taken part in operations in Portuguese Guinea in 1869, and in 1870 was decorated for bravery in the field. As an army captain he had been stationed with 2 Light Infantry on the Portuguese island of São Tomé where, it was rumoured, but never proved, that he had been involved in certain financial irregularities concerning the officers' mess funds. His request to transfer to an operational area had been accepted giving him the chance to demonstrate his worth or at least clear his name.

Naval surgeon Dr José Pereira do Nascimento was designated second-in-command of the force with Lieutenant António Palermo de Oliveira, commanding the Light Infantry detachment, armed with a Krupp field gun and one machine gun. Command of the small irregular cavalry troop was given to Cornet Ramalho. The column's supply train consisted of seventeen Boer wagons with food, ammunition and medical supplies. At Huíla on 27 April 1891, farmer and big game hunter Pete van der Kellen joined the column. Though van der Kellen was born in Holland, his many years in Africa had given him an excellent knowledge of the region and of its different clans, and would be important to the success of the operation. With van der Kellen came his 22-strong Boer commando. Shortly before departing from Huíla, the column was joined by the campaign-hardened Chief Oorlog with 44 Bergdamas, 30 Bushmen and 25 Basters. The column reached Chibia, fifteen kilometres from Huila on the morning on 30 April where they were met by a number of Portuguese colonists. When they entered the Gambos region the column laagered at Munongolo to await the arrival of the auxiliaries, estimated to be in the region of 1,500 warriors. Early on the morning of 8 May the column set out towards Humbe and four days later Padrel laagered his column at Cahama some 100 kilometres away. On 13 May the column halted within sight of the Kakulovar River, close to an abandoned and derelict trading station. They had no sooner outspanned their wagons than Padrel received a message from Humbe district commissioner, Captain Joaquim Luna de Carvalho, telling him of the general unrest in the area and that the column would soon be under attack by the rebel leader Chief Luhuna. Luna de Carvalho's intelligence was correct, as the column was attacked on the following day, 30 kilometres further on at Tchipelongo. The Nkumbi warriors had hidden behind tall ant mounds, baobab and mopani trees, but were beaten off by the mounted Boer scouts and the auxiliaries. In spite of the constant skirmishes, Padrel's punitive column pushed on through smoke blackened kraals covering the remaining 70 kilometres, and reaching *Forte Humbe* on 16 May, to the enormous relief of its beleaguered garrison. A captured Nkumbi warrior told the column's interpreter that Chief Luhuna had made his escape on horseback in a southerly direction toward Dongoena. After resupplying and leaving the sick and wounded at *Forte Humbe*, the column's scouts slowly followed the course of the Kunene towards Dongoena following Chief Luhuna's spoor.

After five days of fighting in and around Dongoena, Padrel's column had inflicted a number of serious defeats on Luhuna's followers, and captured large herds of cattle. The dispirited Nkumbi clans sued for peace, however, Chief Luhuna had already fled over the Kunene River and Padrel was still determined to apprehend him. The column then moved back north to *Forte Humbe* with the captured cattle, in order to replenish stores and ammunition while awaiting the arrival of over 3,000 auxiliaries. By 9 July Padrel was ready to resume the hunt for Chief Luhuna.

Padrel moved south and forded the Kunene at Pembe Drift, entering Kwamato territory for the first time, and marching towards the kraal of Chief Ikera at Greater Kwamato, where Luhuna was rumoured to be hiding. The Portuguese column was now passing through hectares of cultivated mealie fields and great stretches of open savannah. On 12 July, the crooked, high-stockaded kraals of Dombeafungwe came into view. At this juncture, a large number of the recently joined Kwamato auxiliaries fled the column, fearing reprisals from their own clans. In desperation, scouts were ordered out to apprehend the ringleaders but it was a hopeless task, and Padrel was left with disaster staring him in the face; the column was now in an exposed and vulnerable position and any attempt to withdraw would in all probability signal the end for the depleted force.

The watching Kwamato had been emboldened by the auxiliaries' chaotic flight, and came streaming out of their kraals towards the column, with one of Chief Ikera's sons in the lead. In order to stall the mass defection of the remaining

Kwamato, Padrel ordered the column to advance in open order on the distant enemy kraals. The Kwamato impis had previously placed themselves in a position to cut off any possible Portuguese retreat, and now they began to move towards the column to face Padrel and his men head on. At that very moment Padrel ordered the column to about turn and retreat on the Kunene River. The Portuguese and their auxiliaries made an orderly fighting withdrawal from Dombeafungwe, but the rearguard was constantly harassed, and had to repel enemy incursions for most of the rest of that long day. Two firm infantry sallies backed up by telling machine gun fire directed by Lieutenant Palermo de Oliveira, against an enemy attempt to attack and take the Boer wagons, was repulsed with great loss to the Kwamato warriors. One hour before reaching the Kunene River, the Kwamato ceased firing and were seen rapidly moving off through the dust haze. Padrel correctly guessed that it was to give them time to cut off the Portuguese at the river. Padrel ordered a halt and sent part of his horsemen, followed by an infantry platoon, to occupy both banks of the Kunene in order to cover the perilous crossing of the Boer wagons and the main column. Those orders were faithfully and ably carried out by Pete van der Kellen, who with his brother Emile, and Barend Prinsloo, Stephanus Venter, Piet van der Wat and James Stewardson, who from their vantage point, on the left bank among the tall reeds, kept the Kwamato impis at bay with their accurate musketry. By 4:00 in the afternoon, the column had forded the river without mishap. Padrel ordered a short rest and then moved off again towards *Forte Humbe* and eventually to safety. During the campaign Padrel's column has lost more than 100 men; the vast majority died from sickness and among the seriously wounded was the ever-ready civilian volunteer José António Lopes, whose African auxiliaries had been of immeasurable service to the column.

Chapter 14
The Boers Exact Revenge

In the Berlin Reichstag on 1 March 1893, Bismarck's successor, the former military strategist, the unlikely named, Count Georg Leo von Caprivi de Caprera de Montecuccoli, announced that the German Reich was to strengthen both its political and military control over its southern African colony. Chancellor von Caprivi had declared that Germany must become the master of German South West Africa without bloodshed. Those measured words may well have encapsulated von Caprivi's laudable ambition yet the reality was very different.

In 1889 Berlin came to the conclusion that the economic development of the colony would be impossible without regular troops, and a military force had been recruited and trained in Germany before being sent out to German South West Africa in June of that year. Thirty-nine-year-old Captain Curt Carl Bruno von François arrived at Walvis Bay with that first contingent. In August 1893 fresh German troops arrived at Swakopmund on the *Marie Woermann* under command of Captain Joachim von Heydebreck. Captain von François, buoyed up by the arrival of fresh reinforcements, launched an unprovoked attack on the Witbooi Namas at Hoornkrans, causing many of the clans to eventually flee north over the ill-defined border into Portuguese territory.

Captain de Paiva was again called away from his wife and growing family at Humpata and ordered to Luanda. Once at Luanda he was instructed to organise an expedition in his own backyard, the Huíla Highlands. The border clans having been displaced from their lands in neighbouring German South West Africa were now plundering the Portuguese controlled region. The Portuguese government was anxious, as Lisbon interpreted Germany's actions as a direct challenge to the stability and control of its Angolan colony, consequently, de Paiva was charged with re-establishing Portuguese authority in the area.

Artur de Paiva believed that Lisbon had overreacted to what amounted to isolated banditry by small groups of brigands, and gave overall command of the small Portuguese force, and its Boer auxiliaries under Willem Venter, to Second Lieutenant Quintino Rogado. Shortly after Quintino Rogado's column had set off south, Willem Venter was dismayed to learn that the cattle rustlers who had abducted African herdsmen and oxen from Boer kraals at Chibia were nearby, and fearing that they would ambush Quintino Rogado's men, called together nine other Boers and rode out in search of them. On the way Venter had come up with a group of some 50 Africans on a wildebeest hunting expedition. The hunters were initially wary of the mounted and well-armed Boers' reputation but after Venter explained his intentions and promised them a share in the booty, they agreed to follow his commando on foot.

Late in the afternoon, the ever-watchful Boers came across both human and animal spoors and soon discovered their quarry at a stockaded kraal by a vast mealie plantation some three hours' ride from Tabua. As it would soon be dark, Willem Venter had no alternative other than to settle the men down for the night as best he could, well hidden by the elephant grass, to wait for the dawn. After a bone-chilling night, the hungry, huddled men heard a creaking noise and the sound of voices coming from the kraal. A warrior with a rifle slung over his shoulder was seen to slide through the small exit, and then climb a nearby baobab to scour the veld for trouble. Venter and his men held their breath. After what seemed an eternity, the Hottentot climbed back down and ran to the kraal. A short while later the gate was fully opened, and the cattle driven out to pasture, followed by seven heavily armed men on horseback and other warriors on foot. The riders had not gone far before one of the Boers was spotted and a lively firefight ensued. The well-sited Boers initially had the advantage of surprise and soon all seven mounts were riderless. The disorganised and confused warriors fled back to the comparative safety of the kraal, firing wildly at the Boers as they did so. But because of the narrowness of the entrance to the kraal, the desperate men were forced to bunch together; in that exposed position many were shot down. By the time the shooting had stopped, Venter's men had succeeded in advancing to within 30 metres of the kraal, it was only then that the Hottentots were able to regroup and open up a withering fire on the oncoming Boers. The Hottentots were seasoned fighters and had carefully counted the flashes from the Boers' rifle barrels. When the Hottentots realised they were under attack by less than a dozen Boers, they sent out two groups of warriors to encircle them. At this critical moment, the captive herdsmen began to file out of the kraal, causing most of the 50 African auxiliaries to flee, taking all the previously stolen cattle with them and leaving the Boers with only ten men. Venter's men were momentarily caught in two minds and the Hottentots' lively fire forced them to seek cover. Venter, who by this time was severely wounded, gave the order to withdraw to a vlei where the horses were tethered. Fortunately for Venter and his men, the Hottentots fearing the Boers' sharp shooting skills, remained within the safety of the kraal, and the small commando was able to scramble down into the vlei, mount up and slip away without being harassed. The badly wounded Venter's heart sank as he saw a large group of unidentified riders coming towards him and was mightily relieved to recognise a friendly commando. The Boers, who had been sent out to reinforce them, were led by one of the original Thirstland trekkers, Jan Harm Robbertse. After detaching six of his riders to escort Venter's bloodied men back to Humpata, Robbertse and his men rode hard towards the Hottentot held kraal.

Robbertse gave the order to dismount and, after leaving the horses in charge of one of the younger Boers, a tall, fifteen-year-old lad, they warily approached the silent kraal. Once inside, they found a number of dead Hottentots and cattle herders but the kraal was empty of both raiders and cattle.

It had been an altogether unsatisfactory operation for all concerned. The Hottentots had evaded Quintino Rogado's column and both Venter's and Robbertse's Boers. Attacks continued on isolated African kraals and Boer farms, and it was not long before Robbertse's homestead fell victim to the Hottentot raiders. It was the opportunity Robbertse had been waiting for. The Boer leader had been greatly angered that the Hottentots had escaped him, and into the bargain seriously wounded Willem Venter. He wasted no time in saddling up his horse and riding from his farm to the settlement at *São Januário de Humpata* to request de Paiva, as Portugal's authority in the region, for permission to mount a punitive raid against the rustlers. De Paiva was seated at his writing desk when his wife told him that Robbertse was waiting to see him on the stoep of their homestead. After the usual greetings, both men dug deep into their tobacco pouches, lit their clay pipes and began to discuss cattle, the summer wild fires ravaging the region, and the Hottentots' rustling activities. It took the Boer a while to get to the point, but permission was readily given and Robbertse returned to his farm prior to organising a commando. After a matter of days, he rode south with a 34-strong commando, accompanied by fifteen Angolan mounted troops.

After riding through the barren, featureless lands south of Humpata, the force located the fresh spoor of the mounted Hottentots, which eventually led them to their hiding place in the Kaokoveld, hard by the Kunene River, on the German side of the border. The frontier was crossed well before dawn. Leaving their mounts tethered to the sand-swept wreck of an old Boer wagon, they cautiously made their way towards the tell-tale spiralling smoke from the rustlers' laager. The men were still asleep and had not thought to post sentries. Robbertse and his commando gave the cattle kraal a wide berth, fearing the animals would alert the sleeping Hottentots. Once in position on a high, camel-thorn covered dune, overlooking the laager, the Boers and Angolans awaited dawn. The sleeping forms were now clearly visible in the early morning light and on the given command of a single pistol shot, the Boers opened up; only three of the gang were able to escape the slaughter. The Boer commando and its Angolan allies, buried their dead and then recrossed the border into Angola, carrying the wounded back to the settlement at Humpata along with 3,000 head of slow moving cattle and numerous plundered trophies.

Chapter 15
Slaughter at Jambacamufate

In 1897 a grave bovine epidemic reached southern Angola from German South West Africa. In Mossâmedes, the governor, naval Lieutenant Francisco Diogo de Sá requested the district commissioners of Mossâmedes and Benguela to organise preventative measures against the rinderpest outbreak. The Kunene River, though a natural barrier, would not block the disease's advance, and the many drifts could not possibly be policed as it would have required many more soldiers than Angola had at its disposal. The decision was made to vaccinate. A vaccination brigade was set up under medical officer Captain Dr António Bernardino Roque with veterinary Lieutenant Aristides da Silva Guardado, assisted by a small group of Angolan infantry. The Dragoon Troop Mossâmedes, commanded by Captain José Eugenio da Silva with Lieutenant Count Almoster and Cornets Carlos Augusto da Silva and Fernando Augusto da Silva, would escort the vaccination brigade. The dismounted column left Lubango on 20 October - many of the 'unsalted' mounts had earlier died from horse-sickness - and arrived at *Forte Humbe* early in November. After crossing the Tchicusse River they discovered that the rinderpest virus had bridged the Kunene and had begun to decimate the herds of oxen on the right bank of the river. But they were heartened by the news that a number of European traders and cattle owners had moved their herds close to the Kakulovar River, where water and reasonably good pastureland was readily available, and had sent a message to the column to meet them there in order to set up a vaccination station. Among the traders awaiting the Portuguese were José Lopes, and Axel Eriksson who had trekked north over the border to show his Humbe trader friends the method of vaccination practised in German South West Africa.

All was not well at district headquarters based at *Forte Humbe*. The military commander was informed that resistance had been encountered from the *sekulos*- headmen - who feared that the Portuguese had come to Humbe with *milongo* – magic – to treat their sickening herds. The chiefs believed that the herds of oxen had died because of the vaccination brigade's *milongo* treatment. The frustrated Portuguese found many of the stockaded cattle pens empty as the Nkumbi herders had moved their cattle far out of reach. Lieutenant Silva Guardado was dismayed when he learned from his interpreter that the main fear was not really their *milongo* but the presence of Portuguese and African troops now stationed at the fort. The chiefs reasoned that troops and artillery wagons were not needed in order to treat their cattle. Silva Guardado through his interpreter patiently explained that as the rinderpest sickness had come from the south they could very well be attacked by starving Hottentots whose own herds had already died. The *sekulos* were not impressed by the Portuguese officer's argument and countered that if the Hottentots raided northward into their lands they would defend themselves as they had always done. And anyway, the Nkumbi peoples' *kimbandas* – spirit mediums – had prophesied that the Portuguese would attempt to remove them from their kraals and that they must resist at all costs. Lieutenant Silva Guardado had no alternative, other than to pack up his veterinary wares and take his small detachment back to *Forte Humbe*, and report the signal failure of the vaccination mission to Captain da Silva.

As Silva Guardado approached the fort he heard a bugle blast, and a few minutes later, was met on the road by Captain da Silva and Dr Roque. The captain was visibly angered by Silva Guardado's report. He threatened to teach the chief a lesson he would not forget, and swiftly turning his horse, dug in his spurs and rode back alone to the fort. Silva Guardado and Dr Roque looked at each other in silence, at least they understood the enormity of the small vaccination brigade's task, and the risk that they were running, in attempting to convince the chiefs of the wisdom and efficacy of the alien vaccination process. It was then that Lieutenant Silva Guardado confided in Dr Roque of the hopelessness of the mission and the resentment it was stoking up in the Humbe region. After a few days' rest at *Forte Humbe*, Silva Guardado was on the road again, this time to Kiteve in the extreme east of the district. He and Dr Roque had decided that any cattle found en route would be vaccinated – providing their herders agreed. On this occasion he had better luck and by the end of the day had succeeded in vaccinating 50 head of cattle for which he was given one ox for every fifteen vaccinated. Silva Guardado was elated with his day's work – although 50 was such a small number, given the thousands of head of cattle roaming the area – at least it was a start. Silva Guardado ordered two of his men to take the three oxen back to the fort and give Dr Roque the welcome news of his success, and then return with any further instructions from the fort. At 9:00 the next morning, the two soldiers reported back to Silva Guardado, that they had been attacked as they approached the fort by a group of men, one of whom was recognised as being a herder of the recently vaccinated cattle.

Silva Guardado received orders to press on to Cafuntuka. Close by the river he came upon a group of men fighting their way through the thick reeds with an enormous five-metre long, barbed bream swinging from poles carried on their shoulders. The startled men at first refused to speak to Silva Guardado, and the interpreter was forced to tell him they had flatly refused the offer of vaccination, and as their attitude towards the Portuguese officer was very hostile, it would not be advisable to press the argument. Silva Guardado was forced to ride on over muddy lagoons and through dense mopani thickets, interspersed with baobab trees and elephant grass, in order to reach the small settlement of Cafu, two days' march from Humbe. The veterinary officer came across two Portuguese traders busily cooking their late afternoon meal of impala meat. They were close to a mopani tree that had become weirdly intertwined with an enormous ant heap, but that freak of nature afforded them reasonable shade from the glaring sun. The Portuguese traders were pleased to see Silva Guardado and beamingly told him they had already vaccinated their cattle and pointed to the paddock some distance from their camp. Silva Guardado rode over, but to his great consternation, they had placed the 'salted' cattle in the same paddock as the sick ones. Having partaken of the traders' offer of roasted impala meat, the small party trekked on to the shimmering mirage-like lagoons at Pokolo; their eyes were smarting in the fierce afternoon sun. An hour later they reached Pokolo only to discover that its people had fled their kraals taking all the cattle with them. Silva Guardado and his party settled down as best they could in an *omaramba* – a shallow grassy depression - and after a night disturbed by the constant roaring and snorting of hippopotami in the nearby lagoon, Silva Guardado and his men moved on to the large riverine village of Kiteve, where they were met by district commissioner Second Lieutenant Barradas, who commanded a small number of Angolan troops at *Forte Kiteve*. Though Barradas tried his best to convince the chiefs at Kiteve to allow their cattle to be vaccinated, the result predictably was the same. The chiefs asked how injecting them with the bile of sick cattle could cure the herds, as they would die too. It was becoming a futile mission and Silva Guardado thanked Barradas for his attempts to help but now had no alternative other than to head back the way they had come to *Forte Humbe*.

It had only been a few days since Silva Guardado and his men had trekked along the dusty, wagon-rutted road to Humbe but now a scene of utter devastation met their eyes; animals were lying dead everywhere. There were clouds of droning flies surrounding rotting carcasses in shallow pools of water, under trees and even beneath the smallest bushes; the cattle in their death throes had attempted to seek shelter from the burning sun. The stench was indescribable and Silva Guardado and his men were forced to cover their noses with kerchiefs and saddlecloths against the overpowering smell. After some five kilometres of putrefaction, the small party at last was able to remove their makeshift masks and breath freely again. In spite of this gruesome experience, the men who had eaten nothing all day were hungry, and asked Silva Guardado if they could stop and feed. Silva Guardado looked round for shelter and through his binoculars saw a group of mopani trees some 700 metres distant, which would give them welcome shade and a modicum of comfort. As they approached the clump of trees, the men again became aware of a sickly stench, and were repelled by the sight of gorged hyenas their heads burrowing deeply into the fetid corpses. Out of sheer frustration, Silva Guardado loosed off half a dozen rounds at the filth-bespattered hyenas, killing only one of them, while the rest retreated further into the mopani trees, prior to resuming their feast. The Portuguese officer was forced to order his men to cook their food in the open under the broiling sun, while large vultures circled the corpses, screeching hideously and like the hyenas, awaited the men's departure. The smoke from their fire had attracted unwelcome attention, and Silva Guardado warily watched as a group of men approached the camp. To his great relief they were not carrying weapons and after greeting the interpreter, warned him that the chief at Cafuntuka wanted Silva Guardado's head, as he believed the Portuguese officer was responsible for spreading the bovine disease throughout the region. Silva Guardado ordered his men to rest until dusk, when they would set out under the cover of darkness, keeping off the track where possible. The party safely completed their journey and appeared at the gates of *Forte Humbe*, their uniforms torn and bloodied by their arduous trek through the thick thorn bush.

The company commander was not surprised to hear of Silva Guardado's lack of success and even appeared not to be listening to his veterinary officer. A disconsolate and exhausted Silva Guardado was walking towards his quarters, when dragoon Lieutenant Count Almoster stopped him. The thirty-nine-year-old lieutenant, a stoutly built, affable and perpetually cheerful man, was easily recognisable from his small, steel-rimmed spectacles. In fact, he was so chronically short sighted that without spectacles he simply could not see. He told Silva Guardado that there were serious differences of opinion between the dragoon's commanding officer, the head of the veterinary brigade, and the Humbe district commissioner. Detailed orders had been received from Artur de Paiva at Humpata for a general withdrawal from *Forte Humbe*. However, de Paiva lacked the benefit of local knowledge and all were agreed that they had been rendered impracticable, given the situation and the animosity towards the Portuguese. As no telegraph line existed between Humpata and Humbe, the decision would have to be made on the spot and quickly. The orders from de Paiva had caused consternation and heated arguments between the three men with the dragoon captain stating, that as de facto military commander and senior officer, he would not take orders from the others.

Count Almoster confided in Silva Guardado that he feared he had angered his commanding officer by contradicting him in front of the others. Count Almoster looked down at his feet and half whispered that he expected the withdrawal to be a confused affair, which would end badly. After crossing da Silva, he knew he would be left at the fort with the sick, and that his commanding officer would take the two young cornets with him when he left for Humpata. Da Silva wanted to return as quickly as he could, and certainly did not want to be slowed down by taking sick troops with his column. Count Almoster shifted his gaze from Silva Guardado, and after staring at the fort's meagre ramparts, smilingly told him that up to a certain point it suited him not to go. At least he would not make the journey in his commanding officer's company, though it would not be easy remaining in what Almoster regarded as a hellish spot, lacking the most basic resources. Furthermore, it was difficult to defend with a small garrison of mainly sick Angolan troops. Almoster confided that Dr Roque had been alienated by da Silva's boorish attitude. He had decided that rather than travel to Humpata with him, he would remain at *Forte Humbe* with its young commander, Cornet José Felix, and would order Silva Guardado to go in his place, in case of any possible injuries or sickness among the troops en route. In view of the orders received from de Paiva, the dragoon captain began planning the form and timings of the withdrawal of the military forces and the vaccination brigade. It was agreed by all, that remaining at *Forte Humbe* would become untenable; due to the rinderpest outbreak, food was becoming impossible to obtain and bullock transport was now non-existent, as the disease had spread to the Gambos and Huíla regions. Many of the troops stationed at *Forte Humbe* were sick and to compound the problem, the rainy season would soon be upon them.

Da Silva had been instructed to phase the withdrawal by platoons. What de Paiva in Humpata had failed to recognise, was that due to the disease's heavy toll, no draught transport whatsoever was available to the dragoon led force. Da Silva made the decision to take only essential equipment and supplies on the march to Humpata. At the last moment a group of 80 Kiteve men appeared from a nearby kraal and were contracted to serve as bearers to the column. For reasons best known to da Silva, he insisted on taking a bronze Canet breech-loading field gun, though the limber had been detached and there was no ammunition for it. He gave the order that the field gun was to be dragged all the way to Humpata by soldiers of the Angolan infantry.

The withdrawal began on 6 December, with the departure of the first echelon of 3 Troop under command of Sergeant Silveira, followed the next day by the second echelon under command of Captain da Silva, with 3 Troop and 4 Troop commanded by the two young cavalry officers. The rearguard echelon of 1 Troop, was to be made up of soldiers too sick to be moved, and would remain at *Forte Humbe* under command of Count Almoster with medical aid provided by Dr Roque. Before Silva Guardado left for Humpata, he put together a small field medical box and said goodbye to his superior, Dr Roque, district commissioner José Felix, and to the Angolan soldiers who had ably accompanied him on his abortive vaccination missions. Lieutenant Almoster ran up to Silva Guardado and quietly but cheerily explained that a sympathetic local chief had told him of a short cut, which would quickly allow him to catch up with the main column.

Silva Guardado left on horseback with his bulky medical supplies slung over the back of his saddle, to join 3 and 4 Platoons which were to laager at Katekero, fifteen kilometres from *Forte Humbe*. Silva Guardado reached the Katekero laager without mishap and treated two soldiers who appeared to be developing a fever, before bedding down with the rest of the force. They were up at dawn and about to get under way when the dragoon vedettes reported a small group of riders approaching the laager. The force rapidly adopted defensive positions around a group of baobab trees to await the attack. As the riders came on towards the Portuguese position, the vedettes called out to them and heard Dr Roque identify himself and his followers. After reporting to Captain da Silva, the sweating and dust covered Dr Roque, told Silva Guardado that at the last moment he had decided to join him. He had given some of the sickest soldiers quinine injections and informed Count Almoster that they should be fit enough to travel within a few days. The troopers then packed up their gear and set off to cross the Kakulovar River where scouts had found the drift to be quite shallow. They followed the right bank until Captain da Silva ordered his men to laager at a spot chosen by his scouts a little above the Tuandiva settlement. One of the Angolan infantrymen had gone down to the river for water where he had shot a crocodile through the eye. On ripping its stomach open with the point of his bayonet, he had found a woman's bracelets and bangles, which he dutifully presented to his somewhat surprised commanding officer.

On 8 December, the force was again up well before dawn and trekked on towards Tchipelongo where they temporarily laagered during the mid afternoon heat. Three Angolan soldiers stole away from the laager without permission to visit a nearby kraal to obtain food and were fired on by its occupants. When Captain da Silva heard the shots and learned of the incident he was furious with the men and ordered Cornet Fernando da Silva to prepare a written report on the soldiers' claim. However, due to wildly conflicting versions, the matter was held in abeyance and the column carried on to Mutukwa settlement on the riverbank. It was already dark when they reached their laagering point, and the moon was already high as Silva Guardado dismounted. A muffled cry sent him running, pistol in hand, towards Captain da Silva who was trying to hold his shying horse's reins while backing away from an enormous snake. Silva Guardado grabbed a broken branch, which he brought down heavily on the snake, cutting it in two. On examining the still writhing creature, the Angolans told him it was an extremely venomous black mamba and was an evil omen; something untoward would happen before they reached the safety of Humpata.

As the force was now laagered close to Tchicusse, Silva Guardado rode over on the following day to speak to his friend, the Huíla born Portuguese trader José Lopes. He found Lopes busy cleaning an enormous lion skin. Earlier that morning, while following an elephant's spoor, a lion had broken cover and charged him, he brought the lion down with his first shot but in its death agonies it had thrown itself on to his gun bearer and torn out his stomach – the unfortunate man had died shortly after and had been buried on the riverbank. The trader was visibly upset and vowed to Silva Guardado that he would deliver the skin and the lion meat to his dead bearer's family.

On 10 December the column passed through Tchicusse and on the following day laagered without incident at a group of gaily coloured, butterfly-covered water holes close to Cahama. Da Silva was surprised to come across four Angolan soldiers guarding two supply wagons. They had been immobilised in the sand due to the deaths of the draught oxen, which the Angolan wagoners had vainly tried to drag away into the bush. The men had no alternative but to watch as the two carcasses were picked clean by vultures and hawks, then as night fell, the hyenas had moved in. Captain da Silva congratulated the four men on their forbearance. After five days of marching through the heat dust and bush fires of southern Angola, the Portuguese were able to eat and stock up on food and supplies for the remainder of the journey.

As night fell, the column began to cook its newly found supplies, when one of José Lopes' men appeared with a hastily scribbled note; Troop Sergeant Rocha had turned up at his trading post bleeding profusely, the wounded and confused sergeant was unable or unwilling to say what had happened to the rest of his dragoon comrades. Silva Guardado immediately volunteered to return to José Lopes' trading post with the messenger. It was an extremely dark night as the two men warily led their horses through the bush. Suddenly, the clouds parted, and the moon lit up the trading post that could now be made out in the near distance. Silva Guardado checked his pocket watch; it was just 3:00 in the morning. The wounded sergeant was lying on a makeshift bed behind the rough wooden counter of the trader's tin-roofed hut. The sergeant was in pain, a bullet had entered his right leg, but fortunately, it had passed through without shattering the bone, and Silva Guardado was able to clean the exit wound and bandage up the semi-conscious man.

Before passing out, Sergeant Rocha told Silva Guardado that Lieutenant Count Almoster fearing an attack on _Forte Humbe_, had left with his 33 men and two horses during the afternoon of 11 December, with the intention of joining the main column at Katekero. The small column rested for a while on the march, then ate cold rations before moving out again, under cover of darkness, in order to escape the effects of the searing heat. First light found them within sight of what appeared to be a friendly kraal, as they had seen no hostile activity whatsoever. Lieutenant Almoster decided to break their march, post sentries, eat their meagre rations, and then move on at 8:30 that same morning. Meanwhile, he ordered two Angolans forward to look for water as he had been told there were water holes nearby, but forbade any troopers to approach the kraal to barter for food. The Angolans, one of them bleeding from a hand wound, soon returned to Almoster's laager hotly pursued by angry Nkumbi who had refused to allow them near the water. Worse still, more troopers had defied Almoster's orders and were fired on as they approached the kraal. Later in the year another version was propounded; one of the soldiers had come across a young woman and had demanded food, she refused saying that everyone was attending a funeral at *Muene* Dekango's kraal. The soldiers were annoyed by her answer, and roughly grabbing hold of the young woman, threw her to the ground intent upon rape, in the ensuing struggle she managed to break loose and raised the alarm. On hearing the woman's cries for help, those inside the kraal had fired on the soldiers. The enraged Nkumbi appeared bent on exacting their own justice on the hapless column and rapidly advanced towards the outlying sentries who were called back to join the main column. The Portuguese opened a brisk fire on the advancing Nkumbi who retreated into the bush from where they kept up sustained fire on the Portuguese laager.

There were two versions of why there were so many Nkumbi at Chulo, close to the kraal of *Muene* Dekango. One version had it that clans throughout the district had gathered for the funeral of an important chief, the second version was that the Nkumbi had laid a carefully prepared ambush for the Portuguese force along the thick, bush fringed track from *Forte Humbe*.

The ambush had been well sited. The track from *Forte Humbe* to Otokero followed the steep banks of the Kakulovar River and was lined extensively by impenetrable clumps of thorn bush and reed beds. As soon as the column had left the fort, runners informed *Muene* Dekango of the fact, and he immediately sent his rifle carrying impis out to infiltrate the thick thorn bush and await the unsuspecting Portuguese troopers. The Nkumbi were forewarned of the column's arrival by the dust haze rising into the sky above the bush. The clouds of dust were driven into the soldiers' eyes, ears and mouths by a gusting, westerly wind. As the dust-caked force wearily followed the rutted track close to Jambacamufate, on the left bank of the river, it was suddenly fired on from the depths of the thorn bush. The Portuguese were caught on the track in the open and virtually without cover. The dragoon commander's column was now in almost featureless ground and he had to find cover or his force would soon be decimated. He motioned his troopers to take cover in the direction of a small *omaramba*, when his horse suddenly stumbled and his precious spectacles shot off his face, to land in the deep, sandy soil. It was to have fateful consequences for the harassed Portuguese column. The enemy's fire was intense and at the very time when his men needed him, Almoster was on his knees, desperately scrabbling in the sand to find his spectacles. Shouting at the top of his voice, in an attempt to be heard above the sound of rifle fire, Count Almoster motioned to Sergeant Pio. Dodging the bullets, the sergeant threw himself down at his officer's side, to be told that command was being turned over to him. The corpulent yet efficient sergeant ordered António, Almoster's servant, to take the officer's reins in order to guide him along at the head of the column. Sergeant Pio got to his feet and rallied the troopers, motioning them to follow him along the track. After a moment's hesitation, the men began to follow their sergeant but the wounded had to be left behind. The reins of Almoster's horse were quickly handed over to Sergeant Rocha as António had somersaulted over into the sand; the man was in great pain, bleeding profusely from a gunshot wound. The dispirited Portuguese fired wildly into the thick bush, but did very little damage, while being picked off by accurate rifle fire. In spite of Sergeant Pio having ordered his troopers not to waste ammunition firing at shadows, the column quickly began to run short of cartridges; the soldiers' mouths were dry from fear, and now their canteens were almost empty. Sergeant Pio was forced to take up a defensive position among a group of ant heaps and baobab trees. However, the firing was so hot that the sergeant ordered the men to move along the road independently, and defend themselves as best they could. Not a trooper moved. There was nowhere for the depleted column to go. Sergeant Rocha though wounded was told off by Almoster to make for Captain da Silva's column, though the main Portuguese force was some four days' march away.

Ignoring Almoster's order, Sergeant Rocha rode hard for José Lopes' trading post, where he arrived that night with the news of the ambush. At Tchicusse, Guardado came across Ambrósio, the severely wounded Angolan soldier who had been told off to stay with Count Almoster. According to Ambrósio, the Nkumbi had pressed their advantage as more and more of the column had fallen to their rifle fire. Count Almoster, whose mount had been shot from under him, was hit just below the right knee. The shortsighted lieutenant called to Sergeant Rocha to leave him and save himself. Sergeant Pio had ordered Almoster's servant and Ambrósio to help their officer, and not to leave him on his own or let him be left behind. The three men collapsed in a heap as Ambrósio was hit in the leg. Almoster was unable to walk unaided, and slumped down at the side of the track with his back against a baobab tree, with the two men on either side of him. It was midday; the heat was almost more than the beleaguered Portuguese could bear and bullets were singing through the shimmering air. Almoster now bleeding from a stomach wound, turned to the two men and told them to leave him, as nothing more could be done and it would be pointless to sacrifice their lives. However, António was losing a lot of blood and felt too weak to leave his officer's side. Thirty metres away, the Nkumbi had stopped to strip a number of soldiers whom they had cudgelled to death, and at that moment, Ambrósio began to drag himself behind the baobab tree and over the track into the thorn bush, where he remained until the warriors finally tired of mutilating the Portuguese and African corpses. During that temporary lull in the slaughter, a small number of wounded African soldiers were able to crawl off into the thick bush, only to be murdered later as they tried to make for *Forte Humbe*. Almost all the soldiers were now casualties. They no longer had any ammunition, yet the troopers had fought hand to hand, but the odds were overwhelming and their fate was already sealed. The vultures and hyenas would soon begin their grisly work.

From his hiding place, Ambrósio silently watched as the Nkumbi warriors ran yelling towards the officer and his servant, still propped up against the tall baobab tree. A screaming, dancing mob quickly surrounded Count Almoster and António. Single, powerful blows to the head from the Nkumbi warriors' knobkerries killed the two men - it was over in a moment.

Meanwhile, news of the massacre at Jambacamufate began to filter through the ranks of Captain da Silva's column. Though Silva Guardado had been lying on a cot in his tent shaking from the after effects of malaria and still unable to quench a raging thirst, he hauled himself up and sought out Captain da Silva. He requested permission from the dragoon commander, to ride out to José Lopes' trading store in order to gain further intelligence on the events at Jambacamufate. As he rode along he began to regret having volunteered to search for survivors, but José Lopes assured him that they would be able to rest en route, as he knew of the whereabouts of water holes. As it was already late in the afternoon, Lopes advised Silva Guardado to eat with him, and then bunk down for the night at his store. Though distracted by the news, Silva Guardado had previously noted that Lopes had a large scar on his nose and after consuming a generous amount of the trader's *bagaço*, plucked up the courage to enquire as to how it had come about. Lopes laughingly related, how, during an elephant-hunting trip in dense acacia bush, a thorn had become deeply embedded in his nose. On that occasion even his Humbe trackers' ubiquitous, thick, iron tweezers, had been unable to remove the thorn. It had turned septic and Lopes had cauterised it himself. Before turning in, Lopes told him that early next morning after breakfast, they would set out together with four of his most trusted men. The night's sleep and the relaxing effect of the *bagaço* had done its trick and Silva Guardado felt much recovered.

At dawn, the small party rode towards Jambacamufate, armed with repeating rifles and with leather water bags slung from the pommels of their saddles. The group pluckily rode deep into hostile country, in what was to be a vain attempt to rescue survivors of the massacre; there were none. As the small party warily cantered towards the scene of the slaughter, there were many vultures watching them from the twisted branches of the baobab trees. The vultures indicated the presence of the dead not the living. As they moved forward through the sandy ground they came first upon two fly covered bodies that had been almost entirely stripped of their uniforms. After Silva Guardado had carefully searched the bush-lined riverbank with his binoculars, the men slung their rifles over their shoulders and dismounted. On closer inspection, they saw that the two soldiers had been horribly mutilated; the genital organs ripped off, chests slit open and the heart removed to enable the *kimbandas* to make *milongo* - magical potions. Yet, near one body was a bloody remnant of khaki-coloured cloth. It had been part of a torn right sleeve, on which José Lopes could make out the insignia of a corporal of 9 Cavalry Regiment. The second body, was sadly, instantly recognisable because of its corpulence. Both men knew full well that it could only be the remains of Sergeant Pio. The Nkumbi had mistaken the sergeant's insignia for those of an officer's and had set to hideously mutilating the bodies. Close to the track were ten more butchered and mutilated troopers. The veterinary officer noted that all of the men were naked. Their ankles had been tied with cord and by looking at the bloody marks on the sandy soil, he could clearly see where they had been dragged and left in a pile. Silva Guardado soon discovered the body of Count Almoster, and that of his servant, António. Only after the clouds of flies had been partially dispersed did it become apparent that a blow from a knobkerrie had cloven the lieutenant's head, scattering the brains over the sandy ground. The Portuguese nobleman also had two bullet wounds in his body. Next to Almoster was his trusty, elderly servant António, who one early spring day in Lisbon, had volunteered to accompany him on his African adventure. Both men had been completely stripped except for the subaltern's blood encrusted sock, which had proved impossible to remove. This gave Silva Guardado to understand, as the eyewitnesses had related, that Count Almoster had initially been wounded in the leg. The two men fearing the Nkumbi warriors would return to the scene of the massacre, quickly remounted and galloped back to rejoin the main party.

In spite of the danger inherent in such a task, José Lopes was to return to the grim scene with a small escort, in order to bury the Portuguese corpses. His touching, humanitarian efforts were in vain, as the bodies were only to be dug up and again defiled by the Nkumbi, shortly after the Portuguese riders had departed the scene. Much later, a Boer commando from Humpata collected the bleached bones together and reburied them with due reverence. Ironically, had Count Almoster fallen back on Katekero, he would have been able to call on help from José Lopes and his men, who had heard the shooting from the farm. Shortly after the massacre, an official letter arrived for Count Almoster, from the Ministry for War in Lisbon, informing him of his promotion to captain.

It did not take long for news of the massacre to reach Cornet Felix at *Forte Humbe*. Now the young subaltern had to consider its defence. The African soldiers and their families had been housed in lean-to shacks, outside the walls of the fort. Cornet Felix ordered the shacks to be pulled down and his soldiers and their families garrisoned inside the fort. The ground around the fort had to be cleared of obstacles. Water and what few rations were available, were brought in, and the soldiers were issued with rifles and ammunition, and shown their places on the walls. On 14 December Felix and his men watched the silent approach of some 200 warriors, led by Chief Nambonga. The chief walked up to the fort's wooden gate and called up to the Portuguese officer inviting him to open the gate and point out the kraals of those chiefs responsible for the massacre. Cornet Felix, sensing a trap, remained at his post above the gate and refused to parley with the old chief. The chief turned to his warriors and with a wave of his hand the men drew back 500 metres and sat down to await the chief's pleasure. Later that night a spy informed Felix that two messengers who had tried to get through to the fort had been ambushed at Malange and killed. He was also warned to expect an attack that same night. It was rumoured that the chiefs of Mulondo and Kamba intended joining forces with the Nkumbi chief to attack the fort, and the forts at Kiteve and Pokolo. To Felix's surprise and puzzlement, Sergeant Pereira woke him with the news that the area in front of the fort was deserted, the Nkumbi warriors had slipped away before dawn.

Cornet Felix had to wait until 18 January for an answer to the Nkumbi withdrawal. The defenders peered through the darkness as the fort was again surrounded; a piercing cry signalled the onset of the attack followed by sustained and accurate rifle fire. Fortunately the Portuguese officer had made good use of this breathing space and strengthened the fort's defences. He had tasked his Portuguese NCOs to instruct the soldiery in vital musketry techniques, and the attackers were repulsed with large casualties. Sporadic attacks were mounted against the fort on the following night and during daylight on 20 and 24 January. The final attack lasted for five hours before the warriors withdrew. In spite of repeated assaults only one of the defenders had been killed with five wounded, but the siege had only just begun.

Chapter 16
The Relief of Forte Humbe

As a consequence of the massacre at Jambacamufate, the Humbe region was again in open rebellion against Portuguese authority. At Katekero, José Lopes had been told of the siege of *Forte Humbe* and had been warned that his farm would be attacked. On the same day of the first attack on *Forte Humbe*, a small party of Nkumbi were seen in the bush close to his farm but were beaten off by Lopes and his farm hands, however, a number of other European traders and hunters were not so lucky.

Artur de Paiva, now promoted to colonel, had gone on to serve with distinction in military campaigns in Mozambique, but was back on very familiar territory and yet again struggling manfully to put a viable military force together. The Portuguese government had been severely shaken by the massacre at Jambacamufate and feared that the ignominious defeat would encourage not only the warlike Nkumbi and Kwanyama clans but also would be watched with grim satisfaction by their European neighbours in German South West Africa. National prestige now hinged on de Paiva swiftly reoccupying the Humbe region.

Colonel de Paiva's initial concern was the state of the weather – it was the rainy season and the worst time to mount a campaign in the waterlogged Humbe region. That problem was compounded by a lack of ammunition; during the dragoon's shambolic withdrawal from *Forte Humbe* Captain da Silva had contrived to leave most of the ammunition behind. De Paiva had no time to lose, as there had been no news from the defenders of *Forte Humbe*. The clans of Mulondo, Kamba and the Gambos were in ferment and it was strongly rumoured that the Kwamato were preparing for war. So against his better judgement he began to plan the composition of his relieving force. The plan was to establish his headquarters at Chibia and then follow the route of the Kakulovar River, using Kahama as his jumping off point for operations in the Humbe region. On 2 January 1898, the column's advance party, under command of Second Lieutenant José Nogueira, and made up of light infantry, dragoons and auxiliaries plus 27 Boer wagons, left Humpata for the south. The Angolan authorities in Luanda had provided naval gunboats to transport a mixed infantry and artillery force of 130 men down to the port of Mossâmedes. The troops embarked on 20 December but their arrival in theatre was delayed due to lack of ammunition and supplies. The troops finally began their deployment from Chibia on 24 January.

The column led by de Paiva, left Chibia in torrential rain, and was forced to halt and laager at Yoba to await the arrival of the ammunition wagons, which had been bogged down in the cloying mud. The column finally set off in the early afternoon of the next day. The outbreak of bovine sickness meant that fresh draught oxen were being used and the animals were unfamiliar with their drivers, leading to constant accidents and hold ups. As darkness fell, the straggling column halted at the stockaded Tchiongo water holes, only to find the water undrinkable; buffalo spoors led to a break in the fence where it had been heavily contaminated by animal droppings. In order to compensate for the delays, the column set off with the heaviest wagons in the lead, and reached Quihita and its mission station on the Kakulovar River late in the evening on 27 January. The men and animals were exhausted. All the following day was spent resting and repairing damaged wagons and equipment. After a chilling night, the trek recommenced in thick fog, and the column halted to rest at Muchuwakae in order to replenish their water stocks from the river. In the afternoon they left for Beriambundo and after a brief stop at 5:00, the column trekked on in bright moonlight until they reached their objective. Captain Bivar, the cavalry commander, a normally mild-mannered officer, was becoming increasingly irritable with his troopers, and had complained to the surgeon of a blinding headache. Shortly after, as he rode forward to reconnoitre an *omaramba*, he was seen to slump forward on to his horse's neck. Bivar was lifted out of the saddle and carried to the ambulance wagon where his condition began to deteriorate rapidly. Early in the morning on 30 January, the column moved towards Nyoca where the wagons were laagered. The Kakulovar was ten kilometres from the laager and the draught animals had been taken there to water. Unfortunately for the column, the soldiers had failed to count them all back in. They were now short of oxen for two wagons, that had to be left behind under guard while the column pressed on towards Chimbemba – capital of Gambos - and laagered there at 8:15 that night, after a long, hard and tiring day. Due to Captain Bivar's serious condition, it was decided to leave him at Chimbemba, to be removed later to Huíla; de Paiva appointed Lieutenant Costa to command the cavalry. It was not until 4:00 in the afternoon, in searing heat, that the column recommenced its trek, but once again the animals for four wagons had gone astray and had to be rounded up. The column laagered after dark at Mukope and was joined by the missing wagons at midnight.

On 1 February the column laagered at Mulola and saw enemy activity for the first time, but the Nkumbi melted into the bush before de Paiva could call out his scouts. The column passed Enkonde where they learned that José Lopes' mounted patrol had been forced to free a group of Nkumbi, taken prisoner near Jamabacamufate. As it was already dark, they laagered and posted extra sentries. The local people were not impressed by the bedraggled column or by the soldiers' dirty and torn uniforms; some of the infantry were shirtless. De

Paiva was informed that two old men from a nearby kraal had been overheard ironically questioning if these soldiers were really going to defeat the Nkumbi. With Portuguese prestige in mind, de Paiva ordered all his officers and NCOs to remove their rank insignia.

The column reached Lage and set up camp at dusk within a baobab forest. Resupplying the column with water was fraught with danger; the riverbank was teeming with crocodiles that were almost impossible to see in the darkness. De Paiva ordered his commissary officer to break out the water ration and distribute it to the column. Early next morning, the wagons were inspanned and the column set out towards Honkombe, arriving there at nightfall and laagering close to the fast flowing river. On the road from Honkombe, the column came across two mounds topped with crosses, roughly fashioned out of a wooden biscuit box. The wagons continued on to Cahama, arriving in the early evening. There were 500 auxiliaries waiting with the advanced column and they noisily greeted de Paiva and his men. The advanced column was generally in good order, but all the draught animals had died, and de Paiva was forced to purchase costly, vaccinated oxen. It was not the ideal place to laager; all around the wagons were burning carcasses and the cloying stench of putrefaction. No news had been received from *Forte Humbe*, 110 kilometres away, as messengers sent out on the road had been captured, tortured and murdered, and the Tchicusse military post had been attacked.

A reconnaissance patrol went out to search for a site for a military post that would ensure stable communications with Gambos. For two days the column made running repairs to wagons, and checked weapons and ammunition. De Paiva's anger and frustration increased when on a routine inspection, he discovered that to serve as shelter from the rain, the dragoons had removed the tarpaulins covering the barrels of precious gunpowder. On 6 February, 25 scouts and 300 auxiliaries, under Lieutenant Quintino Rogado, reconnoitred the right bank of the Kakulovar, but were forced to abandon their task, as thunder, lightning, rain, and howling winds made further scouting impossible. Next morning, after boiling up their iron coffee pots, shaking out soaked blankets and cleaning muddied weapons, de Paiva held a roll call; three drivers reported sick with high fevers and seven men were struggling against the debilitating effects of dysentery. The scouting party was sent out again and attacked by warriors from kraals at Mutukwa. They had been lying in wait in a large outcrop of reeds, close to their village. The scouts heavily outnumbered the Mutukwa and drove them back into the reeds, where they were quickly encircled. The fighting was fierce though one-sided; 30 dead warriors were counted in the bloodstained outcrop. The survivors, unable now to defend their wives and kraals, were heard splashing into the river, and were shot as they attempted to make for the safety of the opposite bank. Quintino Rogado entered the deserted village and commandeered all its remaining livestock, but he was unable to prevent his auxiliaries from ransacking the settlement. On 8 February a cavalry troop with sixteen soldiers was detailed to Ediva to escort two carts carrying ammunition. During the dragoons' precipitous retreat from *Forte Humbe*, Captain da Silva had abandoned 24,000 boxed-rounds of Kropatschek ammunition.

The skies opened up, and the troops detailed to transfer ammunition to Tchicusse, spent a miserable day battling torrential rain and high winds. The rains continued unabated all night. Soldiers and troopers were soaked and the officers doing their rounds waded through waist high water. On that dreadful night, as Captain Guimarães struggled through the mud and rain to reach the Portuguese pickets, he was struck by the thought that this really could herald the beginning of the end. After a sleepless night everyone was up well before dawn trying desperately to get their cooking pot fires going, and at daybreak the remaining force left Cahama in heavy rain with the wagons' wheels churning and skidding in the deep mud. The column was almost immediately held up by fourteen wagons, which had sunk up to their axles; it took three hours to get them back on the road again and it took a further twelve hours before the column finally reach Tchicusse. They had travelled less than fifteen kilometres. The next five days were spent rebuilding the fort at Tchicusse, repairing wagons and getting supplies and transport over the river. The column departed on 14 February, leaving a sergeant, 30 Portuguese soldiers and 30 auxiliaries, with one 75mm gun and ammunition, to garrison *Forte Tchicusse*. Many wagons had to be left as they lacked draught oxen. The column was now composed of dragoons armed with Kropatschek carbines and a detachment of Portuguese Light Infantry from 1, 2, and 4 companies, armed with the heavy and cumbersome Snider rifles; the Portuguese infantry was still awaiting new issue. The European auxiliaries were a mix of Madeiran colonists and Boers from Chibia and were armed with Martini-Henry rifles; Mukankalas and Bushmen armed with a motley collection of weapons brought the total force to above 1,000 men. The column was now entering hostile territory.

It was Colonel de Paiva's intention to split the column, and have them advance on either side of the Kakulovar River but this would have proved impractical and very dangerous; had one of the columns been engaged by the enemy, the column on the opposite bank of the fast running and swollen river would have been reduced to the rôle of powerless spectator. As the left bank was lined by dense bush and reed beds, stretching as far as Humbe, and the right bank had less foliage for the first 25 kilometres, it would be easier going for artillery and cavalry. De Paiva changed his plan; the entire column would keep to the right bank. After calling his officers together in his command tent to give them their revised dispositions, the column continued on and arrived at Coya Onantana in the early afternoon where they bivouacked. After resting, the column led off with an advanced guard composed of one dragoon troop and two light infantry platoons; fourteen wagons and artillery limbers were in the centre of the column protected by dragoons and infantry, followed by a rearguard of dragoons and two companies of light infantry. Mounted auxiliaries flanked the column with scouts pushing out in all directions.

On 15 February the column headed through Mutukwa, where days earlier, Quintino Rogado's patrol had fought a pitched battle around the reed outcrop, and where his auxiliaries had indulged in an orgy of destruction. Now the spiralling smoke from the devastated kraals at Munyade, two kilometres from Mutukwa, gave notice of de Paiva's intentions. When the column had reached Munyande, he had ordered his auxiliaries not to set fire to Chief *Muene* Dilungo's kraal; it was to be spared the flames. The chief, his wives, children and livestock, had joined the column at Tchicusse. The old chief had feared retribution from the Nkumbi, having earlier, given temporary shelter to two African soldiers who had fled to his kraal, following the massacre at Jamabacamufate. Above the crackling of the flames and the wailing of the womenfolk, the Portuguese heard the faint sound of war chants and drumming carried on the stiff breeze. A scouting party, under Sergeant Francisco Correia, was detailed to advance in skirmish order along the track as far as the kraals at Jambacamufate.

The skirmishers were fired on, and after a sharp engagement, Correia gave the order to withdraw to the safety of the column. De Paiva immediately sent the cavalry forward to cut down the Nkumbi, while the bulk of the African auxiliaries advanced on a wide front. The Nkumbi were pushed back and were now defending their kraals and their families. In sheer panic many women, children and old people tried to make their escape by fording the Kakulovar and were swept to their deaths in the swiftly flowing river or were taken by crocodiles. The Portuguese counted 116 dead Nkumbi warriors on the battlefield, and captured a quantity of weapons and Kropatschek ammunition. After the battle, the auxiliaries noisily celebrated the victory in front of de Paiva's wagon.

Early on 17 February the column slowly rumbled through clouds of acrid smoke from smouldering kraals, on its way to Bandeira. Nkumbi dead were strewn in clumps by the wayside. At times, the smoke from the burning kraals, combined with the glaring sun, became too much for the wagoners who were forced to cover their eyes with bandanas. The column then halted in thick thorn bush, while they awaited the Boer wagons. In the centre of the column, the artillery battery was up to its knees in water. Suddenly, shooting broke out on the left flank and men were rapidly detailed to aid the rearguard echelon in getting the bogged-down wagons moving. Captain Guimarães waded his way through to the ammunition wagons with the intention of fusing the artillery shells, only to find they were empty of powder. Had de Paiva not previously discovered the damp gunpowder, and dried it out, Guimarães' efforts would have been in vain. Crouching on a dry powder keg, in volunteer Kobus Viljoen's wagon, he stoically recharged the shells, before handing them over to the gunners. De Paiva believed that it was cannon fire above all, which had a demoralising affect on the Nkumbi. That night, with the column securely laagered, orders were given to fire a number of harassing rounds in the direction of the kraals at Tchifito. On 18 February as the column headed towards Tchifito, it found the track blocked by a two-metre high thorn bush barricade. The Nkumbi had hoped to lure the Portuguese into a trap by making it impossible for the wagons to turn, but their plan was foiled. The Portuguese advanced guard had thrown its scouts out towards the river, where they had come into contact with the Nkumbi, who had been forced to scramble down the slippery, thorn lined bank into the swift flowing river; few escaped with their lives. A number of Portuguese weapons and cavalry equipment from the massacre at Jambacamufate were captured from the Nkumbi kraals.

By 19 February weather conditions had become unbearable. It took the column eight hours to move the four kilometres to Ongo as the wagons were constantly trapped in the boggy ground. The column had just laagered when a group of Nkumbi were seen in the distance on the far side of the river. There was sporadic shooting during the night but the column was not attacked. Now there were only two kilometres separating the column from the 200-metre-wide Mukope River, but they were dismayed to see an unending vista of glistening swampland, stretching out before them. De Paiva ordered a large fatigue party to backtrack to a deserted kraal and pull up the stakes from the stockaded walls in order to lay down a track across the worst part of the waterlogged ground. With the timbers in place, the wagons began to achieve traction and the column moved to within 1,500 metres of the river, but de Paiva now had to deal with a further obstacle as the river divided into two 100 metre wide forks. At dawn on 21 February the Boer wagons were emptied and the wagoners whipped their oxen down the bank and into the water. There had been a critical miscalculation, and the water steadily began to rise over the axles and upwards; it was a tense moment and the wagoners were about to swim for it, but the river bottomed out and the oxen and wagons were able to cross without further mishap. As with every crossing, shots were fired into the water to discourage crocodiles from venturing too close to the labouring oxen. The soldiers and the ammunition were transported over in small canvas boats while supplies were carried across on improvised rafts, and by a rough Nkumbi bridge, sagging into the swift running river. By the end of the day the majority of the men were lying exhausted on the far side of the riverbank. Just then, a large group of African auxiliaries who had earlier been sent back with the fatigue party appeared loaded down with booty from the Nkumbis' deserted and ruined kraals. That night, in spite of the appalling conditions, bonfires were lit on both arms of the river which afforded the column some security from attack and kept the lions and hyenas away from the draught oxen; though it created difficulties for the sentries who were unable to see beyond the flames. In the middle of the night exhausted officers ate cold beans and downed red wine in the light of the blazing bonfires. By 22 February, the entire column was over the river and laagered at Katekero. As there had been no sign of the enemy, and *Forte Humbe* was only ten kilometres distant, de Paiva suspected a trap en route and sent out a scouting patrol to reconnoitre the road. An hour later shots were heard and de Paiva ordered out a further mounted scouting party; but it returned having seen nothing. He later learned that the firing had been an exuberant greeting from the Mondongo kraals close to Humbe. The Humbe relief column arrived in the early morning and was rapturously greeted by its defenders. The fort had held out against attack but had been so badly damaged that de Paiva's men had to construct a sick bay for the wounded and emaciated survivors. He commandeered a damaged trader's store as the officers' headquarters. The ammunition in the powder magazine was in a deplorable state, and it took hard work to dry it out and refill the shells and repair three damaged French 8cm cannon. The garrison had little food left and was down to its last 6,000 rounds of ammunition.

On 26 February, a runner informed de Paiva that the Kwamato war chief Djimba, *soba* of Jambacamufate, who had fled south of the Kunene in a bid to evade capture, had been cornered with his bodyguard by men of the Mondongo clan, and after a short but bloody struggle, had been taken prisoner and was being brought back to Humbe.

Colonel de Paiva and his makeshift column had ridden out to avenge the massacre with a signal, crushing defeat of the Nkumbi clans, but after exhausting campaigning in terrible weather conditions over inhospitable terrain, against the tactically astute Nkumbi, de Paiva was forced to pull back his now depleted and fever-wracked column to the safety of the Chela Highlands. Jamabacamufate would have to be avenged on another day.

Chapter 17
British and German Designs on Portuguese Africa

The dawn of the twentieth century found Portugal a poor and troubled country. More than 61 per cent of its people worked on the land, in back breaking labour from dawn till dusk, in the drenching rains of spring, and through the searing summer droughts and famine; 78 per cent of Portugal's land was used for farming.

An official government census in 1900 registered more than four million illiterates out of a population of five and a half million, including the remote semi-tropical Atlantic islands of the Azores and Madeira. Educating such a hapless, ragged multitude was far beyond the competence of a rampantly corrupt and inefficient bureaucracy; Portugal boasted a meagre 1,882 schools countrywide. Official government statistics for 1878, recorded an 82% illiteracy rate, twelve years later it stood at 79% and by 1907 it had dropped just one percentage point. Pellagra, a chronic disease of chronic poverty, carried many victims to an early grave; tuberculosis took 45,000 souls annually, while gastroenteritis killed even more infant Portuguese. During the first three years of the new century, 26,494 children up to the age of two years died of malnutrition – their starved and anguished mothers were physically incapable of providing maternal milk.

Squat, raven haired, leathery-skinned peasants, still young yet already physically spent, scratched a living as migratory labourers, working on the cork and olive plantations of the Alentejo - that bleached and cloudless region to the south of the River Tegus. Grimacing in the midday glare, with smooth, goatskin water gourds propped to cushion their aching backs against the rock-strewn earth, they would eat their meagre fare. They were typical of many of their folk; unable to read or write and knowing nothing of life save for the endless struggle to make ends meet at the behest of rich and absent landlords. Men and women of Lusitania caught up in a tragic and perpetual cycle of poverty, hunger and disease. Yet these same people were forced to pay some of the highest taxes on the continent of Europe, due in large part to the total mismanagement of Portugal's finances.

João Chagas, the volatile Brazilian born, sometime pro-monarchist turned republican pamphleteer, had outraged many of his political friends and scandalised the nation, by publicly declaring from the safety of his Parisian refuge, the true extent of his country's enormous financial deficit. By 1892, soaring debt and the virtual mortgaging of customs, railway and tobacco revenue left the government with nothing further to hock. A steady hand on the tiller of state was needed, to guide her through turbulent financial waters but the captain of that metaphorical ship, Prime-minister José Dias Ferreira, aimed to reorganise the country's financial affairs and had openly declared the country's inability to meet the interest on its external debt. He then panicked and issued a government decree drastically reducing the amount owed to Portugal's foreign creditors and bondholders by an incredible two-thirds. It was to signal the last desperate act of a desperate politician. Portugal's heavy debts and obvious vulnerability had led those foreign interests to openly and vehemently press for complete control of its revenues, and the illegal and ill-considered measure, was very naturally, hotly opposed in the teak walled, leather-chaired boardrooms of northern Europe. After much soul-searching, the Portuguese government managed to negotiate a deal with the Council of Foreign Bondholders in London. It was agreed that in return for a number of specific guarantees, the creditors would forego one half of the interest on the loans. However, it proved unacceptable to the Portuguese public. Politicians pressed for a review; the horizon began to clear and a compromise was reached whereby Portugal pledged enhanced terms to her powerful foreign creditors; it became law a year later. In order to fulfil that agreement, Dias Ferreira attempted to push through a number of draconian tax increases to raise further revenue, but even the long suffering Portuguese had had enough and the government slowly sank without trace.

Earlier in 1898, Berlin's proposals for an Anglo-German understanding on issues relating to the spoils of Portugal's distant colonies, should the Portuguese default on their financial obligations, were raised in discussions with the Foreign Office. Britain's envoy at Lisbon, the former Rifle Brigade officer Sir Hugh MacDonell, had informed the Foreign Office that the price of bread, coal and other essentials had rocketed and that Portugal found itself in dire straits with the monarch apparently blind to his perilous situation. Like card players seated around a green baize table playing for Portugal's colonies, it was noddingly agreed, through the thick blue vapour of stout Havanas, that Britain should take for herself all of Portuguese East Africa south of the Zambezi River plus the northern part of Angola. Germany in turn would have southern Angola, all of Portuguese East Africa north of the Zambezi River, and for good measure; the island of Timor would be thrown in to swell the jackpot.

The Windsor Accord had been re-negotiated and signed on 14 October 1899 by the aloof and taciturn Robert Cecil, the Marques of Salisbury, and by Luís Soveral, the Anglophile Portuguese ambassador to the Court of St. James. Soveral had put his signature to the accord on behalf of his sovereign; Dom Carlos I. Portugal agreed to abstain from a declaration of neutrality in the South African War. Portugal further agreed to prohibit the importation and passage of arms and munitions through Mozambique to the Transvaal Republic. In return,

Britain agreed to recognise and guarantee the territorial integrity of Portugal and her colonies, which at that time, the Portuguese were powerless to defend against external enemies.

In 1904 the government and monarchy suffered yet another shock this time military rather than economic. News began to filter through to Lisbon that Portuguese forces, which had been deployed in the vast and still untamed lands of southern Angola had suffered a major defeat. The daily newspaper *O Século* carried the bleak news to the corridors of power and to the armchair intelligentsia of Lisbon. Portugal's reputation was again besmirched by yet more colonial incompetence.

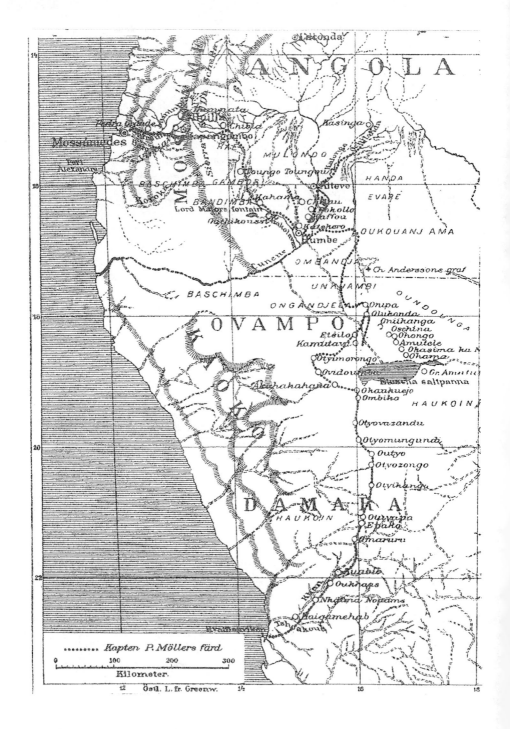

Captain Möller's Map of Angola and Ovamboland 1896 (Struik)

João Teixeira Pinto at Dongoena, Angola 1907 (Agência Geral das Colónas)

Chief Abdul Injai, commanding Auxiliary forces, Portuguese Guinea 1915
(Agência Geral das Colónas)

Nkumbi Hunter, Angola 1896
(Struik)

Kuvale Warriors, Angola 1896 (Struik)

Captain Roçadas at Aucongo in 1907 (Imprensa Nacional)

Kwanyama men and women, Angola 1896 (Struik)

Chief Mandume of
the Kwanyama
(Ilustraçâo
Portuguesa)

Kalibulala at Naloeke in 1907 with
Nephew Samuel and servant
(Imprensa Nacional)

IÇAR DA BANDEIRA NACIONAL NO FORTE DE BAILUNDO

Raising the colours at Bailundo Fort ((Agência Geral das Colónas)

Murdungaz — o célebre e aguerrido Régulo «Gungunhana», préxo em Gaza por Mousinho de Albuquerque, em 1895, depois levado para Lisboa, em 1896, morreu em Angra do Heroismo, onde estava desterrado, em 1912.
Murdungaz — the furious and valiant Chief Gungunhana, captured by Mousinho de Albuquerque in Gaza in 1895, and sent to Lisbon in 1896, died in 1912 at Angra do Heroismo, where he was kept a prisoner.
Murdungaz — le célèbre Chef guerrier «Gungunhana» fut prisonnier à Gaza par Mousinho de Albuquerque en 1895, il fut envoyé à Lisbonne en 1896 et mourut en 1912 à Angra do Heroismo, où il était comme prisonnier.

Chief Gungunyana, 1895 (Fundação Portugal—Africa)

Crossing the Kakulovar River, Angola 1896 (Struik)

Crossing the Kunene River, Angola 1896 (Struik)

Chapter 18
Disaster at Pembe Drift

The governor of Mossâmedes, Captain João Maria de Aguiar, had advocated the occupation of Portuguese Kwamatoland in 1901. But it was not until 1904 that clear strategic objectives were prepared for the establishment of Portuguese authority between the Kunene and Kubango rivers in Kwamatoland. However, all did not go to plan. The Portuguese suffered a military defeat in the Lesser Kwamato region on the west bank of the Kunene River at a crossing known as Pembe Drift.

The governor-general of Angola, naval Captain Custódia Borja, ordered de Aguiar, with Captain Manuel de Oliveira Gomes da Costa, to lead a column of 1,800 troops into Kwamatoland. The column was composed of two Portuguese infantry companies, under lieutenants Salgado and Tamegão, and two African companies commanded by lieutenants Roberto Pacheco and Carlos Fonseca, a dragoon squadron under Lieutenant Ventura, two artillery batteries commanded by Captain Pinto de Almeida, and a naval artillery detachment under ensign Filemon de Almeida. The ever capable, enthusiastic and battle-scarred José Lopes commanded the African auxiliaries.

The Portuguese column was to march south and take on the Kwamato in their homeland. De Aguiar's force concentrated at Lubango at the end of August, before moving in a south-easterly direction towards the Gambos. They marched through waving, mielie plantations, before entering baobab and palm forests, to be slowed down by seemingly limitless, thick, thorn bush. It was a mountainous region with a single, very rough track, and the column's wagons were constantly in need of repair to broken wheels and shattered axles. The troops were relieved to see Mount Tongo-Tongo shimmering mirage-like in the distance; it would provide them with of a good, safe camping place, after labouring up hill under a broiling sun. Later when the troops arrived at Gambos, they were disappointed to discover that the fort was now completely dilapidated. The small barracks was in an appalling state; the walls were crumbling and the doors and windows had been ripped out to provide fuel to warm the kraals during the sharp winter nights. The column left early next day and halted at Forno de Cal where cold rations were eaten before pushing on to Kakolongongo. The column was now passing through a region teeming with elephants and buffaloes; giraffe threaded their lofty way through the dense thorn bush lining each side of the track. The column was critically running short of water and its supply wagons had been slowed down by the deaths of many of the draught oxen, and were still many kilometres behind the foot-slogging column. As the marching men entered a wide park-like plain they were relieved to see *Forte Humbe* through the heat haze in the far distance. In response to a booming cannon shot from the column, Captain Gomes da Costa, the Humbe district officer rode out with a small escort to greet Aguiar and his men. After spending a night laagered under the mud and stonewalls of *Forte Humbe* the column marched out towards the Kunene River, which they reached in the early afternoon.

Through his binoculars, de Aguiar, was able to observe a large group of heavily armed warriors on the far side of the river. On spotting the Portuguese, the Kwamato quickly melted into the thick Mukohimo thorn bush. The Kunene River was now the last obstacle. The artillery was ordered to unlimber and prepare to give covering fire as the African auxiliaries began to ford the Kunene. The infantry were to follow in shallow, collapsible canvas boats, then the staff officers, and the remainder of the infantry. The wagons and artillery would go over last, followed up the rear by the cavalry. However, the crossing was delayed by the heavy Boer wagons that had sunk into the sandy riverbed, and had to be dug out. The first infantry elements to force their way through the thick reed beds and scramble up the riverbank were ordered to take up defensive positions facing dense bush, and protect the wagons and artillery pieces as they struggled to make headway over the drift. In spite of constant sniping, the infantry dug in and returned fire at the unseen enemy. As soon as the artillery was over the river, it began to bombard the line of thick thorn bush. In the distance, well out of rifle range, large groups of Kwamato warriors were seen observing the crossing.

Captain de Aguiar ordered his infantrymen to roll out three lines of barbed wire and dig a defensive trench around the square with the 37mm guns defending it. At its centre, was the command tent with the column's regimental standards and a brass 7.05cm cannon. The sporadic shooting continued into the late afternoon, giving the infantry ample time to identify the enemies' weapons as Kropatscheck, Mauser, Snider and the older Martini-Henry. Shortly before nightfall, sentries were sent out to dig and occupy shallow berms some metres beyond the wire. The soldiers broke out their cold rations after dark to the sound of desultory rifle fire. De Aguiar suspected that the enemy would attack later that night when the moon went down, but although there was almost no sleep for the weary column, the enemy attack failed to materialise. At first light the crossing was renewed. In spite of infantry sorties to the edge of the bush, the sniping continued. Meanwhile, the sick and wounded had remained in the field ambulance wagons on the Humbe bank of the river, they now had to be ferried over under sporadic fire. The Portuguese were laagered on the opposite bank of the Kunene 100 metres from the river. What Captain de Aguiar did not know, was that the enemy facing his column was made up of 1,000 fresh and fit warriors; many were trained riflemen, under Chief Igura of Lesser Kwamato and Chief Shawlo of Greater Kwamato.

On the morning of 20 September, a mixed cavalry and infantry fighting patrol commanded by Gomes da Costa, was ordered out and advanced to the edge of the dense bush before withdrawing to the safety of the Portuguese position without having encountered the enemy. However, almost immediately upon their return, Kwamato sharpshooters fired on the position causing a number of casualties. In the energy sapping heat of the early afternoon, Portuguese vedettes reported movement around a number of distant ant heaps and the square was stood to, and soon a line of disciplined Kwamato skirmishers began to advance and pour sustained and accurate fire into the Portuguese square. The warriors pressed the attack and through the gritty smoke of battle, reached to within 300 metres of the square, falling back towards the ant heaps. Captain de Aguiar then ordered the artillery into action to support the infantry and African auxiliaries, and eventually the Kwamato were pushed back from the ant heaps. In the blackness before dawn on 22 September, enemy rifle fire intensified, sore-eyed sentries reported seeing shapes steadily advancing towards the Portuguese wire. Lieutenant João de Sousa and an infantry corporal, felt their way along the trench to the Hotchkiss machine gun, and then raked the attackers with machine gun fire, but after a long burst, the gun jammed. As dawn broke, de Sousa heard Portuguese voices calling out from beyond the wire. He realised to his horror, that the dead and wounded were African auxiliaries, who had been mown down, after returning from a night patrol accompanied by a small number of Portuguese infantrymen. As a result of the night's bloody confusion, some 400 African auxiliaries lined up in front of Captain de Aguiar, and silently handed over their weapons before recrossing the river and trekking back with their dead and wounded.

From that time on, Captain de Aguiar was gripped by inactivity, while the force remained dug in on the riverbank. The soldiers were now beginning to suffer from the effects of the extremes of day and night temperatures, and more seriously, fever and the ever present enemy; amoebic dysentery. The constant night alarms were taking their toll on the Portuguese defenders' nerves as the entrenchments had been sited directly in the path of the drift, which also served as a favoured watering place for wild animals. Throughout the long nights, the exhausted Portuguese were stood to as ratels, having gorged on kiaat pods, would make for the drift and snag themselves on the wire entanglements. The officers began to complain among themselves as de Aguiar's increasing irritability and critical attitude towards them was becoming intolerable; they were constantly being pulled up for failing to salute him correctly.

On the morning of 25 September, Kwamato riders appeared, dismounted, opened up a brisk fire on the static Portuguese defences, remounted and rode off before the artillery could get their range. Later, scouts on the Humbe bank of the river, informed de Aguiar of an approaching column, which turned out to be a detachment under command of naval Lieutenant João Roby, and naval surgeon Dr Manuel João da Silveira. Twenty-nine-year-old Roby had seen active service in both Angola and Mozambique, and possessed a lively spirit, coupled with an almost boyish sense of adventure. Both men had been on their way from Mozambique and had just received official permission to join de Aguiar's column. Their arrival was a welcome fillip to the static force. De Aguiar had earlier prepared and shelved a plan of action in which he would lead a 400-strong reconnaissance patrol with Gomes da Costa, as second-in-command. Now, Gomes da Costa had been tasked to lead the patrol with Lieutenant Roby and with Second Lieutenant Pacheco Leão in command of the Humbe auxiliaries. The patrol was to be composed of two mixed infantry platoons, a cavalry troop, a naval detachment with one 37mm gun and 60 auxiliaries.

On the following morning, Gomes da Costa's men were up well before dawn and having eaten cold rations, the patrol set out at first light moving parallel with the river towards the Mukohimo bush, from where Kwamato sharpshooters had been harassing the column. The Portuguese warily entered the thick, thorn wilderness, and after three kilometres, came to a park-like clearing, which provided the patrol with a welcome respite from the backbreaking work of cutting their way through the tangled thorn. Two kilometres further on, they reached a second clearing, where they came up with a determined enemy that had to be charged with the bayonet, before fleeing into the bush. The Portuguese then discovered a large kraal, which Gomes da Costa ordered to be razed to the ground, before the patrol made its way back to the main force. De Aguiar was delighted with the results of the reconnaissance patrol.

On 28 September he ordered a detachment of 500 soldiers under command of Captain Pinto de Almeida, with Lieutenant Roby and cavalry Lieutenant, Francisco Resende, to scout ahead of the column and reconnoitre the tangle of thorn bush and mopani trees farther along the trail. No sooner had the detachment entered the bush than the Kwamato warriors fired on it. As the warriors were hidden, Pinto de Almeida ordered his men forward towards a clearing to draw enemy fire, and only then did he begin to form a defensive square. The Portuguese were now completely surrounded and were firing wildly into the bush at unseen targets, while the enemy picked them off at will from their hiding places in the tops of the trees. Captain Pinto de Almeida and the remnants of his detachment attempted a fighting withdrawal but ammunition was running low; their wild firing had cost them dearly. Soon the

Portuguese were fighting with the bayonet, but the depleted detachment was vastly outnumbered and was soon cut up and wiped out to a man. The Kwamato carried off the captured Portuguese weapons and silently slipped away into the deep, thorn bush, leaving a feast for the lurking jackals and hyenas. On hearing rifle fire from within the bush, scouts were sent forward from the defensive position and reported back seeing Kwamato warriors waving articles of Portuguese uniforms in the air. While the Kwamato celebrated their victory, de Aguiar, realising that Pinto de Almeida and his men were beyond help, gave the order for the column to withdraw across the river towards Humbe. To the sharp pistol-like crack of sjamboks and shrill whistles, the wagoners forced their teams down the slippery bank and into the river to eventual safety. The infantry were the last to abandon their entrenched defences and make their way over the drift as best they could, some in the remaining canvas boats, others clinging to ropes slung across the fast flowing drift.

The Pembe massacre had the depressing and predictable affect of lowered Portuguese prestige in the region. The Portuguese dead amounted to 254 soldiers, including sixteen officers. The emboldened Kwamato clans began to commit systematic acts of violence against those whom they believed had previously been friendly to the Portuguese colonists and soldiers. The effects of bloody retribution were to be seen everywhere, and the Portuguese, due in large part to de Aguiar's miscalculations, were once again powerless to stop it. Paramount chief Chietakelo of the Kwamato nation was now able to send his impis over the Kunene River totally unopposed, and begin to harass and murder colonists and traders at will; the clock had once again been turned back on the Portuguese in southern Angola.

Chapter 19
Roçadas in Southern Angola 1906-07

In 1905, in response to the morale-sapping disaster at Pembe Drift, Lisbon ordered José Augusto Alves Roçadas to command an expedition against the Kwamato clans. Colonel Alves Roçadas had served the colours since joining 2 Infantry Regiment in 1879. In 1902 he was posted to Goa in Portuguese India, as chief-of-staff to the Expeditionary Corps, commanded by the Duke of Braganza, and subsequently became governor-general of Portuguese India and later governor of Huíla District. Though he was a less than imposing figure; diminutive, narrow shouldered with a high forehead, receding hair and clipped moustache, he was a highly regarded officer. A colonial administrator of vast experience he had led his country's delegation to the Anglo-Portuguese Conference at Pretoria in the Transvaal.

Captain Alves Roçadas' first priority was to draw up a detailed map of Kwamatoland, and within a six-month period, occupy the Lower Kunene region peopled by the Kwanyama, Kwamato and Evale. Captain Eduardo Marques was ordered to carry out a reconnaissance of the area and also gauge the loyalty of the local chieftains in case of war. Roçadas received intelligence that Chief Dungula of the Mulondo clan, had barred Portuguese officials and traders from entering the region, he further believed that the chief had, in effect, created a state within a state, ruled by fear. Once Marques had completed his reconnaissance, Alves Roçadas held a council of war. Prior to full-scale operations, small military actions would take place to consolidate Portuguese control over the lands on the right bank of the Kunene River. The drifts would be guarded and operations against hostile factions would be put into place.

By the end of August, Alves Roçadas had formulated a plan in which, after defeating Dungula and destroying his power base at Mulondo, he would reinstate Chief João of Gambos, a Portuguese ally, and mount offensive operations in strength against the Kwamato clans.

Captain Alves Roçadas' column, with Captain Marques, as second-in-command, was made up of a half battery of two 75mm field guns with 38 gunners, 60 cavalry troopers mounted on mules, 215 Portuguese infantrymen, 208 men from 12 Company, Mozambique Native Infantry, 25 sappers and 100 Portuguese, Boer and African auxiliaries, with a large supply column made up of ten Boer wagons. The straggling column trekked out of Huíla on 23 September, and marched eastward to Capelongo, where it was joined by the Boer leaders, Andries Alberts, and Willem Venter, of the Humpata Commando. The combined force then followed the line of the Kunene River, 380 kilometres south, towards the Gambos region. On 19 October the column reached the military post at Kiteve, where Alves Roçadas finalised his plans with his officers, prior to the assault on Mulondo Kraal, 23 kilometres distant on the left bank of the Kunene. The date for the attack was to be the 25 October. The cavalry detachment was sent forward but reported back that they had seen no sign of life whatsoever; the enemy had evidently withdrawn to the safety of the kraal. Captain Zacarias Pereira, accompanied by a guide, approached the kraal unseen, and from his hiding place on a low kopje, drew a detailed sketch, which he delivered to Roçadas two days later. The Royal Kraal of Chief Dungula of Mulondo represented a formidable obstacle to the Portuguese commander and his column. The kraal was circular in shape, 500 metres in diameter, with an earthwork-shored stockade of five-meter high, sharpened poles, surrounded by a deep ditch and a natural thorn zareba. The sketch also showed five narrow openings in the zareba, which led to the interior of the kraal. An inner palisade further protected the royal apartments.

At first light on 25 October, the column advanced to within 500 meters of Mulondo without resistance. The artillery deployed with its two field guns and opened up on the kraal, firing over the heads of the advancing infantry. The infantry skirmished to within 50 metres of the kraal but were then forced to take cover as Dungula's men began to fire on them from behind the stockaded walls. After being ordered to fix bayonets, the massed infantry then charged forward, clearing the deep ditch, hacking through the thorn zareba, pushing down part of the palisade that had been smashed up by artillery fire, to stream into the inner sanctum. By 10:00 that morning it was all over. The Portuguese had 32 casualties. The infantry counted over 200 dead Mulondo warriors and estimated the wounded to be well over 300. The only disappointment for Alves Roçadas was that Chief Dungula had fled. Later that day, the Portuguese flag was raised over Dungula's kraal, before Roçadas gave the order to burn it to the ground. With elements of the expeditionary force well dug in, and mounting a round the clock guard against possible counter-attacks, Portuguese army engineers consolidated the column's position by rapidly throwing up a defensive blockhouse, which was named *Forte Mulondo*. Previously, Boer scouts had been sent out deep into hostile territory but reported no sign of the enemy. However, three days later, Willem Venter's men were led to Chief Dungula's badly decomposed body, which was lying in the bush next to a carbine. As proof of the chief's death, his severed head was taken to *Forte Mulondo* by the scouts, and was later buried under its foundations. Before the column left for Humbe on 3 November, Second Lieutenant Francisco Lopes was placed in command of the fort with 60 soldiers, and the two field guns and machine guns used in the assault on Dungula's kraal. Nine days later on 12 November, the victorious force reached *Forte Humbe*.

With the rain rhythmically beating down on Alves Roçadas' command tent, he set to drawing up a plan for the occupation of Greater and Lesser Kwamato. The mission would be to station Boer auxiliaries at Pembe Drift to operate in the Lower Kunene, while Portuguese colonists would operate in Dongoena. The Portuguese forces would execute diversionary movements in order to give the Boer commando and the colonists free rein to complete their respective tasks. Although the Boer commando enjoyed some limited success at Greater Kwamato, the sheer loss of life and number of wounded, dissuaded Alves Roçadas from continuing, and the incessant rains brought the military operations to a close, but not before he had mapped out a revised plan for the military occupation of Kwamatoland. Roçadas outlined his objectives: to capture the *embalas* of the *sobas* of Greater Kwamato and Lesser Kwamato, and to create a series of interlinked military posts throughout the region.

The authorities in Luanda, had ordered the construction of a 73 kilometre-long railway, from Mossâmedes east through the desert to the Chela Highlands. Lubango was chosen as the concentration point for men and supplies, and depots were set up at regular intervals between Lubango and Humbe. Intensive infantry and cavalry training were carried out at Lubango under the eyes of the Portuguese general staff. The infantry had been issued with the latest K.8mm rifle, and the auxiliaries, with the Martini-Henry. Many hours were spent at the firing ranges with troops practising volley fire and skirmishing techniques, backed by live firing from the field guns. The expedition had been provided with supplies for the estimated three months' campaign plus supplies for a further six months of the occupation period. In order to provide support and protection for the troops during the building work, Roçadas ordered his sappers to throw up a small post between Humbe and Mukongo Drift. By 23 August 1907, the 2,212-strong column was already laagered in and around *Forte Roçadas,* and all preparations for the coming expedition were well in hand. The Mixed Brigade was composed of two large infantry battalions, designated 4 Portuguese Battalion and 5 Native Battalion respectively, and 6 Auxiliary Battalion composed of Portuguese nationals, Boers and local peoples. There were two cavalry squadrons and two and a half artillery batteries, made up of ten Erhardt, Krupp and Canet field guns with a machine gun battery. A platoon of sappers plus a large transport train and a well staffed field ambulance provided supplies, ammunition and medical support. On station and anchored close to *Forte Roçadas,* was the gunboat *Cunene,* whose white awnings stood out against the red-banked earthworks of the fort. The sheer size of the column, the noise and activity in and around *Forte Roçadas,* had already begun to make an impression on the Africans in the column's large auxiliary battalion. There had been a delay as the water bowsers had failed to arrive, and as Roçadas was determined not to leave anything to chance, he ordered his sappers to provide an alternative. The sappers, commandeered stacks of iron sheeting, which had been brought to *Forte Roçadas* to provide roofing material, bolted them together and lashed them on to the sturdy frames of stripped-down Boer wagons. The column now had its water supply and was a mobile force to be reckoned with. The strategically sited fort, at the confluence of the Kakulovar and Kunene rivers, was to be the bulwark from where its commander would oversee that troubled region. By occupying the principal entry points to Ovamboland, the Portuguese would be able to control the clans and deny them their former unrestricted movement, and open the way for the development of the region.

The column struck out into Lesser Kwamato and at dawn on Thursday 27 August 1907, after a freezing cold night, Boer scouts reported sighting Kwamato impis moving towards their position; the Mufilo Battle was about to begin. Over 20,000 warriors surged forward through the spiralling dust, rhythmically beating their shields, while the Portuguese officers steadied their troops. For a time, the battle seemed to swing in favour of the massed Kwamato, as they hurled spears and poured accurate rifle fire into the faltering Portuguese-square. The situation was becoming desperate for the sweating, dust caked men, however, a determined sortie by 1 and 2 troop of Angolan Dragoons on their swift Argentine-bred horses, with Portuguese and Boer auxiliaries, followed up by accurate and sustained musketry from detachments of the Naval Brigade within the beleaguered square, turned the tide of battle. By sundown, the badly mauled impis had withdrawn into the darkening bush; the rout was complete. The almost mystical military power of the Kwamato impis was shattered.

One hour's march from Mufilo, were the strategically important *cacimbas* at Aucongo, they were to be the column's next objective. After fighting its way through to the wells, the column was surprised to find the nearby *libatas* – huts - undefended and deserted. Sappers were ordered to construct a fort on a slight elevation overlooking the wells, but their first task was to throw up a lookout tower, which was to become a permanent feature of the fort. The Kwamato guide Kalibulala had told Roçadas there was a large group of *libatas*, one of them belonging to an important spirit medium, three kilometres from Aucongo. Armed with this valuable local knowledge and using Aucongo as its firm base, the force pressed on through the *chana* – clearing - at Makuve. The Portuguese were continually harassed by the Kwamato, but boldly pushed on towards the lands of Aiikar, the uncle of Chietakelo, *soba* of Lesser Kwamato. On 13 September, after a daylong encounter with the enemy, the Portuguese advanced on the water wells at Damequer, where they dug in and formed a defensive position on high ground between two *chanas*. On 20 September the column moved off towards the water wells at Inyoka where they built a further camp with the precious wells at its centre. From the Portuguese position at

Inyoka there were 11 kilometres to the *libatas* at Lesser Kwamato. After bombarding and then assaulting the *embala* they discovered an abandoned smouldering ruin beyond the palisades. The Kwamato had assumed that when the column reached Inyoka, it would push straight on to Lesser Kwamato. From there, the column moved towards Greater Kwamato at Naloeke. On 4 October the Portuguese were fired on as they advanced on the *embala* at Greater Kwamato, but by the time the troops broke through the rough stockades, the enemy had fled. The Portuguese dug in and constructed a post, which was given the name *Forte Eduardo Marques*. Captain Alves Roçadas had attained his objectives; the *embalas* at Greater and Lesser Kwamato had fallen to the Portuguese and a series of forts had been set up throughout the region and most importantly, the power of the *sobas* had been broken.

Chapter 20
Kalibulala – An African Tragedy

Kalibulala had heard the warnings from his *sekulos*; he was not a popular choice as pretender to the crown of Greater Kwamato, Shawlo was the favoured one and Kalibulala had been badly treated by him. Crushed bones and jackals' teeth had been mysteriously strewn on the sandy ground outside his family's *embala* at Naloeke in Greater Kwamato. Witchcraft was in the air. In the dead of night Kalibulala, his family and *sekulos* crept out of their *embala* and headed towards Lesser Kwamato, close to Pembe Drift, where they would seek asylum with distant family members. It was rumoured that Kalibulala had taken no part in the Kwamato victory at Pembe, even though the track past his hosts' kraal was already pockmarked with bleached Portuguese bones. The word was out, warriors had been sent from Greater Kwamato to capture and bring the young royal to Shawlo where he would undergo ritual torture before death. An aged *sekulo* brought the chilling news to the young pretender. First light found him and his retinue riding for their lives towards the Kunene River and *Forte Humbe*. During the previous night, Shawlo's men had surrounded the *embala* at Pembe, and broken down the entrance, only to find it empty. Kalibulala had had a lucky escape.

Kalibulala's frenetic gallop had slackened to a trot and as the morning sun began to burn fiercely in a cloudless sky, he remembered that he had not eaten since slipping out of the *embala*. He heard the sound of voices and looking round saw that he was being pursued by a group of fifteen to twenty heavily armed warriors. As the swiftly running men began to close on his retinue, he could hear their jibes and threats. Ahead, some 600 metres distant was the copper-hued Kunene River, if they could get across before Shawlo's men reached them they would be safe, as the Portuguese were known to patrol the opposite bank. Sensing the young pretenders intentions, the warriors halted and putting their Martini-Henry rifles to their shoulders, took aim at the fleeing figure. When the acrid rifle smoke cleared, the sweating warriors could see no sign of Kalibulala. He had vanished from the face of the earth. His *sekulos* and three mules lay dead, while two mules were running wildly towards them. They warily carried on until they came to a pool of blood which led away from the track and down towards the Kunene. Kalibulala had made good his escape, now they would have to face the uncontrollable anger of Shawlo.

Kalibulala watched the warriors as they frantically searched the thick reed beds and prayed that he would not be snatched and dragged under by the ever-watchful crocodiles. As soon as the warriors were back on the track, he slowly made his way across the Kunene, which was quite shallow at that time of year.

The bleeding young man was given shelter in a nearby *libata* at Cafu. Kalibulala's gunshot wounds were serious, and for a while he hovered between life and death.

At *Forte Humbe*, Luna de Carvalho, now promoted to colonel, heard the news of Kalibulala's escape from Kwamatoland and that he was being sheltered nearby. The colonel visited the young royal with José Lopes, and provided him with basic medical care, while at the same time sounding out his political allegiances. Two weeks later when Captain Eduardo Marques arrived at *Forte Humbe* as part of the column's advance party, he alerted him to the presence of Kalibulala and of his possible aid to the success of the expedition. Marques and Luna de Carvalho rode out from *Forte Humbe* to visit Kalibulala; he was lying on a rough, blood-clotted, straw mat. Through Luna de Carvalho, Marques spoke to him about the coming campaign, offering him medical treatment at *Forte Humbe* and the position as guide to the column. At first Kalibulala demurred, he did not want to be seen as a traitor in the eyes of the Kwamato clans but he eventually agreed to both proposals. The young Kwamatan quickly responded to treatment provided by Dr Bravo. On 26 August, an extremely tall, slim, young man with a handsome, sensitive and thoughtful face stood awkwardly in front of Captain Roçadas, he was wearing a large Portuguese felt hat with a high collared, military jacket that was far too short in the arms, and a pair of dark blue trousers tucked into leather boots. The contrast could not have been greater; Alves Roçadas was an extremely short man whereas Kalibulala towered over him, in fact, he stood head and shoulders above every other man in the column. Through Luna de Carvalho, he informed him that he was ready to serve the Portuguese as their guide in Kwamatoland.

He did his job well, always finding the shortest route and wherever possible, leading them from one precious *cacimba* to the next; his knowledge of local topography was peerless. Never before had the Portuguese such a reliable guide. His trustworthiness gained him many friends among the previously, highly sceptical Portuguese officer corps, and his ability to adapt to an alien European system astounded them. He never lacked courage, being wounded twice, once in hand to hand combat with his own Kwamato clan. On many occasions he had saved much bloodshed by fearlessly going out into the bush and parlaying with his people, who had begun to respect the young warrior; he was now the voice and embodiment of the Portuguese column.

As a reward for his services to the Portuguese, Roçadas told him that he was to be invested as *soba* of Greater Kwamato, but it would take place at Naloeke as the royal *embala* at M'gogo had already been destroyed. Kalibulala was visibly delighted and readily agreed to the codicil of unconditional Portuguese control over his lands. He promised to halt all human sacrifice rituals and curb the warring factions under his control. The *embala* at Naloeke had not been sacked, as the auxiliaries who considered plunder as part of their wages, were ordered to respect the future home of the *soba* of Greater Kwamato, Kalibulala. The *soba*-in-waiting was consulted by Captain Eduardo Marques as to the location of the military post and was given a number of alternatives. For reasons of security, he opted to have the post built as close as possible to his kraal, in order to have easy access to the officer commanding it.

The clans had come from every corner of Kwamatoland to pay homage to the future *soba* and present him with weapons and gifts of oxen. A drum had been placed at the entrance to the *embala* and was rhythmically beaten throughout the day. Small groups of warriors would approach the *embala*, then stop and crouch on their haunches and await the drummer's signal - the changing tone of the beat. Each man carrying a knobkerrie would slowly crawl toward the entrance and halt, three times they would issue cries of praise to the new *soba*, then on the final cry, throw their knobkerries into the dust, as a sign of submission. Having picked up and dusted off their weapons, they entered the *embala* in single file, while the oxen were led off by Kalibulala's *sekulos*. After a short *indaba* with the king in which they were ordered to obey *Muene Puto* – the King of Portugal, they filed out of the kraal promising to return for the investiture.

After the *indaba* with Kalibulala, many Kwamato warriors fraternised with the Portuguese soldiery. Roçadas was quietly pleased with the unfolding events. Former enemies now had the opportunity to see the bustling fort, Portuguese weaponry, and industry close up. They would return to their *libatas* with a very different impression of Portuguese power.

After discussions between Roçadas, Luna de Carvalho and Kalibulala, 8 October was chosen as the date for the investiture. It dawned a cool, bright, blustery morning, but by midday the sun was scorching. With the sweating troops formed up on either side of the track leading to the *embala*, more than 1,000 Kwamato *sekulos* and warriors watched as the Portuguese flag was run up the black painted pole, which sappers had recently erected on top of the king's royal kraal.

On the day of his investiture, Kalibulala appeared at the entrance to Captain Marques' tent and asked to speak to him. Kalibulala was both nervous and angry. He told Marques of his fears; many of the younger warriors had openly refused to acknowledge him as their future king. Captain Marques did his best to reassure Kalibulala and after the young, crestfallen *soba* had returned to his kraal, he rushed to Roçadas' tent with the unwelcome news. The investiture had to go ahead as Portuguese authority and prestige were at stake.

A single shot rang out from the kraal and a cry of anguish was quickly carried away on the blustering wind. Lieutenant Colonel Luna de Carvalho and two of his men charged into the *embala* revolvers in hand. Once their eyes had become accustomed to the darkness, they found Kalibulala in a pool of blood, writhing and kicking the ground in agony. The young *soba* had taken a carbine, and had attempted to place it in his mouth, prior to pulling the trigger. Only a despairing lunge from his nephew Samuel had saved him from certain death. Kalibulala's lower jaw had been carried away and he was bleeding profusely. He was dragged out of the *embala* and taken, against his will, to the tented hospital for emergency treatment. Kalibulala violently refused treatment and as medical orderlies held him down, doctors struggled to place a chloroform pad over his face. With Kalubulala finally subdued, doctors began to operate on his smashed jaw. Meanwhile the massed Kwamato clans watched in indifferent silence.

Kalibulala had been the target of an assassination attempt by Shawlo and had been shunned by his Kwamatan clan. For a time his life had been in great danger and he had been severely wounded while trying to outrun Shawlo's men. Circumstances had forced him into the arms of the Portuguese where he had tried to make the best of his situation. He had loyally served Captain Roçadas against his own Kwamato people, and had led them safely through the bush and sandy wastes of Kwamatoland, where the soldiers of *muene puto* had been victorious. He had been driven by revenge, due the hurt suffered at the hands of his own clan, yet when finally confronted by his people, he realised that in their eyes he had become nothing more than a puppet of *Muene Puto*.

Chapter 21
João de Almeida and the Dembos Campaign in 1907

At the beginning of 1907, Angola's governor, Eduardo Ferreira da Costa, ordered Captain João de Almeida Fernandes Pereira, to Luanda to discuss the deteriorating situation in the troublesome Dembos region, 273 kilometres east of the capital. It had been reported that Portuguese and other European traders were being refused entry to the region, as were many Africans. Governor Ferreira da Costa could not and would not allow the Dembos clans to bar free passage to the colonial authorities, and tasked de Almeida to prepare a covert reconnaissance, prior to sending a Portuguese column into the region.

João de Almeida had no hesitation in choosing Lieutenant Melo Vieira to accompany him on his secret mission into the Dembos. At Cabiri, a small settlement a few kilometres distant from Luanda on the banks of the Bengo River, the two officers carefully packed away their uniforms in a large, brown, leather trunk and donned civilian clothing. They were now hunter-traders, taking with them only those pieces of equipment that could be carried on their horses' backs. They headed out towards Sala Mubemba close to the right bank of the Dande River, which they forded; entering the forbidding lands of the Dembo clans. The two riders slowly picked their way up through the steeply rising track towards the Quibaxi. From the heights of Quibaxi they were able to survey below them the extensive Sasse valley, and in the far distance, through the heat haze, they could just make out the shadowy shapes of the kraals at Nabuangongo, Quipuengo and Ambuila. Having carefully detailed the locations on their map, they awaited nightfall, before skirting the kraals and heading towards Encoge, which they reached on 2 March. The two men were not used to hunting for their rations and food was growing short, so they determined to remain close to the settlement in order to supply themselves with game for the pot.

On the afternoon of 2 March, the Portuguese trader Manuel Pinto Furtado had ordered his two wagons to be outspanned and while his men were busy skinning and preparing a gemsbok for the evening meal, he had spread an old kudu hide out on the sandy ground under a clump of mopani trees. Having lit his pipe, he was just about to remove his boots when he saw mounted figures approaching from the direction of the rapidly setting sun. The Portuguese trader was surprised to encounter two European riders who appeared to be travelling light, especially when they introduced themselves as fellow traders. But the custom of the trek required him to invite his visitors to share his meal. Pinto Furtado's suspicions were confirmed when he heard the younger man refer to Almeida as 'sir.' After a moment of embarrassing silence, Almeida let

Pinto Furtado into his confidence, and then asked him his views on the present situation. Pinto Furtado told the two officers that the Dembos clans had set their faces against all but their own people, and anyone entering their lands would be stopped by heavily armed warriors demanding a payment under threat. He explained that even those brave souls who had paid the toll were warned to keep well clear of the Dembos highlands on pain of death. The first hand information from Pinto Furtado confirmed Almeida's view, that only a large and well-armed force would be capable of reimposing Luanda's control over the Dembos. After a good meal and a sound night's sleep, only once broken by the distant, echoing roar of a lion, the two men set out early next day on the long journey to Gulongo Alto, where they duly arrived some two weeks later. After covertly mapping the strategic heights at Gulongo, they rode down to the Zenza River and then on to Cabiri where they bathed, shaved and exchanged their sweat stained and thorn ripped traders' clothing for their uniforms, which were still neatly folded in the brown leather trunk, which the younger officer laughingly admitted, he believed he would never see again.

Almeida and his young companion were amazed on meeting not Ferreira da Costa, but the new governor-general, the energetic and popular Paiva Couceiro of Gazaland fame. During the animated briefing, Almeida stressed his opinion of the need to send a large, heavily armed and well-supplied column into the Dembos, where if necessary, it would take them on and defeat them in their own back yard. It would not be an easy task and careful planning would be absolutely essential if the Portuguese were not to meet the same fate as Oliveira's column in the Dembos War of 1872. Enemy warriors besieged Second Lieutenant José Inácio de Oliveira and his eighteen soldiers at his post at Sasse. The Portuguese force's ammunition had become critically low and rations had already run out; fearing slow starvation and eventual death at the hands of the Dembos warriors, they broke through the enemy line and his depleted force withdrew to the Zenza River.

By the end of August, Captain João de Almeida had completed all his preparations. The column was ready to fulfil its tasks; it would reconnoitre the Dande River, maintain free passage through the Dembos and re-establish Portuguese authority in the region.

On 11 September, the youthful Crown Prince Luís Filipe, who was on a royal visit to Angola, was asked to review the column's troops, formed up before him in Luanda's main square. The column was composed of 271 European soldiers, 319 African Infantrymen and 296 auxiliaries. Lieutenant João Teixeira Pinto, who was later to distinguish himself in Portuguese Guinea, commanded the auxiliaries, with the ever-present José Lopes and the Boer leaders, Venter and Alberts. A further 150 men were detailed to guard the column's staging posts.

The armaments included artillery and machine guns. Ammunition, provisions and medical supplies were carried in ox-drawn wagons. On 20 September the column slowly trekked out of Luanda. Four days later, the first staging post was established at Casal and on 12 October the column reached the *banza* – kraal - of Gombe Amukyana, which although heavily fortified, and containing some 1,000 huts, surrendered to the column without offering any resistance. There then followed a long and exhausting trek to the enormous *banza* at Pango-Alúquem, where to the immense relief of the struggling column, its powerful chief welcomed them to his kraal.

The situation began to change and on 15 October, the column found itself surrounded by warriors from Gombe and Imbundo, hiding in thick thorn bush and deep defiles, in exactly the place where the Portuguese had suffered their initial setback in Dembos War of 1872. It had been a dispiriting experience and history was now in danger of repeating itself. The going was very difficult and the Portuguese were forced to move in close file, but their superior firepower kept the warriors at bay, and the column was able to longer and fight off the warriors who withdrew towards their kraals. Almeida's column regrouped and pursued them, and on 16 October, the massed impis faced the Portuguese column on the treeless savannah in front of their kraals. After a spirited fight the enemy fled and the Gombe and Imbundo kraals were taken and burned to the ground. On 17 October the column halted at Kichona, where they laagered in order to rest and reorganise. The Portuguese casualties were extremely light given the ferocity of the enemy attacks against them; four soldiers had been killed plus six porters with two officers and 24 soldiers wounded. However, during the advance on the kraals, Almeida had been hit by a rifle bullet and was receiving treatment from the medical officer. On 19 October he ordered the column to march on the *banza* at Cazuangongo, the most feared in all of the Dembos. In spite of his wound, Almeida's courage and enthusiasm bolstered the column, which carried the kraal after fierce fighting. The bloodied Portuguese then marched on towards Gimbo Alúquem. In the distance they could make out spiralling columns of black smoke, which they eventually recognised as the kraal at Gimbo Alúquem - the enemy warriors had fled, but before doing so, had set their huts on fire. After laagering overnight close to the smoking ruins, the column marched on Cazuangongo. João de Almeida's wounded arm showed no signs of healing and the worried medical officer diagnosed tetanus. Almeida wanted to know how long he had before the tetanus completely debilitated him. The medical officer's curt reply was, four days, at best, In Almeida's opinion that would be time enough to take Cazuangongo. The column advanced on the massive kraal, which surprisingly, put up only a limited resistance before its defenders fled into the bush. The column then withdrew to Kichona and on passing through Kilemba; Almeida halted the column, and ordered two platoons to build a post at Maravila next to the *banza* at Gimbo-Alúquem, which his officers called *Forte João de Almeida* in his honour. Fortunately for Almeida, the medical officer's diagnosis proved incorrect, and though his wound was slow to heal, tetanus had failed to set in. The column then went on to attack the strongly defended kraals at Zongue, Bambi and Muando.

Almeida and his officers soon realised that the biggest confrontation of the Dembos campaign was yet to come. Ahead of them the enemy warriors were massed, rhythmically beating their assegais against their ox hide shields while others, armed with captured Portuguese army rifles, had taken up defensive positions around the kraals and in the thorn bush. To slow down the column's advance and increase its casualties, sharpened stakes had been placed at the bottom of many freshly dug, deep, funnel-like holes. By nightfall on 28 October, the column with the infantry in the van had fought its way through the kraals at Mukumbi, Kissemo and Kibombe. At Mukumbi the Portuguese built a small fort to guard the river crossing towards Maravila. On 31 October two more kraals were invested and taken at Kimbungo and Gombe do Sasse.

By 7 November, the defenders of the massive *banza* at Cazuangongo who had fled during the column's assault had made their way to the *banza* at Mandele to join their allies and await the column. But even the Dembos impis were unable to halt the column's momentum. The enemy was totally beaten and the kraals burned down to the ground. It was the final victory of the Dembos campaign. The chiefs then surrendered to the Portuguese and among them, the most powerful of them all, Paramount Chief Kakulo Kahenda, who at the start of the campaign, had boasted that he had ordered his people to dig an enormous hole close to the Xinge River; when the Dembos clans had killed all the whites, their bodies would be flung into it.

On 24 November, after building a post at Cambela, Captain João de Almeida's column began its long withdrawal from the Dembos towards Luanda, leaving a chain of ten military posts from Maravila, to Luango and Casal.

Chapter 22
Regicide and Revolution in Lisbon

Saturday 1 February 1908 had dawned bright and freshly warm when Dom Carlos I and Prince Luís Filipe set out to return to Lisbon. The king and his eldest son had spent a convivial hunting holiday together and had lodged at the ancient palace of the Duke of Braganza in the sleepy village of Vila Viçosa, not far from the Guadiana River, hard by the Spanish border.

Crown Prince Luís Filipe was to enter the navy as a midshipman, and it was agreed that he would return early to Lisbon, in order to brush up on the subjects he would need to study while at the naval school. Prior to leaving for Lisbon, Dom Carlos had been informed that the police had uncovered a plot against the monarchy, and the ringleaders had been arrested. The king was shown a document, which gave the government the power to exile the plotters. After perusing the decree, the king gave it his royal assent.

As the *Dom Luís I* rode at anchor, the royal passengers were smoothly transferred to the royal launch, which swiftly carried them through the light swell of Lisbon water to the quayside. The royal party was over one hour late and the waiting crowds in Black Horse Square were filled with a sense of expectancy. The queen was presented with a large bouquet of flowers as she stepped from the boat on to the jetty. From there, they climbed into a waiting open landau drawn by four horses, which the king had specifically requested, in spite of being advised to travel by motorcar. The queen was seated on her husband's right; the two royal princes dutifully faced their parents. As the royal party turned to enter the vast, arcade fringed Terreiro do Paço Square, facing the post office building, a small figure in the crowd sprang on to the landau's running board and fired point blank at the uniformed king, who suddenly raised his forearm against his attacker, and then slumped back against Dona Amélia, as she reflexively rose from her seat, her dress already blood spattered. The bullet had passed through the king's neck severing the carotid artery and struck Crown Prince Luís Filipe. Though grievously wounded, the crown prince lunged at the assassin, who ran to the opposite side of the carriage, and as the liveried coachmen fought to control the frightened horses, levelled the muzzle of the rifle at the crown prince's face and pulled the trigger. Prince Luís Filipe's black, silk top hat bounced against the tramlines and rolled to an uncertain halt under the hooves of a mounted officer, who charged the assassin and ran him through with his sabre. There was blood everywhere, and some of it reddened Dom Manuel's sleeve, as he toppled forward clutching his arm in agony and shocked disbelief. Shots were now coming from the direction of the arcades mingled with screams of anger and anguish from the packed crowds. The lead coachman cracked the reins over his horses' withers and set them off at a desperate gallop towards the open gates of the Arsenal to escape further carnage, while his blood soaked companion lay moaning at his feet. It is an irony of history that the small, pleasant looking professor had actually met the king on a number of occasions, and the rifle he used to kill the king and the crown prince, had been presented to him by Dom Manuel for winning a musketry competition.

Now, at the age of nineteen, the nervous and hesitant Duke of Béja, had assumed the mantle of king of Portugal, after the assassination of his father and brother. Dom Manuel was ill prepared for kingship, and revolution was in the air. His reign was to usher in a period of monarchist apathy and republican discontent.

On 19 August 1910, police agents warned the young monarch of a possible military and naval insurrection. The greatest danger was clearly posed by the Italian-built cruiser *Adamastor*, and *Dom Carlos I*, which were anchored in the Tagus close to the Terreiro do Paço. In the airless admiralty buildings, the fraught, heavily perspiring minister for the navy and former colonial administrator, Marnaco e Souza, panicked and immediately signalled the captains of the iron-clads to get up steam. The *Dom Carlos I* was ordered to sail for the distant Atlantic islands of the Azores and the *Adamastor* – which had been bought as a consequence of the British *Ultimatum* - to Madeira; anywhere other than remain in Lisbon. In the sultry evening heat, hurriedly dressing senior naval officers were seen commandeering carriages and careering over glistening, cobble stones, down to the murky quayside, to tumble aboard launches and jolly boats in the failing light.

The awning covered plates of the twin-funnelled 4,186-tonne Armstrong-built cruiser; *Dom Carlos I* had sizzled all day long, as she rode at anchor on the tidewaters of the Tagus River, close to the royal palace. Now, between decks the heat was suffocating as the crew hastily took station. As she had insufficient fuel to steam even halfway to the Azores, her captain was signalled that the ship would have to refuel at sea; filling her holds with 289 tonnes of coal while pitching and rolling in the Atlantic swell was not something to be desired, but she had to get up steam and weigh anchor with all possible haste. The signal was immediately countermanded by the admiralty, and the captain of the *Dom Carlos I* was ordered to steam due south then enter the Straits, in order to coal at the British naval base in Gibraltar, thus the revolution was postponed.

Less than two months later on Monday 3 October, the new Vickers's-built Brazilian dreadnought, the 19,000-tonne, *São Paulo*, dropped anchor in the Tagus River. She proudly carried her country's president elect, Marshal Hermes

Rodrigues da Fonseca, who was to attend an official state banquet as the guest of honour of Dom Manuel II at the Palace of Belém. At 1:00 in the morning on Tuesday 4 October, uniformed naval commissary António Maria de Azevedo Machado Santos, adjusted his cutlass belt and with a nervous wave of his hand, led a group of revolutionaries through the deserted, cobbled streets of the capital in an assault against the barracks of 16 Infantry Regiment. The insurgents met with very little resistance, and the regiment quickly caved in to the rebels, after murdering their colonel and two senior officers, they made straight for the barracks of I Artillery Regiment. At the same time, the crews of the *São Rafael* and *Adamastor* mutinied while the *Dom Carlos I* vacillated. The strategically important naval headquarter at Alcântara on the banks of the Tagus close to the royal palace was attacked and its occupants quickly surrendered.

The insurrection followed a pre-established plan; the revolutionaries were swiftly organised into two columns; one was told off to storm the Necessidades Royal Palace and capture the young king who would be spending the rest of the night there after returning from the state banquet. The second column was tasked with the capture of the headquarters of the municipal guard in Carmo Square. However, both groups met stiff resistance from I Infantry Regiment, skilfully commanded by Colonel Sousa Dias, and withdrew north towards the Rotunda. Rotunda Square became the focal point of the revolution, from where the insurrectionists were to engage the monarchists in sporadic artillery duels until daybreak.

As the first light of that October dawn reddened the sky over Lisbon, the monarchist forces led by the Africanist hero, Paiva Couceiro, who had located an artillery battery at the palace in order to protect Dom Manuel II, began to realise that militarily their position was quite untenable. The navy had cast its lot with the insurgents; revolutionary troops still held Rotunda Square, and the naval barracks had already hoisted the green and red republican flag. The Portuguese high command had failed to muster sufficient forces to combat the insurrectionists; railway links with the provinces had been sabotaged thereby stopping military reserves getting through to the capital. In the distance, in the direction of the yellow-hued Necessidades Palace, the heavy crump of a naval bombardment could clearly be heard.

The early morning mist hung heavily over the grey bows of the iron-clad cruisers *Adamastor* and *São Rafael* as they weighed anchor and with screws foaming, slowly ploughed through the still waters of the River Tagus; two dark shapes against the brightening autumn sky. The tension aboard the *Adamastor* was palpable. Her task was to lead the *São Rafael* down the wide estuary and together turn their German-made Krupp 150mm guns, against the royal residence. On that morning, the royal standard of Dom Manuel II hung limply against its white flag staff on top of the ancient palace. The guns, which Paiva Couceiro had heard, booming out over the Tagus, not only brought the royal standard tumbling down in a shower of splinters and dust, but also brought Portugal's royal dynasty to an equally abrupt end.

Agitated ministers advised the king to leave the palace, as it was the principal target for the iron-clads' guns; though the palace had suffered little damage, other residential buildings had been badly hit and the number of casualties was rising alarmingly. Just at that moment the heavy whine of a naval shell rent the air and the palace shook, as it slammed into the royal apartments, showering plaster and splinters over the monarch, and severing the telephone wire on his desk. Dom Manuel speedily vacated his apartments and made for the garden, where he saw that many of its palm trees and been sliced through by shrapnel splinters. The king, dressed in civilian clothes, climbed into a waiting car while the sound of heavy gunfire rang in his ears. The car sped off through the turbulent streets, carrying Manuel to the weather-stained mass of the Convent-Palace at Mafra, 64 kilometres from Lisbon, where he was to spend his last night in Portugal. Early on the following day, his mother, Dona Amélia, arrived and brought with her the news that the republic had been proclaimed. By 2:00 in the afternoon, the order was given to raise the green and red republican flag on all public buildings in the former monarchy. Two hours later they were at the coastal village of Ericeira from where the royal party boarded the yacht *Dona Amélia*. Dom Manuel told the ship's captain to make for Oporto, but as the rebel fleet had blocked that route, the captain's advice was to sail to Gibraltar. King George V immediately offered Manuel and his party passage to England on the royal yacht, and after a short stay on the 'Rock' Manuel was greeted in Plymouth Sound by the London born Duke of Orleans. Dom Manuel was to live out the rest of his life in Britain at Fulwell Park in leafy, suburban Twickenham. In 1913 he married his cousin, Augusta Vitoria, Princess of Hohenzollern-Sigmarigen, and devoted himself to charitable works and to his private library. Dom Manuel died in 1932 and was given a state funeral in Lisbon by the Salazar regime.

Chapter 23
Clinging on in Portuguese Guinea

In the new republic's West African colony of Portuguese Guinea, the situation was far from good. Apart from the capital, Bolama, Bissau, and one or two villages guarded by blockhouses, massacres and regular large-scale Portuguese defeats, at the hands of the Guinean clans, had made Portuguese sovereignty purely symbolic. The colony covered 36,125 square kilometres. Its climate could be divided into two seasons, one dry the other rainy. The dry season began in the middle of November, and lasted up to the middle of May. For the rest of the year, the colony was at the mercy of prolonged, torrential downpours.

In 1868 the population of Bissau was only 537. Of those, sixteen were Portuguese born, and the rest were Cape Verdians and local peoples. As to the indigenous clans of the interior, the Portuguese could only estimate their numbers, and it was not until the completion of the military campaigns in 1915, that the authorities came up with the figure of 350,000. Bissau was tightly squeezed between, a canal, a muddy beach, and the fortress wall, creating a stiflingly unhealthy atmosphere for its inhabitants. This unprepossessing evil smelling place was eventually to become the colony's capital.

On 23 February 1891, Bissau Region was in a state of armed conflict, as the rulers of Intim, Bandim, Samfim and Bor, had risen against Portuguese control. The Portuguese put together a makeshift force to counter the insurrectionists, using part of the Bissau fortress garrison, and troops from the island of Cape Verde. Command of the force was given to Lieutenant Colonel Pedro Moreira da Fonseca, with naval Lieutenant Filipe dos Santos and Sub-Lieutenant Álvaro Herculano da Cunha, providing gunboat support and supply services in the *Flecha* and *Zagaia*. Colonel Fonseca left Bissau leading a column made up of five officers and 120 men of 1 Light Infantry and an artillery battery. The majority of the soldiers were totally unfamiliar with the terrain and most had never before encountered their formidable enemy the Pepel clan. Native scouts were sent out ahead of the main column to reconnoitre the dense jungle. They walked into an ambush, the rest of the column panicked, and fled towards Bissau, abandoning their officers and their weapons. The slaughter included the column's second-in-command Lieutenant Azevedo.

In order to instil confidence in Portugal's ability to defend the coastal region, the corvette *Mindelo* and the gunboats *Flecha* and *Zagaia*, were placed on station. Another column commanded by Captain Joaquim António do Carmo Azevedo, with 140 soldiers and 200 Mandingo irregulars, set out for the Intim clans' jungle stronghold, from the fortress at Bissau in early April. The column, like its predecessor, suffered a crushing defeat, losing four of its officers and many of its soldiers and Mandingo irregulars. Due to the column commander's death in battle on 19 April, Lieutenant Júlio César Barata Feio assumed command of the depleted and demoralised force, which quickly retired on Bissau. The clans living close to the Geba River had keenly watched the effects of the rebellion; they now felt emboldened by the Pepels' success.

The principal threat to Portuguese authority in the colony was from the Pepel, who had repeatedly attacked the fort at Bissau between 1891 and 1893. In December 1893, *Forte Bissau* commanded by Captain Zacarias de Sousa Lage was only saved from destruction by the timely intervention of the gunboat *Rio Ave*, commanded by Lieutenant Artur José dos Reis, laying accurate gunfire on the rebels as they advanced towards the fortress. Captain Sousa Lage was given command of a column tasked with finding and destroying the hostile Pepel and Balanta of Nyakra. After a sustained naval and artillery bombardment of the *tabankas* – villages - at Bandim and Contumo, to the southwest, the Pepel replied and attacked Bissau in a desperate attempt to take the fortress and silence its guns. The Pepel were thrown back into the jungle suffering enormous losses. In 1894 governor Vasconcelos e Sá, ventured deep into Pepel territory, and as a consequence, was able to parley with the Pepel and eventually sign a peace treaty. The first Oyo campaign mounted by the Portuguese began in 1897, with the task of securing the left bank of the Farim River, and in 1902 a new expedition was mounted to destroy the rebel forces in the region.

It was decided in Lisbon, that fresh impetus and energy were needed to lift the spirits of the war weary Portuguese forces stationed in Guinea; Captain João Teixeira Pinto, was chosen by Lisbon to fulfil that task. He was born at Mossâmedes in 1876, the son of Major Teixeira Pinto. In 1899 he joined 5 (Emperor of Austria Franz Josef's Own) Infantry Regiment as a second lieutenant and was posted to Angola where he served with the mountain artillery and infantry until 1904. On returning to Angola he continued to serve throughout numerous campaigns until posted to Portugal in 1912. He was a stocky man, with an incredibly large beard, which became the envy of many of his Muslim irregulars.

In 1912 Teixeira Pinto was appointed commanding officer, Portuguese Guinea, arriving there on 23 September 1912. His first view of that troubled colony was of small, flat, green islands, palm trees and mangrove swamps. As his ship nudged towards the harbour, the Atlantic Ocean began to shade brown as the Geba River poured forth its red earth. Vivid green foliage dipped languidly into the water, exotic birds shrieked and cackled. But the abiding impression was the smell, the sickly-sweet stench of the jungle and of tropical decay. Bolama was nothing more than a steaming, former slave-station with one or two administrative tin-roofed huts. It was not an auspicious beginning.

Teixeira Pinto began to reorganise the miniscule military and police forces at his disposal, and created a platoon of rural police, two artillery troops and two African infantry companies. Yet this was hardly enough, as the armed bands of the far northern Oyo jungle region, ravaged the countryside at will, while the Portuguese clung desperately to a few fortified coastal villages and had been too wary to venture into that mysterious and often deadly green maze. Teixeira Pinto's military options were limited; he commanded a handful of Portuguese officers, hardly amounting to more than a dozen men. Military supplies and spares were equally limited. In the past, columns had tried to take the war to the jungle but lack of planning and preparation had led to disasters; bloated, fly-blown bodies in Portuguese army uniforms floating down the Geba and Mansoa rivers, told their own grim story. After studying the chaotic military situation, and thumbing through the scant intelligence available, Captain Teixeira Pinto's first concern was to see the jungle region at first hand. Though the Convention of 12 May 1886, had fixed the limits between Guinea and the surrounding French colonies, the total number of its inhabitants remained a mystery. Leaving sealed instructions with his second-in-command, Lieutenant Augusto José de Lima, he readily accepted the help of the French trader and Soller employee, Charles Pierre Magne, and donning civilian guise, passed himself off as a commercial inspector for the Soller Trading Company, which had a station at Port Mansoa. With Magne's help, he secretly reconnoitred the hostile area from Mansoa headwaters to Farim on the River Cacheu in the extreme north. It was a river journey fraught with danger. He knew only too well, as his boat slowly steamed up river, sometimes only metres from the fetid, mosquito infested, river bank and its settlements, that recognition by the warlike and deeply suspicious Balanta and Oyo peoples, would lead to torture, mutilation and death in the primeval tropical forests of Guinea; lost without trace like so many Portuguese before him.

From intelligence painstakingly gained from his journey, he formulated a plan of action. Using Port Mansoa as a firm base for his operations against the Oyo jungle region, he would mount a two-pronged thrust through Port Mansoa, 17 kilometres north to Bissoram, while simultaneously laying siege to the *tabankas* of Geba on the Geba River in the east. First of all he needed to build a military post at Port Mansoa to link with similar posts at Bissoram and Karanke-Kunda. The wooden frame was built at Bolama in the south, from where it was transported up the Geba River and then erected at Mansoa where on the bank of the Mansoa River, Teixeira Pinto established a permanent Portuguese presence.

Lieutenant Augusto de Lima, the military commander of Bissoram region, was tasked to lead the advance to Bissoram. The district commissioner, Vasco Calvet de Sousa Magalhães, was given responsibility for securing and holding the Geba region with the Fulanis under his and Chief Mamadu Sissé's command. Captain Teixeira Pinto's 200-strong column included two youthful Portuguese officers, Lieutenant Artur de Sampaio Antas and Second Lieutenant Pimenta, with the powerful Senegalese chief of Cuhor, Abdul Injai, leading the irregular forces of Fulanis and Mandingos. Teixeira Pinto had been advised to trust Abdul Injai, and over a period of time, he came to acknowledge him as the embodiment of military competence - vigorous, far-sighted and extremely brave. Abdul Injai, a Wolof, had served in the colonial French army in the rank of sergeant, and after leaving the army, moved to Portuguese Guinea in 1894, as an employee of a French company. He soon tired of civilian life, and with his military experience, was welcomed into the Portuguese colonial army; he was to become a firm friend and ally of Teixeira Pinto. In 1914 Abdul Injai was promoted to lieutenant. In recognition of his loyal service to Portugal during Governor Oliveira Muzanty's 1908 campaign, he had been given the title of Chief of the Cuhor region.

Chapter 24
The Oyo War in Portuguese Guinea

Military operation in Mansoa and Oyo began on 29 March 1913. To provide sustained firepower and mobility, the small river-draught gunboats, *Flecha* under command of Sub-Lieutenant Queimado de Sousa, and *Zagai* commanded by António Raimundo da Costa Santos Pedro, were pressed into service.

The small force was being transported up the Geba River, and had reached a point close to the Soller Trading Company station, when an armed Balanta was spotted on the left bank of the river. He was only 30 metres away from a launch crowded with irregular troops and already had his weapon in his shoulder when he was brought down by machine gun fire from the *Flecha*. Teixeira Pinto's greatest fear was that his river borne force would be attacked while disembarking, but fortunately it was carried out without further hostilities.

Charles Magne, who had been Teixeira Pinto's travelling companion on the Mansoa reconnaissance, willingly placed the station's resources at his disposal, and promised to provide valuable medical facilities and food supplies to the column. On the morning of 30 March the irregulars were put to work clearing the bush directly in front of their position; entrenchments were deepened and sandbagged, and the officers and NCOs were given their dispositions in case of attack. Abdul Injai's forward sentries reported they had seen shadowy figures moving through the jungle. The column was stood to and then shots followed by taunts, echoed through the mass of tangled foliage lining the cleared ground in front of the position, however, nothing could be seen of the enemy. Teixeira Pinto had ordered his men to maintain complete silence and not reply to the insults being hurled at them from the jungle. It was Teixeira Pinto's intention to let the enemy get as close as possible to the Portuguese before opening fire. Shots began to fly over the defenders' heads, showering them with leaves. Suddenly, Oyo warriors appeared from beyond the palm fringed jungle, and swiftly advanced towards the entrenchments. The irregulars held their fire. The warriors advanced to within 50 metres before Teixeira Pinto gave the order to open up with volley fire, which was directed by whistle blasts from Abdul Injai. Lieutenant Pimenta, from his exposed observation post on the Soller station's roof, directed the *Flecha's* cannon fire on to the open ground close to the jungle's edge. After almost four hours of battle, the enemy pulled back and Abdul Injai's irregulars were ordered out to harry them. The attack had been a costly one, many of the dead and dying lay out in front of the Portuguese position, yet the defenders had not lost a man.

At dawn on the following day, the *Zagaia* replaced the *Flecha* on station in the Mansoa River, close to the Portuguese position. The Oyo warriors had again advanced to the edge of the jungle without being detected and begun firing at the sandbagged defenders. Within minutes, the *Zagaia* was sending high explosive rounds crashing into the jungle, and the rifle fire stopped as abruptly as it had begun.

Teixeira Pinto noted the Oyo clan's lack of fight and ordered Abdul Injai to send scouts out into the jungle to gauge the enemy's mood. Three days later they returned with the news that the Oyo had lost heart when the full extent of their losses sunk in; the dead were being mourned at nearly every *tabanka*. The Oyo clans had decided to halt their costly attacks against the Portuguese in order to call on fresh warriors, and the frenzied beat of the *bombolom*, began to reverberate through the dark jungle. The news was a fillip to Teixeira Pinto, who immediately began to work out a plan of attack, while on 9 April Abdul Injai's irregulars came up against the enemy and defeated them decisively in an hour-long battle.

District commissioner Sousa Magalhães, at Port Gole on the Geba River, 25 kilometres south east of Mansoa, signalled Teixeira Pinto that irregular reinforcements were on their way to Abdul Injai. The Portuguese commander ordered the *Flecha*, to protect the irregulars' crossing of the left bank. On 14 April the Portuguese position was again under attack but was repelled by gunboat fire. That evening, small boats arrived carrying a party of Grumete people – detribalised Guineans - from the Mansoa region, and others from nearby Braia and Bambi, and from Encoche and Echeia, 22 kilometres due west of Port Mansoa. They were ordered to hand over all their weapons, and in return, those that had played no part in the conflict, would only pay the hut tax for the present period, whereas those, mostly Mansoa clans, who had resisted would be forced to pay three years' worth of taxes. But the 'incentive' had a negligible effect, and although they promised to return with their chiefs, the Portuguese waited in vain. Teixeira Pinto learned that they were unable to keep their promise because the *tabankas* at Mantefa and Encala were blocking the chiefs' passage through their lands. On 16 April, Teixeira Pinto ordered the irregulars, under Abdul Injai, to occupy the region but postponed the order on hearing that the Mansoa clans of Sana were massing to attack his force. On 21 April, the Portuguese gunboats provided covering fire, while the column forced its way across to the left bank of the Mansoa River, and entered the eerie and hostile world of dense unmapped jungle, causing panic and fear among the Balantas. Chief Jugudul of the Balantas, sued for peace, telling Abdul Injai that he would return the following day with his chiefs. As the chiefs failed to appear, Teixeira Pinto ordered the push through the jungle to continue.

On 3 May, Teixeira Pinto heard the sound of rifle fire coming from the direction of the Mansoa River. He clambered up onto an enormous *baga-baga*, and with his binoculars picked out a large group of warriors with distinctive red headgear. He recognised them as members of the Balanta clan. They were attacking the irregulars with the intention of stopping reinforcements from fording the river and entering their territory. He had to act quickly, and as the gunboats had gone further up river, he ordered Chief Samba-Ly to take 30 men and extra ammunition and reinforce the irregulars at the river crossing point. Later, Abdul Injai told Teixeira Pinto that the attacking Balantas and Pepel clans had wanted the irregulars to expend their ammunition, prior to massacring them on the riverbank, but they had been foiled by the arrival of Samba-Ly and his men. Abdul Injai and his irregulars pushed on to Bindoro where they inflicted another defeat on the enemy. The Chief of Jugudul reappeared, this time he handed over two unused Snider rifles and begged the Portuguese to cease their attacks as the jungle clans had suffered enough.

The left bank had been cleared of the enemy and its rebellious clans quelled but the heavily armed Mansoa of Sana continued to resist in the Oyo, where they were threatening those who had sued for peace with the Portuguese. But there was to be no rest for Teixeira Pinto, as news was brought to him that the Fulani warriors, under command of Sousa Magalhães, had deserted en mass on their way to Gendum. The column had been dramatically reduced in strength and its commander left with little alternative other than to withdraw. Abdul Injai brought better news; many of the inland clans had no stomach for continued warfare and would be prepared to surrender without a fight. Teixeira Pinto now felt the time was ripe for an audacious attack against the heart of the Oyo, and avenge the all too frequent massacres of Portuguese led troops, that had created a legend of Oyo invincibility.

**Gunboat "Flecha", Portuguese Guinea 1910
(Fundação Portugal-África)**

Chapter 25
The Cacheu Column

On 28 December 1913, Teixeira Pinto arrived at Cacheu with a 387-strong force comprising of six artillery and infantry NCOs, 42 African infantrymen, 339 irregulars under Abdul Injai plus an ammunition train carrying 175,000 rounds, and a 75mm mountain gun with 40 rounds. On 2 January 1914, two gunboats steamed up the Pelundo River as far as Xuroenque with orders to fire on any *tabankas* that showed open hostility to the Portuguese presence. The column then set out in file formation with 40 irregulars in the lead, followed in turn by the African infantry and the 75mm mountain gun, and in the rearguard, Abdul Injai's irregulars. The going was hard due to the absence of a clearly marked track, and water was scarce. At times, when the track became impassable, the mountain gun had to be disassembled and carried on the soldiers' backs. When they reached the *tabankas* at Capó they found them empty, but it was all too obvious that a large force had camped there on the previous day. On entering one of the huts, the Portuguese disturbed two armed warriors who attempted to make off into the bush; one was shot down and his weapon captured, while the second made his escape, leaving his weapon behind. In the early afternoon the column warily entered thick jungle and almost immediately came under heavy attack with the enemy moving to outflank them. Teixeira Pinto ordered his column to press on, as experience had taught him that to halt meant to die. The push continued, but the enemy was so close that two irregulars standing next to Teixeira Pinto were shot dead by the same bullet, spraying him with blood. The column was halted when a group of Fulani irregulars sat down on the ground and refused to go any further. Teixeira Pinto made his way to the head of the column to find that only two of the 40-strong vanguard remained unscathed; they had borne the brunt of the attack. Abdul Injai, angrily ran to the Fulanis, and began dragging them up off the ground. It took all of Abdul Injai's formidable strength of character, and a long quarter of an hour of arguing, before he was able to induce the 50 irregulars to get back into the fight.

The column broke through the jungle and into a clearing. The shaken and exhausted men were ordered to check their weapons and ammunition before regrouping. Though the fighting-push through the dense, humid jungle had been terrifying, the enemy losses had been enormous, due to the column's superior firepower. The column pressed on and set up camp at Xuroenque, 14 kilometres from Capó, where they had to fend off attacks well into the night; in total they had suffered seven dead and 27 wounded. During the engagement 80,000 rounds of Snider and Kropatschek, and 21 artillery rounds had been expended. The column set out under cover of darkness, arriving at Xuroenque jetty on the Pelundo River, just after first light. The column formed all round defence as the enemy was seen massing at the edge of a mangrove forest 1,500 metres away. Teixeira Pinto ordered his gunners to lay down shrapnel fire to cover the irregulars' advance, the bush was soon occupied and the enemy driven out. On the following day, the column turned eastward and invested the Pepel settlement at Xurubrique, bivouacking close to its moss-covered jetty, where the gunboat had dropped anchor. With Abdul Injai providing cover, he oversaw the building of an entrenched military post, which was completed on 22 January. During further battles stretching into February, the Portuguese captured a total of 223 warriors.

The clans of Pecixe and Jetá islands and clans at Buramos, Pelundo, Costa de Baixo and Xuro, had jointly planned to move northward and attack Cacheu settlement. So confident of victory were they, they had already divided up the womenfolk and trading stores between them. The attack was to have begun in early January but the arrival of the column averted a certain massacre.

On 3 February 1914, the column continued its eastward march to Pantufe, where they came up against its warriors who fled after a spirited fight. Teixeira Pinto learned that the Xuro clan had captured a wounded and unarmed irregular, and had tortured him, by slowly and agonisingly, opening his wounds with a rifle-cleaning rod. Two days later the Portuguese leader sent out a heavily armed patrol to Xuro to capture and punish the perpetrators. Teixeira Pinto knew that the Brame clans were very wary of his column and unlikely to attack, so he sent an emissary under a white flag informing them that if they handed over their weapons and gunpowder, he would not make war on them. The chiefs of Greater and Lesser Brame at Bula and Ko, 50 kilometres from Cacheu, told him they owed the government nothing as they had bought their own weapons and powder, and consequently, refused to hand them over. Teixeira Pinto decided to push on through their lands and provided they did not show any hostile intention, would not harm them. It was an eerie experience; they did not attack the Portuguese, rather they completely ignored them. But at the door of every straw-thatched hut stood a man armed with a rifle and sword. When he got to the chief's *tabanka* the old man was impassively seated in his doorway and pointedly ignored Teixeira Pinto, who noticed that the *tabanka* was empty of women and children. Through his interpreter, he warned the chief they had to turn in their weapons and when this did not happen, ordered two men to be held hostage, on hearing this, the rest fled into the jungle. It transpired that the chiefs of Bula and Ko had ordered the *tabankas* not to hand over their weapons. Teixeira Pinto captured the chief of Ko and ordered the Bula chief to surrender himself. He answered that the track had been befouled with blood and would need to be cleansed first. It was the same excuse he had given to the administrator of Bissau when told to pay the hut tax. With the Bula chief's capture, the clans began to return to their *tabankas* and surrender their Kropatschek, Manlicher and Snider weapons. The two captured chiefs were then, inevitably, deported from Portuguese Guinea.

With the successful completion of the campaign, the decision was taken to push on deep into Balanta territory but Teixeira Pinto had serious doubts; south of the Pelundo River, the clans were still in a state of armed rebellion and were threatening the *tabankas* of Costa de Baixo, which had already surrendered to the Portuguese. To advance, leaving hostile areas in his rear, given the probability of wholesale revolt, would have been an act of sheer folly. Teixeira Pinto decided to regroup the Cacheu column with the intention of neutralising the rebellious clans. The column composed of seventeen soldiers of 2 Company Native Infantry under Sergeant João Rodrigues Faria, and 325 irregulars commanded by newly promoted Lieutenant Abdul Injai, began the move towards Pelundo on 3 March. On the way the column came up with the Bagulya *tabanka*, which appeared deserted. A patrol was sent forward of the main column and was fired on; the battle for Bagulya had begun. The fighting lasted for three hours until the enemy fled leaving the *tabanka* deserted except for the dead. When the Portuguese column filed out of Bagulya, many of its huts were already ablaze. Two days later the *tabankas* at Tema and Canyoba sued for peace and on the following day, returned to the Portuguese camp, and surrendered their rifles and swords.

On 12 March, Teixeira Pinto was shocked by the news of the massacre of a Native Police patrol under Second Lieutenant Pedro, close to Port Mansoa. He immediately sent a gunboat up river with orders to reinforce Port Mansoa. The Costa de Baixo could not now be quitted without first quelling the rebellious Basserel. Spies told him that in his rear at Basserel, on the south bank of the Pelundo, the Manjako were massing for an attack and boasting that the Portuguese column would be easily beaten as the jungle was too thick and dangerous to penetrate. Teixeira Pinto left Capol as news reached him of attacks on the military outposts at Brame and Bula; he ordered 25 irregulars to bolster the outposts' defences. On 17 March, the *Flecha* unloaded eight bronze cannon, which had been captured during fighting in the Costa de Baixo region. He sent the *Flecha* to the port at Basserel, and the motor launch *República*, to Bianga at the mouth of the Pelundo, to cut off any possible enemy retreat. Two days later the column entered the Manjako region. Simão, the guide, was leading them through thick tamarind groves when shots rang out; the irregulars had walked into a stockaded area, the Manjako were firing at them from behind a parapeted, one-metre deep trench. In the initial confusion Simão and six irregulars were shot down, but the advanced guard managed to drag the seven men back towards the main body of the column. Teixeira Pinto's 'Kwanyamas' surrounded the trench, killing all of the 80-strong Manjako force defending it. The Portuguese pushed on through the jungle while being constantly sniped at; the Manjako bravely stood their ground and many died fighting back to back against the Portuguese column. The column broke through the jungle and after a sharp encounter with the Manjako, destroyed the chief's *tabanka*. The Manjakos' resistance had been so dogged, that Teixeira Pinto had been forced to move to the head of the column and lead his exhausted men from the front. With the battle over, he was told by the chief at Catigi *tabanka* that in spite of the many casualties, the Manjakos were so confident of victory, they had ordered the Costa de Baixo clans to have their canoes ready, so that as soon as the Portuguese column was destroyed, they would cross to the north bank of the river and sack Cacheu. On 21 March the villagers from the *tabankas* at Bó, Timato and Calequisse perched on the banks of the Calequisse River, launched an attack, but were heavily repulsed. Fortunately for the column's sick and wounded, gunboats were available to take them off to Cacheu.

News came through that Balantas had attacked Bissoram settlement, 50 kilometres east of Cacheu. Teixeira Pinto whose column had completely run out of Snider ammunition, sent the *Flecha* to Bissoram with 10,000 Kropatschek rounds, and in return received 15,000 Snider. When Sub-Lieutenant Queimado de Sousa's gunboat reached Bissoram, the skipper, whose legs had given way, was carried ashore with a raging fever, and was taken to the sick bay, where the medical officer ordered him to bed, but in spite of the doctor's strictures, the skipper had resumed command of the gunboat and steamed back to unload the desperately needed ammunition.

On 27 March Teixeira Pinto's men captured the Chief of Basserel, which precipitated a general surrender of all the region's Manjako warriors. As the Manjakos had handed in their weapons and agreed to pay the hut tax, he began to plan the construction of two military posts, one at Basserel and the other at Cayó in the far south, at the mouth of the Mansoa River facing Jetta Island. The column marched back though Bula to Bolama where he replaced the former rebellious chiefs with those amicable to Portuguese authority, and set about planning the occupation of the Balanta region.

Chapter 26
Taking the War to the Balanta

Over a period of years the Balanta population had rapidly expanded into the Mandingo area in the east and into the Pepel and Brame regions in the west; the Farim and Geba rivers had failed to act as a natural buffer to their expansion. The subject clans were absorbed by the Balanta and gradually adopted their masters' identity and customs. Unlike other Guinean peoples, the Balanta clans were not based on a hierarchical system therefore; each family took responsibility for its own affairs. The Balanta were a hard working people living on Guinea's swampy, rice growing plains, yet they had often proved to be more than a match in battle against their would-be colonisers.

Second Lieutenant Manuel Augusto Pedro commanded a platoon made up of three Portuguese NCOs, António Pereira, António Augusto de Sá Morais, Francisco Martins and 15 Rural Policemen. The Rural Police force had been set up two years earlier in August 1912, and was led by Portuguese officers. Pedro had been ordered to reconnoitre an area to the north of Port Mansoa on the Bambi River and choose a site for building a bridge. The platoon left Port Mansoa at first light in thick mist, on the morning of 5 February and crossed the northern arm of the Mansoa River. On reaching the *tabanka* at Brai, they discovered that the villagers had fled into the jungle. Pedro told his guide and interpreter Salim, to bring them back and tell them the Portuguese meant no harm, but the villagers refused to listen, and according to Salim, they were calling other villagers to join them in the jungle. Salim, realising the situation had reached a dangerous point, begged the subaltern to withdraw, telling him it would be foolhardy to go on. Pedro ignored his guide's advice and pushed on towards Bambrinas. Close to midday, the Brai and Biambi warriors who had been tracking them through the jungle broke cover and attacked. After close quarter fighting, the platoon was forced to withdraw towards the Bambi River. But the Biambi now blocked the platoon's escape route as they had been hiding in the mangrove bush close to the river. Pedro needed to get his men over if they were to survive. Unfortunately for the platoon, the river was at its widest and muddiest point. Salim knew of a better crossing point but before he had the opportunity to speak to Pedro, the subaltern collapsed shot through the chest. Martins and a native policeman were also hit. The leaderless platoon panicked, and in desperation, attempted to wade through the thick mud towards the river, where they were shot down. Only four of the platoon were able to escape and were led to safety by Salim.

In May, Captain Teixeira Pinto was to launch a campaign against the Balantas in the Mansoa region. His two-phase campaign was designed to neutralise the clans between the Cacheu and Geba rivers, then build a military post at Nyacra from where he would begin operations to avenge the death of Pedro and his men.

The first phase of the plan was to concentrate at the friendly *tabankas* of Bula and Binar, mount an attack seven kilometres south against Paxe and Intenté, push on along the right bank of Mansoa River, seventeen kilometres to Encheia, and from there, as there was no crossing point between Encheia and Biur, march to Bissoram and then to Port Mansoa. In the second phase, the Portuguese would cross to the left bank of the Mansoa and Geba rivers, advance the 28 kilometres to the Impernal River, and occupy Nyacra where a military post would be established.

The campaign began on 13 May 1914 with the column concentrating at Bula. Teixeira Pinto had chartered the ageing steamer *Kade* from the *Compagnie Française* to tow the launches, irregular troops and horses from Port Mansoa via the Mansoa River and the Brame Grande River to Bula. However the French rust-bucket broke down and the force had to be towed by the two underpowered gunboats *Flecha* and *Zagaia*.

The order of march was to remain unchanged throughout the campaign; 25 mounted irregulars would be in the vanguard, with the main body, composed of 200 of Mamadu Sissé's irregulars, Teixeira Pinto's 30-man platoon of 2 Company, Native Infantry, 100 porters carrying the column's ammunition and baggage, ten irregular riders under command of Sergeant Faria, followed up the rear by Abdul Injai's 636 irregulars.

Having reached Binar, the column marched on towards Paxe close to the Mansoa River and came under intense fire but the Balantas were beaten off. Having attacked and destroyed the *tabankas* at Bérá; Rume; Xangué and Intenté, the column bivouacked in the early afternoon at Unche. During the night, a plucky Balanta warrior slipped through the sentries and fired his ancient flintlock weapon at the Portuguese camp, without causing any injuries. A sharp-eyed sentry spotted the considerable flash of his weapon, and the Balanta was shot down before he could make his escape. From Paxe on 14 May, an attack was launched against the settlements to the north at Fauqué and Tampé. The *tabankas* were set alight and many of the fleeing Balantas killed.

Teixeira Pinto was greatly concerned for the well being of the troops under his command, and had ordered the gunboat *Flecha*'s sickbay to be enlarged, and its captain to keep her on station. Every night, the captain of the *Flecha* would anchor and fire a signal rocket to show his location, and the column would answer with one rocket, if there were no casualties and two rockets if casualties needed to be transferred to the gunboat's sickbay. At Paxe, Teixeira Pinto and Sergeant Vilaça were setting up a maroon in an open area close to their trenches when an enemy bullet grazed the sergeant's cheek, knocking him over. The unconscious sergeant was dragged to safety by two of Teixeira Pinto's men. On 15 May the column began the return journey to Binar, bivouacking at Nyengue in order to give the Balantas the opportunity to surrender the eighteen Snider rifles, which Teixeira Pinto knew were hidden at Paxe and Unche. In a nearby *tabanka* at Cuboi, a large box of Portuguese ammunition had been hidden in a now blazing hut. It suddenly exploded, showering rounds over the village and setting other huts on fire. Two of Abdul Injai's men ducked into a nearby hut to escape the blast, and discovered a large conical hat decorated with a grey horse's tail hanging from the thatched ceiling; the irregulars recognised it as coming from Second Lieutenant Pedro's mount.

On 16 May the column heard the drumming of the *bombolom* – a message delivered on drum telegraph - calling the Balantas together to attack the Portuguese bivouac. The column was then thrown into near panic; in the rush, a number of horses galloped off before the sentries had time to stop them. Chief Abdul Injai was ordered to lead a patrol to search for the mounts. In the late afternoon, the position was attacked, but the Balantas were repelled; the attack was resumed an hour later just before nightfall. Abdul Injai and his men returned leading the jittery horses, and the remounted Portuguese routed the Balantas with their machetes. On 17 May, the *bombolom* ominously drummed out the call for another attack but it failed to materialise.

Two wounded prisoners were tied to a yohimbe tree and then interrogated as to why they had taken up arms against the government. At first they refused to speak, but eventually admitted they had been told that the Portuguese authorities did not know how to deal with the Balanta and besides, Portuguese government officials had never visited their *tabankas* to discuss and explain what they wanted, consequently, they refused to recognise the Portuguese administration, but would do so now as the Portuguese were much stronger.

On 19 May, Abdul Injai's spies reported Cussano, 22 kilometres to the southeast, to be the centre of enemy activity; Balantas were gathering between Xalé, Cussano and Encheia, close to the Mansoa River. To Teixeira Pinto's great exasperation, a lack of willing porters was holding up the column at Binar. At 8:30 on the following morning, rifle fire was heard coming from the direction of the advanced guard, Teixeira Pinto galloped forward to reconnoitre the area; the enemy was occupying a sturdy, half moon-shaped redoubt, with five raised strong points, two kilometres from the Portuguese column. Large Balanta reserves were believed to be at Xalé and Encheia, so Teixeira Pinto split his force into five smaller groups, as he estimated the enemy to be 20,000 in number. Although he was unfamiliar with Balanta warfare, he guessed at their plan; they would make a frontal attack, and then withdraw towards the river, followed by flanking attacks from the reserve at Xalé and Encheia.

He quickly issued his orders; the right flanking column, which he commanded, was to surround the enemy reserve at Xalé and stop any possible flanking attack; on Teixeira Pinto's right would be another column, commanded by Braime Dan; on the left, a column commanded by Abdul Injai; on his left, a column commanded by Mamadu Sissé, and on the extreme left Modiadi, the Fulani chief, was to halt any flanking attack and wrap up the Balanta reserve at Encheia. The columns were ordered to maintain mutual contact at all times, and push towards Encheia, forcing the enemy to retreat on the river, where the gunboats would come into action. The manoeuvre went to plan; the Balantas' right flanking attack was forestalled, and they were forced to retreat to the centre of their line-of-march. All the columns followed the plan except for Modiadi's, which had swung too far left, and lost contact with Mamadu Sissé. The Balantas surrounded Modiadi, and twelve of his men were cut down. The column would have been completely annihilated had Teixeira Pinto and Abdul Injai's columns not come to the rescue. The *Zagaia* and *Flecha* patrolled up to Xalé and Encheia where they engaged the enemy with machine gun fire.

When the battle was over, an amulet belonging to a Rural Policeman killed at Brai was found around the blood-spattered neck of a dead Balanta, and in a hut, a horse's rusted bridal from Pedro's ill-fated platoon was discovered under a pile of rotting straw. The battleground was covered in enemy dead, and the interpreter was later told by Balanta captives, that this had been a decisive battle – after which they realised they could not beat the Portuguese government and its forces.

On 21 May, the battle scarred column bivouacked close to deserted *tabankas* at Encheia. It was a long night and although the sentries heard noises and saw fleeting shadows, the Portuguese were not attacked. The assault came late the following morning and was repulsed with heavy Balanta losses. The two gunboats' machine guns stopped the Balantas from crossing a large, open area, leading from Biur to Encheia. After the battle, the *tabankas* were thoroughly searched, and rations belonging to a member of the Rural Police patrol were found in one of the huts. The following day, the column invested and razed a cluster of *tabankas* within a fifteen-kilometre radius of Cussano. On 23 May, the Portuguese and irregulars began moving north towards Ompaba on the Binat to Bissoram track, away from the river; consequently, Teixeira Pinto sent the two gunboats to Bolama and Bissau.

The rigours of soldiering in Portuguese Guinea were beginning to have an adverse affect on the column; a soldier serving with 2 Native Company went down with sleeping sickness. The medical orderly was powerless to remedy the effects of a parasitical worm, which painfully infected the men's legs. The night of 23 May heralded the first torrential rains, which lasted for five hours. The ground turned to mud and the men were soon soaked to the skin and shivering in the driving rain; there was not one tent in camp. As it had been too wet to light fires, the troops' clothes had to dry on their bodies during the march. Unfortunately, as the sun did not appear until midday, it was a long and wet morning. As the column continued toward Ompaba, Balantas from Minyome came out to meet them, and after a short parley, agreed to pay the required government hut taxes. Teixeira Pinto ordered the bush telegraph to be beaten, and sent the Balantas out to the *tabankas* to tell their occupants that he would not harm them, provided they all appeared at his camp. Only 22 of them came and a tall, grave, old man, promised they would return and surrender their weapons to show they did not want war. However, shortly after the meeting, the Balanta from nearby Biambi *tabanka* ambushed a 24-strong Fulani foraging party sent out by Teixeira Pinto.

On 25 May, yet another enemy, mosquitoes, attacked the column. The biting insects made sleep impossible, and the plague was to continue and intensify during the journey from Mansoa to Nyacra. On the following day, the column continued towards Bissoram and having reached its objective, decided to move at once to Naga, as spies reported that Balantas there were preparing to attack the column. On 27 May, the column attacked Naga, 31 kilometres west of Bissoram, routing the enemy; the Portuguese suffered only one casualty.

The Bissoram post told Teixeira Pinto that Balantas on the right bank of the river had begun to surrender their weapons, and had agreed to pay the Portuguese government hut tax. The column remained at Bissoram until 1 June, when it was joined by more irregular troops from Mansoa. The evacuation of the sick and wounded left Teixeira Pinto with 620 irregulars. The column began the march from Bissoram in a south-easterly direction, through Uatiner to Bunyi, eight kilometres distant. In the late afternoon of 2 June, it crossed the Armada River where it was attacked; the enemy was thrown back and neighbouring *tabankas* were destroyed. On 3 June, a reconnaissance patrol was sent out toward Cobonche, it was attacked and as a reprisal, the women and children were driven out and the *tabanka* was sacked and burned to the ground. According to the column's guides, the *tabanka* at Cobonche had taken part in the massacre of Pedro and his platoon. On 5 June, while marching on the track to Nagate, the column came under harassing fire, which lasted for two hours. The irregulars returned fire, and many of the Balanta sharpshooters hiding high up in coconut palms, were brought crashing to the muddy ground, while two irregulars were wounded; one dying of his wounds on the following day. As the column set up camp, it began to rain heavily. The Balantas advanced towards the Portuguese position under cover of the driving rain, but the attack petered out and none of the defenders was injured. During the rest of the night, heavy rain chilled them to the bone, and mosquitoes made the men's lives a misery. The first rays of daylight picked out Balanta dead lying in hideous positions around the bivouac. The Balanta corpses were collected together and hurriedly buried in a pit 40 metres from the Portuguese entrenchments.

It was reported that Balantas were gathering at Biur and on 7 June, after cleaning and oiling their weapons, the column left fully prepared for an enemy attack. The advanced guard skirmished with the Balantas who began falling back eastwards towards Brai. Later, the column came up with thick jungle – as the Portuguese officers had no maps, they had to rely on local knowledge, which held it was the Unfaré Jungle, and not more than one-kilometre deep. The left flanking section of the column sent out vedettes, which were fired on, but the column had to press on through the jungle whatever the cost. Teixeira Pinto led the way, commanding his platoon of 'Kwanyamas'; they had been with him since the previous January. Sergeant Faria rallied his men and charged the enemy with fixed bayonets, half an hour later; the column began to emerge from the jungle. The Balantas fled ahead of the Portuguese as if to entice them to follow. On the right, Abdul Injai and his irregulars were fighting their way through enemy *tabankas,* which were taken one by one. The Balantas turned and attacked and then retired, their shooting was ineffectual but not their swordsmanship; 40 irregulars had been wounded by sword cuts. In the early afternoon, the weary and bloodied column finally bivouacked in Brai where the massacre of Lieutenant Pedro's men had taken place. Shards of human bone and skull were still visible on the ground, having been brought to the surface by the torrential rain. The *tabankas* were thoroughly searched and yielded up articles of uniform and cavalry equipment. Patrols were sent out but found no sign of the enemy. Teixeira Pinto estimated that 15,000 warriors had faced them that day. Torrential rain followed and afforded the Balantas cover as they fled towards the left bank of the Mansoa River. The Portuguese commander took his exhausted column to Port Mansoa, in order to give them the chance to rest and repair weapons and clothing. Teixeira Pinto had worn the same clothes for many weeks, and like the rest of his column, he and his uniform were sorely in need of a good wash.

Teixeira Pinto was exultant; the deaths had been avenged without the costly use of a Portuguese expeditionary force. Everyone had told him European troops would be needed and that he would not be able to wage war with irregulars alone, but by using the mainly Islamic coastal population, he had been able to take on and defeat the clans of the interior.

The men remained at Port Mansoa until 13 June. Teixeira Pinto was now fully up to strength with 800 irregulars, however, he learned that large groups of Balantas had recrossed the Mansoa River, believing that the Portuguese had withdrawn, and were about to attack those clans living close to Port Mansoa, who had been friendly to the Portuguese. On 15 June, he marched toward Encheia and ordered the *Flecha* and *Zagaia* on station. The column found Brai and Unfaré completely deserted, and moved on towards Endasse, where they arrived in the early afternoon in torrential rain. The enemy was massing in large numbers and the column deployed within the *tabankas* to await the attack while the gunboats prepared to engage the enemy with their machine guns. Many of the Balantas were armed with swords; their ancient flintlocks being rendered unserviceable due to the rain, but others were armed with Kropatschek and Snider rifles. By late afternoon the battle was over; many enemy dead and wounded were lying out in the driving rain in the clearing in front of the *tabankas*. The Balantas had pressed home their attack, and had got in among the defenders, slashing them with their swords, causing many hideous, gaping wounds, which soon turned septic in the tropical conditions. Of the two rifles taken from the enemy dead, one of them had belonged to Second Lieutenant Pedro's platoon, and a dead Balanta was found with a Native Police issue haversack containing Snider ammunition.

On 17 June, the victorious column marched to Biur where they were fired on from Encheia on the opposite bank of the creek. Womenfolk were crying for the dead, and the men appeared unwilling to attack the Portuguese. Teixeira Pinto ordered the *bombolom* to beat out a message that the government had no wish to harm them. If they came to sue for peace and handed over their weapons and swords, he would let them return to their *tabankas*. A few warriors appeared saying that many others were too afraid to come forward, and were hiding deep in the jungle. As the Balanta clans lacked a hierarchical system, every family would have to decide for itself and it would take time for them to reach a consensus. Teixeira Pinto realised that his request was unlikely to bear fruit and told the warriors to present themselves at Port Mansoa.

Teixeira Pinto then shifted his focus north to join up with Mamadu Sissé, who he had ordered to Basserel with 80 men, having been told that the Manjako had murdered an old chief who had long been friendly to the Portuguese. Early in the morning on 20 June, the column slowly filed out en route to Nagate. When the column passed close to the *tabanka* at Queré it was fired on, but the enemy fled, and eventually they encamped at Nagate. From Nagate, they followed Mamadu Sissé's trail to Basserel via Bula and on to Mansoa, where they arrived on 21 June after an exhaustive march. The whole area between the Armada and Mansoa rivers was now under Portuguese control. Due to the continuous, torrential rains, the men were forced to remain at Port Mansoa for three days, it was now impossible to ford the swollen, fast flowing river; the first phase was over.

The second phase began on 25 June, with the crossing of the Mansoa River. En route to Sugune, the column attacked and destroyed the settlements at Ganye, Psenche and Jugudal. Since 1912 the left bank of the Mansoa River, apart from a small section of Jugudal, had been under the sway of a Balanta chief, who now styled himself 'Pegman King of Jugudal.' One of his nephews, Ensassa, regularly appeared at the military post between Ganye and Psenche, where he would provide detailed information on Pegman's movements. He secretly carried letters and official correspondence to Bissau on behalf of the military post's commander, and in doing so risked his life. Ensassa was twice held by his own people, only his lineage saved him from death. On 26 June, the *bombolom* echoed through the bush and over the waters of the swift flowing Mansoa, calling the warriors to mass for an attack on the Portuguese column. Teixeira Pinto realised that to push on would be a serious, perhaps, even fatal mistake, and instead prepared the column's defences and awaited the expected attack. Just before midday, a tornado, accompanied by heavy rain, blew through the expectant column. The Balantas appeared in the eye of the storm and threw themselves against the defenders but as evening drew near, the attacks began to lessen in intensity, and Teixeira Pinto decided to take the fight to the enemy. The battered attackers fled through the rain, leaving their dead on the waterlogged ground.

Next day, the column reorganised and set out on the seventeen-kilometre march towards Xugué and Munssul, close to the Geba River. The column met with limited resistance on entering Xugué which they invested, burning its *tabanka* to the ground. On the following day, the column struck out to Munssul where two obstacles: a flooded *bolenha* and a fast flowing, deep-sided creek, held it up. Horses and men were soon floundering in the thick mud; it took eight exhausting hours to get through the double obstacles before reaching Rocene where the soaked, mud-spattered column made camp close to a foul smelling mangrove swamp.

The men spent a miserable, cold night, encamped in torrential rain at the mercy of tens of thousands of mosquitoes. On 29 June, the dispirited column continued its way to Ábuto, close to the Mansoa River, where the *Flecha's* cannon engaged and drove off the enemy. After another sleepless night, the column turned south towards Nyacra where Teixeira Pinto observed the enemy fleeing towards Pepel territory. The Balantas feared to attack the column because of its proximity to *Forte Bissau*, fourteen kilometres away. It was only when the column reached the thickly wooded heights of Oko, south of Nyacra that they were fired on by enemy warriors; fortunately the column sustained no casualties. The Portuguese pushed on after the enemy as far as the Impernal, where many threw themselves into the river and were drowned in the seething waters. Teixeira Pinto's guides interrogated a number of prisoners and learned that they were Pepel from Antule, on the west bank of the Impernal, who had unwisely decided to test the column's strength. The victorious column returned to Nyacra where Teixeira Pinto sited a sandbagged, military post, garrisoned by fifteen irregulars under command of nineteen-year-old-Second Lieutenant Jaime Fonseca.

Early in the afternoon of 2 July, six irregulars were ordered out to forage for food in the direction of the *tabankas* at Xangué in Balanta territory. It was a fruitless task. Soon darkness had overtaken them and the jungle was now alive with night sounds. The men became jumpy; a buffalo was heard crashing through the bush. The corporal in charge of the fatigue party ordered one man armed with a Snider rifle, to cover their withdrawal, while keeping in contact with the rest of the group; he was never seen again. Early the following morning, eighteen mounted irregulars were sent out to search for the missing man, but when they reached Xangué, a group of Balantas appeared under a white flag bringing hay for the irregulars' horses. The search party began to parley with the Balantas, and in a show of traditional hospitality, the men were invited to sit down in the shade of a mango tree and share the villagers' morning meal. A band of Balantas hidden in the bush fell on the unsuspecting irregulars and butchered them. Only one of the irregulars managed to escape the slaughter, and after hiding in the jungle for three days, alerted Second Lieutenant Fonseca at the Nyacra military post. Abdul Injai immediately led out a heavily armed foot patrol of handpicked, men and soon found the irregulars' remains. Abdul Injai was no stranger to the cruelty of war but the discovery both angered and appalled him; the bodies had been hacked into pieces, burned and then stuffed into shallow holes in the ground. They followed the Balantas' trail through the bush and on climbing up a muddy, root-covered slope, suddenly came face to face with a large band of armed men resting just off the track in sight of the *tabankas* at Nagwe. A furious fight ensued but Abdul Injai's men had the advantage of cover and fired down on the band from the top of the slope. The Balantas attempted to charge up the incline but their leader, a short, hefty man, was shot through the head, and as his body slithered down the slope, the band lost heart and fled leaving 49 of their dead on the track. It was yet another nail in the Balantas' coffin. By 14 August 1914, the war against the Balanta was largely over, leaving only isolated pockets of resistance.

Chapter 27
The Pepel and Grumete Campaign – Bissau Region

On 12 May 1915, Teixeira Pinto was at Bissau gathering troops for the coming campaign. After drawing up his plan of action, he put Lieutenant Henrique Alberto de Sousa Guerra in command of 2 Company Native Infantry, which was composed of two sergeants and 30 of Teixeira Pinto's handpicked irregulars – the so-called 'Kwanyamas.' At Rei Island, the troops were put through rigorous manoeuvres and musketry practise. The captain of the cruiser *São Gabriel*, Alberto Celestino Ferreira Pinto Basto, generously provided the embryonic force with a Hotchkiss 8mm rapid-fire machine gun. The training of a machine gun crew was given over to Sergeant António Ribeiro Mões. At *Forte Bissau*, its commander, Major José Xavier Teixeira de Barros, organised the stronghold's defences. Teixeira Pinto left aboard the motorboat *República,* and disembarked artillery Sergeant Rodrigues with ten soldiers who were to march to Nyacra to meet up with the irregulars. As the irregulars had failed to appear, he went by the *Flecha* to Port Mansoa where Abdul Injai arrived on 27 May. Teixeira Pinto then boarded the *República* and steamed to Nyacra sending the *Flecha*, which had developed engine trouble, back to Bolama. Abdul Injai and 1,600 well-armed men, 119 of them mounted, made for Nyacra arriving there on the following day. At Cumeré, Abdul Injai and Teixeira Pinto reconnoitred suitable embarkation sites for the mounted irregulars. The small motor launch *República* was fired on. Pepel and Grumete marksmen, hiding in the mangrove bush, by the banks of the Impernal River, close to Bissau, peppered its plates with bullet holes. The *República* returned on 30 May, escorted by the newly repaired *Flecha*. The two boats were again fired on by the enemy hiding in the bush, and in the irrigation channels close to the Impernal River. The intense and accurate fire from the two gunboats caused the Balanta and Grumete clans to flee, dragging their dead and wounded off into the bush.

Through his binoculars, Teixeira Pinto had seen Pepel and Grumete warriors running away from Antule to their straw hutted *tabankas* after attacking the boats. He ordered the 75mm bronze cannon at Nyacra - the Antule settlement was 3,000 metres away on the west bank of the Impernal - to fire two shrapnel rounds which landed in the middle of the *tabanka* killing and maiming many of its inhabitants. But resistance to the Portuguese only increased. The *Flecha* was repeatedly fired on while resupplying the irregulars with ammunition, and the motor launch *República* was damaged. Next day, Teixeira Pinto heard the welcome thunder of a 105.5 Krupp gun, which cheered up the Portuguese force, and made its leader even more determined to push on to Bissau as quickly as possible. Teixeira Pinto ordered the *Flecha* to open up on a group of Pepel and Grumete 2,500 metres distant. The gunboat's 75mm cannon took a heavy toll but, she was hit by rifle fire; luckily it caused only superficial damage and none of her crew was injured. At dawn on 1 June, Teixeira Pinto was awakened by the sound of beating wings as thousands of noisy, emerald starlings whirred overhead showering the column with bird droppings. The disgruntled and bespattered irregular troops then tramped down to the jetty at Cumeré in order to embark for the journey to Bissau. The *Cacheu* towed the barges' 500 irregulars and 39 horses, while the *Flecha's* harassing fire kept the Pepel well clear of the riverbank.

On 3 June, the column was to begin its advance from Bissau fortress toward the interior. Sentries reported spotting Pepel and Grumete warriors massing in large numbers on the heights of Intim. The enemy had earlier attacked a fatigue party who were foraging in the bush, and was now advancing in strength towards the fort, in half-moon formation. Teixeira Pinto and Lieutenant Sousa Guerra rapidly joined the hard-pressed fatigue party. The small group began to withdraw to within 100 metres of the fort, leaving their dead behind. The Pepel warriors from Biombo, believing the Portuguese were panicking, came out into the open armed only with spears and shields, this gave the retreating men fresh heart and once re-supplied with ammunition, they pushed the poorly armed Biombo back up the wooded hill towards Intim. The Biombo suffered many casualties, as shields and spears were no match for modern rifles. For Teixeira Pinto, the legend of Pepel invincibility was forever dispelled. The way was now open to the occupation of Bissau Region. It had been a costly battle; eighteen men had been killed, two were nephews of Abdul Injai, and a further 73 wounded, including Chief Mamadu Sissé. Yet the engagement had been a success and was a far cry from 1891 and 1894 when Portuguese troops were massacred, the town sacked, and the women raped and abducted by the victors. During the night, the Pepel could be heard removing the wounded and dead, but daylight still showed more than 200 bodies spread out over the steeply rising battleground.

On 5 June, Teixeira Pinto began the advance towards Chão, with the first day's objectives being the stone-built redoubts on the heights of Intim and Bandim, seven kilometres from Bissau. At first light the artillery bombardment began as seven guns fired on the heights. A careful advance followed the bombardment. Mamadu Sissé's irregulars, backed up by Fulanis under Alfá Mamadu Leilu with Teixeira Pinto's soldiers, and the machine gun section, took the lead. Abdul Injai and his men formed the rearguard. Just before midday, the Pepel who had taken cover among the thick roots of mango trees, or were lying in *bolenhas*, rose up and rushed towards the Portuguese. Teixeira Pinto's men met the attack head on and the Pepel faltered and were steadily pushed back over the heights. When the heights were gained, Sergeant Mões and his section brought up the machine gun. Just as he was about to take aim at the fleeing Pepel, he was hit in the chest by a rifle bullet and thrown backwards down the hill, coming to rest in a thorn bush outcrop. By the time Abdul Injai's men reached the sergeant, he was already dead. However, the advance was a complete success; the column's casualties were five killed and 35 wounded.

The road between Intim and Bissau was finally open, and with the victorious force now securely encamped on the heights, they were soon being supplied with wine, cakes and other delicacies by a happy and extremely relieved procession of Bissau townsfolk. On 6 June, a reconnaissance patrol was sent out and discovered a large number of dead warriors hidden under enormous fronds within a tamarind grove. On 7 June, the hilltop redoubt was attacked by the enemy but after two hours the Pepel were beaten back leaving many bodies on the slopes. The Portuguese losses were four dead and 27 wounded, including war chief Aliburi, the son of Abdul Injai.

The indefatigable Teixeira Pinto then planned to advance north on the settlement at Antule. An hour-long artillery barrage was to begin at dawn followed by the main attack, which would go in a half hour later. The column's troops were excited and confident, yet Antule was considered by the Pepel and Grumete to be sacred ground, which had never been sullied by government forces in time of war. The bombardment began on time but a heated discussion broke out as to who would have the honour of leading the attack. It was fast approaching zero hour and Teixeira Pinto was seriously concerned, lest his own men should be machine gunned, if they delayed their attack too long. Teixeira Pinto was forced to intervene and order the attack to get under way. Mamadu Sissé would lead, followed by a platoon of soldiers and a machine gun, with Alfá Mamadu Leilu, left flanking, and the lightly wounded Aliburi, right flanking. Behind them the rearguard riflemen under Abdul Injai advanced in extended line. The irregulars encountered little resistance, as most of the enemy fled leaving 107 dead and wounded on the battlefield. The *Flecha*, which had been shadowing the column, steamed into the Impernal firing on the Pepel as they attempted to gain Balanta territory by canoe.

Between 9 and 10 June, the column was encamped at Antule, when on the following day it began to rain heavily, followed by tornado-like winds. Teixeira Pinto moved on, and followed the Ondalo River, entering the lands of the Saca clan. The Saca were driven out and their *tabankas* destroyed after the column was fired on. The Portuguese then pushed on towards Cuju but were slowed down by a combination of thick jungle and torrential rain. The sound of heavy rifle fire was heard coming from the direction of the rearguard, and a breathless runner from Abdul Injai, told Teixeira Pinto that Grumete and Pepel warriors were attacking them, and he desperately needed reinforcements. The column was halted to give the rearguard time to catch up, and then pressed on towards Jaal, arriving there in the early afternoon. The Jaal *tabanka* was located on a bare hill, with an enormous rice *bolenha* to the south, and surrounded on three sides by thick jungle. The column moved to the *tabankas* to deploy and organise their defences. The guides told him that Samfim *tabanka* was 22 kilometres away, and they feared the force might find itself fighting a large enemy on difficult ground. The heavy rain made the march to the *tabankas* difficult, and crossing the wide *bolenhas* became nightmarish, as men and horses floundered in the mud. The Portuguese had to beat off repeated enemy attacks and were forced to bivouac on the rain soaked ground. While the column adopted all round defence, the medical orderlies tended the nine wounded men and a burial fatigue dealt with the dead.

On 12 June the enemy began to advance through the jungle under cover of the blinding rain. The irregular's chief, Braime Dan, brought Teixeira Pinto the unwelcome news that a number of heavily armed Pepel had infiltrated their position. Teixeira Pinto was taking a wash in a cracked gourd when the alarm was sounded, and without having time to put on his shirt or cap, shouted to the machine gun section to follow him, and led six soldiers against the attackers. It took the Portuguese three successive charges with the bayonet before they broke and fled back into the jungle. Teixeira Pinto noticed that a warrior armed with what looked like a Mauser rifle, was trying to get him in his sights and moved to a safer position behind a tree. While he was watching the irregulars through his binoculars, he felt a terrifically heavy blow against his side. Spinning round, he collapsed on to the ground. The medical orderly dragged the heavily bleeding officer back to the hospital wagon; it was a dangerous moment for the column. Having regained his senses, he ordered Abdul Injai to press on to Samfim. The march took three and a half hours and for Teixeira Pinto it was sheer agony, as he swung to and fro in a ground sheet, carried by two irregulars. Teixeira Pinto hoped to remain with his men at Samfim even though the medical orderly had advised him to return to Bissau. When the column reached Samfim, Teixeira Pinto was already delirious. As he appeared to be deteriorating, the decision was taken to evacuate him to Bissau in the *Flecha*. A bullet had hit his right arm and ricochetted off his shoulder but had not smashed the bone, and by late June Teixeira Pinto was back in command.

On the morning of 28 June, two irregulars who had managed to escape from Bór west of Bissau, reported to Teixeira Pinto, with a message that Pepel and Grumete warriors were attempting to surround their position. The column was almost out of ammunition and they had had nothing to eat or drink all that day. As there were no reserves at Bissau, and the few soldiers stationed at the fort were purely for its defence, Teixeira Pinto decided to withdraw the column. He ordered the gunboat *Flecha* to steam up the Mansoa River to Bijiminta to re-supply Lieutenant Sousa Guerra prior to the withdrawal. In spite of the swollen rivers, the skipper of the *Flecha* weighed anchor and sailed, carrying ammunition and Teixeira Pinto's orders. On 29 June Teixeira Pinto was relieved to hear of Sousa Guerra's safe arrival at Bissau.

Only later did he discover that one of the Portuguese civilians who had joined the column, Professor Moreira, had been kidnapped on the orders of the Biombo chief, and after three days of torture, had been brutally murdered, and his body quartered. After resting and resupplying, the column marched out of Bissau in heavy rain on 10 July. They met with some resistance but pushed on towards Prabis where a fierce fight took place. The column was forced to call a halt, tend to its wounded and bury the dead. Teixeira Pinto sent a message to the warring Pepel and Grumete under a flag of truce, inviting them to present themselves to the column, sue for peace and surrender their weapons. If the warriors refused to comply, then the war would only end with their total defeat. The enemy was not completely convinced by Teixeira Pinto's threats and it took the battle at Pelundo, to finally decide the campaign in Portugal's favour. The Grumete and Pepel warriors were soundly routed, and on 17 July emissaries appeared at the Portuguese camp, where they were ordered to surrender their weapons. On the following day, the Papel Chief of Bór in the west arrived saying that as he had not heard from the Chief of Biombo, he would lead the Portuguese to him. The young chief was seated under an enormous tamarind tree with his counsellors, and on seeing the Portuguese, got up and greeted them warmly. The young chief was the clans' choice and wanted peace but the Chief of Biombo had another more bellicose young pretender in mind. The chief handed over a small number of weapons and ordered the people who had fled to return to their *tabankas*. On 19 July the Portuguese received news from Biombo that the chief wanted to open peace negotiations. When they entered his *tabanka*, they came upon a large baobab tree where 80 rifles had been piled up and a white flag placed on top of them; the chief and some of his elders were standing to one side. As the Portuguese advanced towards the *tabanka,* rapid rifle fire broke out from a group of Pepel hidden behind a mud wall. The Portuguese returned fire, which demolished the wall in a cloud of dust, killing most of the sharpshooters. In the confusion, the chief attempted to escape, but was taken by the Portuguese, and many of the warriors were chased into the jungle or shot down before they had time to make away. The chief defiantly declared that he would never accept Portuguese rule as he hated whites and would fight on, and were he to meet whites in another life, he would continue to kill them there too. He said that his people had lost 1,307 warriors in battle with the Portuguese. However, his clan was the bravest and most warlike and had refused to flee. He also admitted giving the order to kidnap, torture and kill Professor Moreira. With the resounding defeat of the Pepel and Grumete clans the column was finally stood down.

By the end of July 1915, the Oyo War, an audacious and meticulously planned operation in extremely difficult strength-sapping tropical conditions, led to the military conquest of Portuguese Guinea. It was not without justification that the clans of his native Angola had earlier dubbed Teixeira Pinto *Kurika* - lion.

Chapter 28
German Machinations - Angola 1913

In 1913, the German ambassador, Prince Karl Max Lichnowsky, was busy attempting to negotiate a secret agreement between Britain and Germany. The Anglo-German negotiations were opened following the ratification of clauses contained in the thirteenth century Anglo-Portuguese treaty. The treaty between the allies had been renewed and re-written over a period of six centuries. Those clauses were sanctioned on 15 March 1912, by Lisbon and were approved on the same day by Westminster. Little did Portuguese parliamentarians know, as they avidly debated the publication of the text, which they took to be a revitalisation of the ancient Alliance that in London and Berlin a web of intrigue was being woven around Portugal and her African colonies.

In the 'secret article' of 1660 England promised, to defend and protect all conquests or colonies belonging to the crown of Portugal, against all its present and future enemies. According to the Reich ambassador, the negotiated Anglo-German Accord would have admirably assured 'in appearance', the integrity and independence of Portugal and its colonies. The accord expressed no more than the intention to aid Portugal financially and economically. Consequently, it did not run contrary to the Anglo-Portuguese Alliance. The Anglo-German Accord was more valuable to Germany when Portugal's complete dependence on Britain was taken into account.

The treaty on the Portuguese colonies would have had far-reaching importance for Germany. Berlin would have gained central Angola, which with German South West Africa, would have greatly increase its sphere of influence, and provided a single colonial possession with access to good ports and fertile highlands.

The German ambassador to London was insistent upon the signing of the accord before August 1913. However, it was never initialled, as Sir Edward Grey stipulated that it would have to be published together with the 1898 and the 1899 treaties. The treaty determined the form of assistance to be provided by taking into account the countries' preparedness. Although Sir Edward Grey appreciated the German government's misgivings, and appeared to understand that the simultaneous publication of both treaties would produce a negative impression in Berlin, he argued that treaties made with the Portuguese bound the British government to make it public.

The 1913 accord would have been much more advantageous to the Germans than the 1898 version. It contained specific situations in which Berlin was authorised to take whatever measures its government might judge necessary to safeguard its spheres of interest, but were expressed in such terms, that only Britain and Germany could decide on their relative importance. As Portugal was largely dependent upon Britain, it was only necessary to cultivate good relations with Whitehall, in order for the German government to carry out its real plans. But those plans, according to Count Lichnowsky became yet another casualty of the First World War.

From a German political standpoint, the ill-fated Anglo-German Accord, ended in failure. Yet when the first echoes of war were heard in Angola, the groundwork had already been laid; Foreign Minister Freire de Andrade, on behalf of the Portuguese Government, had earlier approved a proposal to create a Portuguese-German Commission to study the joint economic possibilities of the southern Angolan region. Colonels Manuel Maria Coelho and Carlos Roma Machado led the Portuguese mission, with Dr Schubert, representing German interests. German engineers, doctors, agronomists and traders, had already hacked their way through the pitiless, thorn bush, past mopani and hideously twisted primeval baobab trees, braving the heat and the clouds of swarming, biting insects, in order to document the colony's bountiful resources, while innocently assisted by compliant Portuguese district commissioners following Lisbon's dictat.

Heinrich Ziegler was a tough, leathery-skinned German colonist, from Streitfontein Farm in the Grootfontein district of German South West Africa. He had journeyed by ox-wagon through southern Angola in 1913, and was enviously impressed by what he saw. He reported in his meticulously kept diary, that travelling from the 1,700-metre high railhead at Huambo in the Benguela Highlands, south to Vila Pereira de Eça, through Galangue, Vila da Ponte and Cassinga, he had, in over 377 kilometres, met no more than 300 European colonists; they were mostly district commissioners, traders and missionaries. Ziegler knew how short Portugal was of manpower, and surmised that because the colonial army had enormous difficulty in policing southern Angola, governor Norton de Matos, had excluded all potential settlers whether Portuguese or foreigners from the region. Furthermore, de Matos was firmly against the building of a railway line from Pôrto Alexandre on the Atlantic coast to Gambos and Cassinga; locations which had been suggested by the German half of the joint study commission. Ziegler recrossed the Kunene River south to Grootfontein and after lengthy discussions with interested farmers, traders and miners, formed the *Angola Bund*, which came into being on 29 August 1913. The *Bund's* aim was to promote the idea of the incorporation of southern Angola into German South West Africa by purchasing unoccupied government land, and making it available as farming areas to German, Boer and Portuguese settlers. Yet, in a news article in the German colony's press, Ziegler had written that southern Angola would be an asset because of its abundance of wheat, and the Bay of Tigers would provide German South West Africa with the port it lacked.

Many colonial officers in Angola realised that it had been a great mistake to allow the setting up of German missions at Ondjiva, Matemba and Namakunde in the 1880s, as it had caused stirrings against Portugal's administration of the region. The Reverend Charles Bourqui, of the Portuguese mission at Cassinga, had visited Kwanyamaland in 1908. He had stayed for a time with King Nande, and noted that the Germans were in the habit of making large purchases of Kwanyama cattle in exchange for rifles. Reverend Bourqui had inspected one such weapon, a German-made Mauser. On his return north, he had visited Paiva Couceiro, and requested him to make representations to the German Imperial government, regarding the inadvisability of bartering weapons with the Kwanyama clans. Portuguese intelligence had long been aware of the porous nature of the border and patrols had been gradually increased to counter the possible threat.

German South West Africa 1900
(Deutsche Kolonialgesellschaft)

Chapter 29
Portugal Considers War in Africa and Europe

Portugal felt seriously threatened by German and British machinations in Africa. The Lisbon government was undecided as to its course of action; many widely differing opinions were loudly voiced both for and against intervention in the world war.

Patriotic fervour was all very well for the young blades strutting around the Empire's capital in their light blue uniforms, proudly displaying subalterns' stars on the tailored sleeves of their high-collared jackets. But in the more pragmatic corridors of power, cooler heads focused on the weighty implications of the Anglo-Portuguese Alliance; Whitehall was entitled to request aid consonant with the stipulations of the treaties, and consequently Lisbon was obliged to provide such aid, but that request clearly could not go beyond Portugal's capabilities, nor place its security at risk in Europe or in its vulnerable African possessions. The normally, genial and urbane, Bernardino Machado agonised over his government's position; there were many who took an extremely dim view of the obligations of the Anglo-Portuguese Alliance after the humiliation of the *Ultimatum*.

Many former monarchists, soldiers and politicians, actively supported non-intervention in the European war. Colonial officers, who had loyally served the Portuguese crown in Mozambique, felt especially aggrieved. In 1891 Portuguese colonial administrators and officers had been astonished to witness the journey to London on the *Roslin Castle* of two of Gungunyana's envoys: Huluhulu and Umfeti - also known as Umteto and Inteni. Huluhulu was over 60-years-of-age, and during the long sea journey to England, had become quite ill. Umfeti, some 30-years younger, had encountered no such problems. The *indunas* were lodged with their South Africa-born interpreter, Dennis Doyle, on Oxford Street. One Sunday, they were taken to Westminster Abbey, where the older *induna* was offered the use of a bath chair, which he refused, saying that he had not yet become a child, and on the following day they visited Madame Tussaud's Exhibition. At Tussaud's, Huluhulu asked Doyle if the figures on display were dead bodies preserved in some unknown way, and on being told that they were waxwork, seemed disappointed that the modellers were unable to put breath into the figures.

The two men visited the Duke and Duchess of Fife, and from that courtly atmosphere, they found themselves next day, having breakfast at Park Lane with Albert Grey MP, assorted business men interested in commercial ventures, and other parliamentarians with links to Southern Africa. Huhuluhu had told the group of his chief's dislike of the Portuguese. Looking at Doyle, he told him to tell Queen Victoria that Gungunyana begged to be taken under the protection of the British Empire. Huhuluhu warmed to his subject, saying that the Portuguese had caused great problems for Gungunyana, forcing him to move his kraal and his people nearer the Limpopo. During the trek many thousands of his subjects had died from starvation, and Gungunyana wanted the protection of the 'Great White Queen.' After translating this into English, Doyle told the group that in his opinion, the Portuguese were attempting to corrupt the Gazaland people with strong cheap Portuguese alcohol. On his way to the coast he had come across over 200 men laden with demijohns of *bagaço* making their way to the king's kraal. Grey asked Huhuluhu to repeat his request to Queen Victoria into a gramophone, which was played back to the astonished *induna*, who then listened to a recorded military band. Meanwhile, Doyle had held an interesting interview with Lord Salisbury. The prime minister had recognised that, as part of Gungunyana's lands had been included within the British South Africa Company's sphere of influence, the king of Gazaland had, 'to a certain extent come under British protection.' It was planned that the two *indunas* would remain in England until the end of August, and visits to Birmingham, Manchester, Liverpool, Glasgow and Edinburgh, were organised. When Lobengula's envoys had visited England, they had not moved out of London; when they returned home, they told their king that in England there was only one big kraal. Doyle and his business friends did not want that to happen with Gungunyana's men. Next day Huhuluhu and Umfeti found themselves entering the gates of the London Zoological Gardens. After being introduced to the zoo's superintendent and renowned taxidermist, Abraham Dee Bartlett, they were guided to the Deer House, where to their pleasure, they viewed animals they knew well from Gazaland. Huhuhlu volunteered that the animals could smell the two men - instantly recognising them as sworn enemies, who had killed so many of their like. Just around the corner, Umfeti came face to face with the zoo's one and only rhinoceros. He became agitated and threatened to kill it with his tlhari. In spite of this, Umluhulu, through interpreter Doyle, thanked Bartlett, who smiled through his long, white beard at the possibility of an invitation to visit his king in Gazaland; they would hold a magnificent feast in his honour, and the women would be very hospitable and supply him with plenty of beer.

Gungunyana had earlier been approached by Dr Jameson, Dr Schultz and Doyle, who had persuaded him to make a verbal treaty giving the British South Africa Company all of the mining rights throughout Gazaland, in return for the promise of 1,000 rifles and 20,000 rounds of ammunition. Paiva Couceiro, one of the few Africanist officers, who had actively manned monarchist barricades in Lisbon during the republican revolution, had sustained a bullet wound from a British-made and supplied Martini-Henry rifle, fired by a warrior at the battle of

Magul. That simmering bitterness against Britain was to be a continuing source of friction between the anti-interventionists and their pro-allied opponents.

The Portuguese were angered to learn of the *indunas'* return to Mozambique carrying a gift for the 'King of Gazaland' bearing Queen Victoria's rubric. In March of that year, the British steamer *Countess of Carnaervon* had been seized on the Limpopo River, and escorted to Lourenço Marques, where she was found to be carrying weapons and ammunition to be supplied to Gungunyana, with a nod from Cecil Rhodes.

Against the backdrop of monarchist anti-interventionism, Portugal's amiable leader, wealthy, grey-bearded, Brazilian born, former Coimbra University professor, Bernardino Machado, penned the first passage of a lengthy text addressed to plenipotentiary minister in London, Teixeira Gomes. It would lay the groundwork for Portugal's entry into the war. In order to determine Portugal's conduct as Britain's ally in the eventuality of war, the diplomat and sometime author, Teixeira Gomes, was requested to obtain declarations from Whitehall, which would serve to guide Portugal's actions in terms of the Anglo-Portuguese Alliance. Article seven stipulated that in case of aggression against either Portugal or Britain, mutual aid would be rendered, should either country request it. It could therefore, be interpreted as a purely defensive alliance, and Portugal wished to know whether a declaration of neutrality would be appropriate. Teixeira Gomes agreed with Lisbon that such an interpretation would be acceptable to the Portuguese.

A letter from Alexander Eyre Crowe, the assistant under-secretary of state for foreign affairs, to Teixeira Gomes, followed by a telegram from Sir Edward Grey to Britain's minister in Lisbon, Sir Lancelot Carnegie, referred to 4 August, as the date of Britain's request for Portugal to abstain from making a formal declaration of neutrality. Teixeira Gomes affirmed that whatever the case, Britain would have Portugal as its ally. The Portuguese diplomat informed the cabinet that he had asked Britain to study the defence of the African colonies in the event of a German surprise attack, and also declared that any such attack would be covered under the terms of the Anglo-Portuguese Alliance. For the time being, Britain would be satisfied with the Portuguese abstaining from a declaration of neutrality. The British government secretly told Portugal, that if in future it needed to make a request incompatible with its neutrality, then as a justification for such a request, the Alliance would be invoked.

On that basis, Bernardino Machado made his declaration to the packed, five-tiered, balustraded, House of Deputies, on a stifling hot summer's day on 7 August 1914; just three days after Britain had entered the war against the Triple Alliance. Bernardino Machado reminded his listeners that after the proclamation of the republic in Portugal, various nations had hastened to affirm their friendship, and one of them, Great Britain, her alliance. Machado emphasised that Portugal had done everything to correspond to Britain's friendship, and was ever mindful of the obligations of the Anglo-Portuguese Alliance, which had been freely entered into, and with which it would not fail to comply.

On that airless, August day in Lisbon, almost universal approval and enthusiasm within the House greeted Bernardino Machado's measured words. As Machado descended the steps leading from the House, he was applauded all the way by the cheering staw-hatted citizenry. The Portuguese were satisfied that they had struck a dignified posture. As the months rolled by and the war intensified, Portugal began to suffer from the ambiguous situation in which as Britain's oldest, and weakest ally, the country found herself. On the surface, peace with Germany continued both in Europe and in the African colonies, however, the Portuguese colonial administration in Angola maintained an acrimonious distrust of their German neighbours.

Chapter 30
Blockade Breaking in Angola

At the onset of the war the Royal Navy had closed the vital Atlantic sea-link between German South West Africa and Europe. The British embargo had effectively imposed a stranglehold on Germany's sea-borne economy. Faced with the threat of gradual economic starvation of the colony, which was surrounded by potential enemies, the governor of German South West Africa, Theodor von Seitz had secretly requested the German consul in Angola, to purchase food supplies, and as exports were now forbidden from the Portuguese colony, to transport them clandestinely over the border into German South West Africa. The man chosen by Governor Seitz to meet the German-purchased supplies, coming by wagon from Angola to German South West Africa's northern border, was Dr Schultze-Jena.

Forty-year-old Dr Schultze-Jena was the district commissioner and magistrate for Outjo   place of coned shaped mountains   south of the Etosha Pan in the frontier region of Damaraland, in German South West Africa. The town of Outjo had been made a magisterial district by the German administration in 1894, and it was Dr Schultze-Jena's duty to oversee an enormous area running from the Ugab right up to the Kunene. Hans Schultze-Jena had joined the colonial service in November 1906. His first posting was to Windhoek where he was appointed to the bench. A year later in May, he was posted north to Grootfontein as district commissioner and magistrate, moving from there to the town of Outjo on the Ugab River.

On 8 October 1914, Dr Schultze-Jena set out northwards on the 300-kilometre trek to the Angolan border with Captain Alexander Losch, commanding Survey Company North. It was made up of Police Sergeant Braunsdorf and Constable Schaaps of the Outjo police post. Volunteer Pahlke, Volunteer Kurt Roder - a farmer from Cauas-Okava in the Outjo district, Volunteer George Kimmel, who had served with the naval field artillery at Germany's China Station between 1910 and 1913, and Carl Jensen, a Danish farmer, who had lived in the area for many years and fought under Alves Roçadas with the Boer auxiliaries in the Kwamato campaigns of 1907. Jensen was fluent in Portuguese, German and the Ovambo language. The German force was followed up the rear by a wagon pulled by a four pair span.

At Lubango, Colonel Alves Roçadas received an urgent telegram from the Humbe district commissioner. It informed him of an incursion, which had been reported that day by scouts, who had been drawn to the thick clouds of red dust thrown up by the Germans' Boer wagon as it creaked and trundled its way across the veld.

189

Second Lieutenant Manuel Antunes Sereno, commanding the dragoon troop, stationed at Otokero north-east of Naulila, was relaxing over a bottle of beer, when a runner from the telegraph hut brought him the order to saddle up fifteen Portuguese dragoons and fifteen Angolan horsemen, and make for the border. Second Lieutenant Sereno was at 37, a very mature junior subaltern; he had first enlisted in 3 Cavalry Regiment in his native Portugal in 1897, and served as a warrant officer with 1 Cavalry Regiment before being commissioned into the colonial army. A veteran of Angolan campaigns against the Kwanyama and Kwamato peoples, he was known for his brusque manner and direct approach; he had won the Military Medal for bravery a year earlier in 1913.

The troopers soon located the German laager at Calueque Drift, close to a clump of moringa trees, on the Portuguese side of the border. A dust-caked Sereno invited the Germans to accompany him and his troop to military headquarters at Humbe. Schultze-Jena declined, telling the stocky, Portuguese officer, that as it was almost sundown, he would inspan at first light the following day. The German told Sereno that they were on the spoor of an army deserter who had attempted to flee into Portuguese territory. The going had been more difficult than they had anticipated, therefore, they had decided to laager and await permission to continue from the Portuguese district commissioner at Humbe. The Angolan troopers retired leaving the Portuguese officers and NCOs to feed and bed down for the night in the German laager.

The two groups sat round a blazing fire, which afforded some protection against the unwelcome attentions of legions of mosquitoes, and talked as best they could through Carl Jensen, of the common experiences of soldiering in Africa. The camaraderie was marred only by a discussion that became increasingly more heated. It centred on a report in a well-thumbed, three-month-old copy of the Lisbon daily newspaper *O Século*, concerning the reasons for the despatch to Angola of a Portuguese expeditionary force. The newspaper was waved in Sereno's face by an agitated Schultze-Jena; no matter how hard Sereno tried, he was unable to convince the German that Portugal's intentions were motivated solely by unrest among the rebellious clans of southern Angola. Sereno spent a sleepless night listening to the howls of vexed hyenas, prevented from slaking their nocturnal thirst at the drift, by the presence of the laager's fires. But it was not just the myriad sounds of an African night on the veld, which made sleep impossible. Sereno was only too aware that he had earlier impounded a number of German victual wagons in Portuguese territory, and now feared that Schultze-Jena and his tough looking comrades were intent upon making good their compatriots' losses.

In the chilling air before dawn, the laager was alive with noise and movement. As the southern sun suffused the eastern sky, the Germans under Portuguese escort, slowly moved off in the direction of Naulila from where they were to proceed to military headquarters. Portuguese troopers, who were told off to set up camp and brew up close to Naulila, preceded the column. At 9:30 in the morning, the small column halted, dismounted, and began to lead their horses and mules to the makeshift laager. The sweating mounts were unsaddled on Sereno's orders. The Germans were nervous that morning; one of the Portuguese troopers had been overheard muttering darkly that no one would ever leave that laager. While still on foot, the German leader approached Braunsdorf and nodded; the police sergeant quickly picked up his saddle and ran towards his mount. Schultze-Jena had become alarmed by what he thought was a possible Portuguese threat to his party; the Germans were unaware that the contraband wagons had already been confiscated and believed that Sereno was drawing them into a trap at Naulila. They had secretly decided to make a break for it across the border back into German South West Africa. As soon as Sereno was informed of the incident, he reminded Schultze-Jena that the Germans had agreed to go under military escort to Humbe, and that they would have to depart immediately after their long-delayed brew-up. The German paid no heed; he hoarsely barked out an order and strode off towards his mount, placing his boot in the stirrup. Sereno's temper snapped and he ran after the German. Sereno firmly gripped the reins of Schultze-Jena's mule, and told him to dismount, while ordering his close arrest for the duration of the trek to Humbe. The German pointed his rifle at Sereno, while other officers covered him with their pistols. He let go of the mule's reins in alarm when he heard a sharp warning cry from dragoon Corporal Botelho. Schultze-Jena sprang into the saddle, turned his mule's head, dug in his heels and made to get away with the rest of his comrades. He was brought tumbling down on to the stone strewn, red earth, by a well-aimed shot from the carbine of the dragoon's previously jittery corporal. Lieutenant Losch and volunteer Roder were also knocked out of their saddles by accurate Portuguese fire; Losch was badly wounded, and though the shaken Portuguese did all they could for him, he died of his wounds two days later. Jensen the interpreter and old Africa-hand, was lucky to have been taken prisoner without injury when his mule was shot from under him.

Meanwhile, the Germans laagered close to Calueque Drift, became aware of approaching riders when plumes of dust began to spiral into the sky. After being given the order to stand to, the Germans awaited a possible enemy attack. As the riders came fully into view, the Germans were relieved to see that one of them was wearing a light brown uniform. It was Dr Paul Vageler, of the Joint Luso-German Commission. The Humbe district commissioner spurred his horse forward followed by his interpreter. The German scientist had been arrested earlier while making his way towards the safety of the German colony's border, and now was being escorted south on parole by the Portuguese officer. He was no stranger to the region; while lecturing at the University of Königsberg, he had led a number of German scientific expeditions into Angola and German South West Africa between 1909 and 1911. Meanwhile Police Sergeant Braunsdorf, who had been left in charge, told them of the departure of Dr Schultze-Jena, and his officers for Naulila. The German detachment had decided to wait, but as time went by, and the officers had not returned, the sergeant had ordered one of his men to ride to Naulila with a note stating that they had remained laagered at Calueque Drift. When Police Sergeant Braunsdorf learned of the shooting of Dr Schultze-Jena he exploded with anger, and had to be restrained from attacking the Portuguese officer. Dr Vageler sharply ordered the sergeant to control himself, and informed the Portuguese that he would personally take the German detachment back over the border. As they drew away Vageler turned in his saddle and shouted, 'C'est la Guerre!'

On 31 October, news of an attack on a frontier post by Germans and *askaris* led by Police Sergeant Wilhelm Lehmann, the post commander at Kuring-Kuru, and Police Sergeant Oswald Ostermann, was reported to the Portuguese commanding officer. The surprise attack was launched against the Portuguese fort at Cuangar on the left bank of the Kubango River. The Germans, aided by ex-chief Ananga, turned their machine guns on to the fort. The militia commander in Lower Kubango district, Lieutenant Joaquim Ferreira Durão, holder of the prestigious *Torre e Espada* and bar, decoration for services to that colony, ran out of the fort and loudly demanded to know who was firing without his permission; he was instantly shot down. The Angolan troops, who were running toward the fort, were mown down in cold blood. The massacre was soon over. The Germans set fire to *Forte Cuangar* and left the bodies of Ferreira Durão, his second-in-command, a Portuguese sergeant, five soldiers, six Angolan levies and one civilian, lying outside the smouldering fort. Through the smoke and flames, the Imperial German eagle, fluttered over the carnage. Prior to the attack, Police Sergeant Oswald Osterman had maintained excellent relations with the Portuguese on the opposite side of the Kubango River, and they had exchanged letters to the effect that should relations change dramatically between their two countries, they would inform each other before taking any precipitous action.

When Roçadas learned of Lieutenant Ferreira Durão's death, he proudly described him as being an outstanding officer, who had contributed greatly to the success of the 1907 Kwamato Campaign.

To make matters worse for the Portuguese military command, after the bloody massacre at *Forte Cuangar*, an attack was launched against another lightly manned frontier post by a small detachment, again under Police Sergeant Oswald Ostermann. The officer and men holding *Forte Cuanavale* were able to repulse the marauding Germans, as the Portuguese defenders were well prepared having been forewarned by friendly cattle herders. However, along the winding Kubango River, the Germans destroyed the posts at Bunja, Sambio, Dirico and Mucusso; built by Captain João de Almeida in 1909.

Meanwhile, Dr Schubert, the leader of the German half of the Joint Luso-German Commission, had been lodged at Lubango's only hotel with his compatriots when he first heard of the grim news of the unprovoked attacks on the Portuguese border posts. The Germans decided to leave immediately, and make for the safety of the German South West Africa border, before being interned or worse by the Portuguese. Not unnaturally, the enraged townsfolk of Lubango had observed the Germans' hurried departure. Dr Schubert and his group were stopped by well-armed vigilantes and escorted back to town. The Germans were searched and maps of southern Angola were found, as were lists of local arms caches, and locations where agents were to store hidden supply dumps for the possible invasion, along with other detailed documents relating to German espionage activities. The Germans were sent under military escort to Mossâmedes to be repatriated by steamer to German South West Africa.

Chapter 31
Defending the Angolan Border

On 14 August 1914, a German military detachment had crossed the border south into Cape Colony at Nakob and dug in, but the German presence was purely symbolic. In September, a Union force under Brigadier-General Henry 'Harry' Lukin, made up of five regiments of South African Mounted Rifles, Witwatersrand Rifles and three batteries of Transvaal Horse Artillery, sailed from Cape Town to disembark in German South West Africa, and occupy a military post at Raman's Drift. Meanwhile in Angola, Portugal's meagre forces were once again put on the alert in case of a German push into the Kunene region.

In view of Germany's bellicose stance, and the possibility of threats to her overseas possessions, the Portuguese government decided on 18 August 1914, to sanction military expeditions to Angola under the direction of the colonial department in Lisbon. Colonel Alves Roçadas commanded the First Expeditionary Force. The force totalling 3,178 officers and men, embarked at Lisbon on the troopships *Moçambique* and *Cabo Verde* on 11 September 1914.

On 27 September, after a long, uncomfortable and sickness-ridden voyage, the encouraging sight of land gladdened the weary troops. From the brazier-like deck of the stinking troopship, standing out in the wide bay, they could make out what looked like a pretty Portuguese coastal hamlet; it was the southern port of Mossâmedes. Due to the lack of billets, the soldiers of 14 Infantry were forced to remain aboard ship until they were finally disembarked on 1 October. As the exhausted, grubby soldiery moved slowly out of Mossâmedes their fond comparison with home was cruelly dispelled by the desert - wave after wave of banked sand as far as the eye could see. On 17 October, after a 168-kilometre march through scrub and steep, jagged, granite highlands, the column at last trekked into Lubango, a pleasant township with a mild climate and lush vegetation, not unlike the Douro Valley in northern Portugal; yet they were greeted by Madeirans. More than 200 of the townsfolk were the children of hardy colonists who had first arrived from the island of Madeira in January 1884, to set up Sá da Bandeira settlement. The Portuguese government had provided them with assisted passage from Madeira to Angola on the understanding that they agreed to remain in the colony for at least five years. For the tired and dusty troops, Lubango the capital of Huíla district offered a welcome respite and a chance to savour good red wine again. Alves Roçadas then took over governorship of the district and began to prepare his force for possible hostilities.

On 19 November 1914, Portuguese troops were concentrating at *Forte Roçadas*, on the east bank of the Kunene River, 80 kilometres north of the border with German territory. Roçadas' hypothesis was that the Germans would have the Huíla Highlands as their objective; consequently, his force would have to defend all the drifts on the Kunene River that would give the enemy access to the tableland. On the other hand, the Germans could even cross the Kunene River from the west, using the drift located almost at its mouth, to gain access to the Portuguese uplands, or even enter Portuguese territory through Swartboois Drift some 64 kilometres from the Ruacaná Falls. Swartboois Drift was little used by the Portuguese, but had often been used by the Germans as a covert entry point to Angola. For at least 1,000 years, the drift had been a crossing point for peoples migrating south. Those daring to live close by the drift were the Swartbooi Hottentots, for many years, their mounted bands, had ravaged the region as far north as coastal Mossâmedes. The drift took its name from a Swartbooi leader, who when returning from a raid in Angola, had been dragged from his mount into the shallow water by a crocodile. Although his companions shot the reptile, by the time they were able to pull him to relative safety, it was already too late to save his life, and he died of his hideous wounds on the riverbank. From that time on it became known as Swartboois Drift. It was possible to walk across the drift to Angola with water coming up to the knees, though the non-Swartboois were always in fear of the crocodiles and kept well away from the river.

Roçadas realised that should the Germans cross the drift unopposed, they could easily come up with the Otchintoto-Otchinjau-Pokolo road; Calueque Drift would give them access to the Dongoena road and to Tchipelongo, and then on to Humbe itself. Highly decorated, 44-year-old infantry officer, Major Alberto Salgado, a most experienced soldier, who had previously campaigned in both Angola and Mozambique, was laagered close to *Forte Roçadas* with his men. A runner sent by the Kwamato district commissioner, warned him of the entry into Angola of a detachment of German troopers moving in the direction of Naulila. General Alves Roçadas, who had reached *Forte Roçadas* on 23 November, ordered Salgado's column, made up of three companies of 14 Portuguese Infantry, an artillery battery of three Erhardt field guns and a dragoon squadron totalling 900 men, to move out to intercept them. On 26 November, Roçadas received a request for gunpowder and ammunition from Chief Ipumbu of the Kwambi clan, who informed him that a German force was laagered at Tamanke close to Kwambi, some four days' march from Naulila. Roçadas at last had firm intelligence on German strategy in Southern Angola, and that the objective was either the occupation of Naulila or Humbe.

Roçadas now concentrated his force, initially under command of artillery Captain Esteves, on a line from Naulila to Dongoena. Captain Esteves was then ordered to relinquish command in favour of infantry Captain Mendes dos Reis. His force was composed of an Erhardt artillery battery, a machine gun company, and elements of 1 Dragoons and one company each of 14 Infantry and of 16 Mozambique Light Infantry. At the same time, Roçadas ordered the creation of a Dongoena-Calueque Drift detachment, commanded by Major Salgado, with a division of Canet 75mm field guns and two companies of 14 Infantry and a troop of 9 Cavalry. Roçadas needed better lines of communication with his forces now deploying against the Germans, consequently he ordered his headquarter company to Naulila just twelve kilometres from Calueque Drift. With headquarter company now hastily established at Naulila; Roçadas had to give some thought to its defence. It was a largely flat expanse of tall, waist-high, yellowing grass, almost totally devoid of trees and consequently difficult to defend. Roçadas ordered his sappers to build a redoubt on a slight incline with the Kunene on its right, and gave its defence to a company of 14 Infantry, commanded by Captain Aristides Cunha, whose soldiers were deployed behind an area of sand dunes facing south. Just to the rear of 14 Infantry's position, Captain Esteves had dug in his Erhardt artillery battery, supported by an infantry platoon under command of Second Lieutenant Vale de Andrade. Two platoons of African Infantry, commanded by Captain Rodrigues Sepúlveda, plus a platoon commanded by Lieutenant Fernandes, were in support of the machine guns deployed on either side of the Onkankwa-Kalundo Drift track facing southeast and east. The Portuguese position was thinly stretched over three kilometres. The two detachments were tasked with defending limited areas close to the right and left banks of the Kunene, and of deploying the cavalry to gather intelligence on the Germans, and appose any possible enemy thrust against Naulila or through the right bank of the Kunene towards Ediva or Humbe.

On 12 December, Lieutenant Francisco Xavier da Cunha Aragão's dragoon scouts made contact with a German patrol in the Calueque Valley. Shots were exchanged and two Portuguese cavalrymen fell from their mounts, but as fire from the German patrol was intense and sustained, Lieutenant Aragão's small patrol was forced to retire leaving the two men to their fate. Once Roçadas was informed of the skirmish, he ordered Lieutenant Aragão's dragoons to join Salgado's force at the Dongoena-Calueque Drift position. On 13 December, Lieutenant Aragão's patrol rode out to try and locate the cavalrymen's bodies, and to their great relief, discovered the two wounded troopers, who had managed to crawl into the long grass and remain undetected. Aragão's men came across a German sentry, who attempted to flee on foot but was no match for the mounted patrol; the German was taken back to Major Salgado at the Calueque Drift position. After interrogating the German sergeant, the Portuguese learned that considerable enemy forces were gathering for a concerted attack on the Portuguese. Portuguese scouts were daily patrolling the veld around Calueque Drift but were unable to locate further enemy activity until 17 December, when a group of friendly Kwamato informed Lieutenant Aragão that men and wagons had been seen moving east in the direction of Naulila. Roçadas ordered his second-in-command, Captain Maia Magalhães, to prepare contingencies for offensive operations against German thrusts either on the Dongoena-Calueque Drift position or Naulila itself; in either circumstance, the Portuguese positions would provide mutual support.

On the evening of 17 December, the order was dispatched to Major Salgado to attack the Germans laagered close to Calueque, and for Lieutenant Aragão to make contact with the enemy and determine his line of march. However, the orders did not reach the respective officers until the following day, and when Major Salgado's force moved on Calueque, they discovered that the Germans had already broken camp and the area was deserted. Roçadas was greatly concerned by the lack of firm intelligence on the movement of the German forces, and ordered Second Lieutenant Matias, and a small patrol made up of dragoons and auxiliaries, to probe in the direction of Onkankwa. The Portuguese were unable to find any signs of German activity, but reported back to Roçadas, on the surprising and suspicious absence of Kwamato cattle or herdsmen in the area around Onkankwa. At daybreak, Portuguese forward patrols heard the cracking of sjamboks and saw the tell-tale clouds of dust; the German force totalling some 1,958 men with six field guns and two machine guns, led by Major Erich Franke was on the move.

Chapter 32
Major Franke - The Victor of Naulila

Forty-eight-year-old Major Erich Victor Carl August Franke was an officer with eighteen years' experience of soldiering in German South West Africa, having first taken part in punitive campaigns against the Swaartbooi Hottentots in the Kaokoveld in 1898. In 1900, the then Captain Franke, visited the Kwanyama chief Wejulu, travelling as far as *Forte Humbe*, where his presence, in German army uniform, caused great annoyance to the Portuguese authorities in southern Angola. In 1903, while commanding 2 Infantry Company, he was awarded the *Pour le Mérite* for actions against the Herero. In 1907 he had been given command of 6 Infantry Company at Outjo.

Major Franke had been ordered to lead a German force into Angola and had made contact with Dr Vageler and the Boer Jan Duplessis, who agreed to guide the Germans. Captain Baron von Water had been sent forward in command of an infantry company to search for water on the way, and take supply wagons up through Ovamboland ahead of the main force. Dr Vageler's supply column reached the Kunene River close to Calueque Drift on 12 December, to be joined by the main force three days later. Franke ordered Second Lieutenant Vahle to reconnoitre the area and probe the Portuguese positions. On 17 December, Franke's column laagered close to Onkankwa, five kilometres from Naulila. From this position, Franke was to order the column to attack the Portuguese left flank, which his patrols had told him, was the weakest point in the Portuguese defences. A diversionary attack against the right flank, to be led by von Water, was due to begin at 4:30 that morning, however, when Franke checked his wristwatch, he noted that it was already 4:40, and by now he should have heard rifle and gun fire coming from von Water's men. Von Water had miscalculated the distance to Naulila, and when the attack should have begun, was still laagered at Nangula Drift, and on advancing along the riverbank, had come up against a spirited defence led by Second Lieutenant Amadeu de Figueiredo, commanding a platoon of 14 Infantry, at Cabelo Drift. With Figueiredo wounded and most of his men dead, von Water secured the drift, and finally began his much delayed attack towards Naulila. The last thing that Franke had wanted was to order a German attack over open ground, in daylight, against the Portuguese defensive positions. There was no time to waste. Franke would have to commence the attack without von Water, and as dawn was breaking, the Germans would soon be exposed to enfilading machine gun fire. He ordered his infantry forward against the weak Portuguese left flank and southeastern positions.

General Alves Roçadas had earlier been instructed by Lisbon to take only defensive action against the Germans, due to Portugal's ambivalent neutrality in Europe; the Germans however, were under no such constraints. At 5:00, a platoon of 9 Company 14 Infantry holding entrenchments on the Portuguese left flank came under heavy attack, and the soldiers abandoned their position. Company commander, Captain Homem Ribeiro, was shot dead while desperately trying to rally the fleeing Portuguese infantry. The Germans rapidly occupied the abandoned trenches and bringing up two field guns, began to bombard the main Portuguese position. With the death of Captain Homem Ribeiro, the platoons held in reserve had broken; leaving the wounded Lieutenant Carlos Marques, in charge of the platoon holding the trench forward of the main position, to temporarily delay the German advance. The Portuguese had to relocate two field guns to lay down fire on the German held, former Portuguese trenches. Captain Aristides Cunha took the initiative and moved his men from their right flanking defensive position, over to the left, where the Mozambique African irregulars were beginning to give way under intense German field gun and rifle fire. The Portuguese line gradually began to steady, giving the machine guns and the field guns time to pull back and regroup. A spirited Portuguese infantry, left flanking movement, covered by a field gun barrage, enabled them to advance to within 250 metres of the German held trenches. With a further Portuguese machine gun out of action, the infantry began to withdraw under cover of the remaining two Portuguese machine guns. Naval Lieutenants Varela and Bettencourt's machine gun sections continued to put up a dogged resistance until their guns became inoperable.

Lieutenant Aragão had spotted an advancing German infantry company supported by two field guns. As the infantrymen were now in danger of being surrounded, he ordered a troop to dismount, and provide covering fire for Sereno's dragoons to charge over rising ground on the left, and get in amongst the Germans. Sereno that gritty, no-nonsense African campaigner was one of the first to fall from his horse, mortally wounded. Lieutenant Clarim Augusto dos Reis, was hit in the arm and thrown from his mount. The attack petered out, and Aragão's men were ordered to mount up and withdraw towards Naulila. Aragão pulled up his horse on seeing one of his wounded men being stripped by a German Kwamato auxiliary. As he galloped toward the Kwamatan his horse was brought crashing to the ground by German machine gun fire. Menacing Kwamato auxiliaries armed with stabbing spears quickly surrounded Aragão. Fortunately, he was taken prisoner by a German soldier who recognised his officer's insignia. Seriously wounded Lieutenant António Rodrigues was also captured in the mêlée.

The decimated Portuguese infantry broke and retreated in disorder, leaving the injured Major Franke the victor. Of the Portuguese force, 66 soldiers lay dead on the veld with 76 soldiers wounded; 40 of them were taken prisoner by the Germans. Major Franke had been wounded early on in the attack and was relieved by his adjutant, Captain Georg Trainer. The Germans lost twelve soldiers with a further 30 wounded. With his commanding officer out of action, Captain Trainer chose not to exploit the German victory further, and withdrew over the border into German territory. Meanwhile, General Alves Roçadas had crossed the Kunene River, taking his shattered column minus much transport and weapons, up through Dongoena and Humbe to Gambos.

When dragoon Lieutenant Clarim Augusto dos Reis came to, the battle had passed him by, leaving the rising ground littered with dragoon dead. Even though he was in agony from a badly bleeding arm, he managed to drag himself into a shallow, reed-covered *omaramba*, and from there made his escape. Three days later, he was found and transported to Humbe, where medical officers amputated his gangrene-infected arm.

The shambolic withdrawal of Portuguese troops from Humbe caused panic among the Portuguese settlers and coincided with outbreaks of robbery, arson and murder. The chaos and anarchy in southern Angola was a direct result of the level to which Portuguese authority had sunk in the eyes of the African clans, and such news travelled fast.

In order to counter the new strategic threat, Alves Roçadas urgently requested fresh reinforcements from Lisbon. His request went largely unheeded. Although some badly trained marine, infantry, cavalry and artillery contingents had embarked from Portugal in late November, it was not until 28 December, that the government finally decreed the mobilisation for Angola of 4,800 officers and men. The reinforcements comprised elements of I, 2, and 7 Artillery, with 18 Infantry, plus cavalry and machine gun companies. As military operations were planned to begin in the Humbe region, the port of Mossâmedes was chosen as the disembarkation point for the troopships from Lisbon. The force's arrival in southern Angola coincided with the change of command at the top. The Lisbon government had formulated plans to mount a campaign in the southern Angola region, Alves Roçadas requested that the coming campaign be prosecuted by a more senior officer, and asked the war ministry to discharge him from a command inappropriate to his rank.

Chapter 33
Trouble Brews in Portugal and Africa

In the early hours of the morning, the heavily armed raiding party forded the Rovuma River, and made its way through thick, reed beds, and up the slippery bank towards *Forte Maziua*, a remote and lightly manned post in Cabo Delgado District, on the southern bank of the Rovuma River frontier. The stockaded post was surrounded by a thickly overgrown ditch, and was sited on a slight incline within view of the Rovuma. Close by, were the huts of a small *boma*, where a number of African soldiers lived with their wives and children. Two German officers led the surprise attack, backed by a detachment of *askaris* and armed irregulars. The Portuguese post commander, Sergeant Emilio Costa, was awakened by the sound of rifle fire, and shot down in cold blood as he emerged from his sleeping quarters to investigate the disturbance; six of his African soldiers were shot, while others who had been living in the *boma* escaped certain death by taking refuge in the dense undergrowth which lined the banks of the Rovuma. The German-led attackers then looted all the kit and stores they could carry, turning out the women and children, before putting the huts to the flame, and withdrawing across the Rovuma River. The Portuguese government immediately sent a strongly worded protest to Berlin, and learned in reply, that colonial military officers in German East Africa had been under the mistaken impression that Portugal had entered the war on Britain's side; the date was 24 August 1914.

Six days earlier, the Portuguese government had issued orders to send an expedition to Mozambique. Due to Portugal's lack of tonnage, 1 Expeditionary Force destined for Mozambique, embarked on the British contracted troopship the *Durham Castle*, escorted by the Portuguese warship, the former *Dom Carlos I*, now renamed *Almirante Reis*. The force was made up of elements of 3 Battalion 15 Infantry Regiment and totalled 1,500 officers and men. Fifty-two-year-old artillery officer, Lieutenant Colonel Pedro Massano de Amorim, was given command of the Mozambique Expeditionary Force. Massano de Amorim had seen active service in Mozambique with Mousinho de Albuquerque, and had been made governor of Gaza in 1897. Shortly after returning to Portugal, he was recalled for service in Africa, and disembarked at Luanda in 1900. From Luanda he was sent up to Santo António do Zaire, where he explored and mapped the Mussorongo region. At the outbreak of the Bailundo War in 1902, he was given command of the Benguela column and at the conclusion of hostilities was awarded the *Torre e Espada*.

The Portuguese troops felt very uneasy, as they doubted that German submarines would see the *Durham Castle* as anything other than a British merchant ship and therefore, a legitimate target, even though Portugal was not at war. The *Durham Castle* first put in at Lourenço Marques on 16 October and at Pôrto Amelia on Pemba Bay, in the Niassa Chartered Company lands on 1 November. The Expeditionary Force was made up of 300 troops of 3 Battalion, 15 Infantry Regiment from the garrison at Tomar, where the brooding fourteenth century convent-castle of the 'Knights Order of Christ', dominated the hill above the town. Another 1,200 men were dispatched to Lisbon to swell the numbers: artillery from Portoalegre and Evora, and infantry from Viseu. Such was the glaring lack of preparation that cavalry from Oporto and Viseu, only reported for duty at Lisbon, some six days prior to embarkation for Mozambique. Serious training at company and platoon level in Portugal had been impossible in such makeshift conditions, and so the ill-prepared force set sail, with Massano de Amorim and his officers in an apprehensive mood.

During the journey, the cavalry's horses suffered greatly from the cramped conditions below decks, and many dead horses were heaved over the side by dejected cavalrymen, to bob and twirl in the troopship's wake. The different units suffered from a lack of cohesion; esprit de corps was almost non-existent. The situation was aggravated by the soldiers' extremely poor physical fitness, coupled with an almost total lack of basic hygienic care, and the scarcity of preventative medicines. Due to lack of communication between Lisbon and the Niassa Chartered Company, almost no preparations had been made for the arrival of the expedition and consequently the troops were forced to resort to tentage as no provision had been made for quartering them; it was the beginning of the rainy season.

Due to Lisbon's ever changing political imperatives, the Mozambique Expeditionary Force's operational limitations were steadily increased during its first six months in the colony. Initial orders from Pereira de Eça to Massano de Amorim, had carried instructions to restrict movements to purely defensive actions. Now the colonel had no option but to comply with Lisbon's orders. Its commander, forging new roads through the bush and jungles, put the Mozambique Expeditionary Force to work. Telegraph lines were set up along the banks of the strategically important 730-kilometre long, Rovuma River. Captain Neutel Martins Simões de Abreu, an engineering officer with vast colonial experience, had reconnoitred and constructed numerous military posts in Portuguese East Africa between 1900 and 1914. After prolonged negotiations with the agricultural Makonde clan, they agreed to provide labour for the Portuguese under the leadership of Captain Neutel de Abreu. Sappers built 146 kilometres of road from Mocimboa west to Chamba, in order to provide passable roads for Portuguese military transport and troops.

After the Revolution of 14 May 1915 had deposed General Pimenta de Castro, Massano de Amorim, received orders to mount offensive operations and re-occupy the so-called Kionga Triangle. Kionga, an administrative centre, was located in the extreme north of Cabo Delgado District, close to the mouth of the Rovuma River. In 1890, Great Britain and Zanzibar had agreed to cede lands to Germany, which had previously been acknowledged as Portuguese territory by an Anglo-Portuguese convention. However, not satisfied with this, Germany protested to Portugal in 1892, criticising its northern limits in Mozambique, and refused to accept mediation proposed by the Portuguese. As a consequence, Kionga Bay had been illegally occupied by the Germans, and was duly incorporated into German East Africa in 1894.

On 15 June 1915, Massano de Amorim sought an immediate conference with the governor-general of Mozambique. The Portuguese colonel alluded to the stream of orders and counter-orders - the root problem of troop inactivity. He explained that in order to comply with Lisbon's latest instructions to invade Kionga, reinforcements would be needed, as he only disposed of 1,200 officers and men, and a great number of troops had been stricken down by disease. However, Massano de Amorim came away from the conference empty-handed. He repeated his request directly to the War Ministry in Lisbon on 27 June, and again on 8 August. In reply he received a signal relieving him of his command.

Yet there were others who wished to reconcile Portugal's non-combatant role with British interests. The pragmatic view prevailed and the Portuguese were requested by London to sanction the passage of British troops through Portuguese East Africa. Bernardino Machado, General Joaquim Cerveira de Albuquerque, and General Pereira de Eça, along with other military and naval experts were called to the War Ministry, where the Portuguese Admiralty produced a detailed chart to the waterways of the East African colony. Machado was able to follow the dark blue line of the Zambezi River, as it snaked inland from the Chinde Estuary on the Indian Ocean, through the northern region of Zambézia District. Then his eyes followed the fainter blue thread of the Shire River, as it turned ever northward to Zomba in the Shire Highlands close to Lake Shirwa, in the British Protectorate of Nyasaland. Machado's naval minister, Admiral Augusto Eduardo Neuparth, explained that steamers sailing to and from British territory could leave or enter the Indian Ocean without touching Portuguese East Africa. Twenty-three years earlier in 1891, the Portuguese Crown and Britain had signed the Chinde Concession, which gave Whitehall a 99-year lease on a 40-kilometre area around the mouth of the Chinde Estuary, at the cost to Britain of £200 per year. In return, the Portuguese had been granted a lease on land on the shores of Lake Nyasa, but because of uprisings and banditry in Lourenço Marques and Inyambane Districts, the Portuguese were never able to utilise the lease. In 1908, the last sleeper on the railway line from Blantyre down to Port Herald in the south had been laid. Yet, the Chinde Estuary remained strategically important as all military reinforcements, equipment and munitions had to pass through it in order to reach Nyasaland. Machado could clearly see that in the eventuality of an aggressive southerly push from German East Africa, through the lightly defended Cabo Delgado and Zambézia districts, the loss of Chinde would put a stranglehold on the Nyasaland Protectorate and totally neutralise British military operations against the German colony. Machado readily understood Britain's anxiety over the vulnerability of Nyasaland, and General Pereira de Eça was instructed to dispatch a cipher to the governor-general of Mozambique, authorising the passage of British troops through the Chinde. He also gave the governor-general the authority to provide the men, artillery and munitions requested by the British Consul in Lourenço Marques.

In November 1915, 2 Expeditionary Force, under command of artillery officer, Major José Luís Moura Mendes, began the long and dangerous sea voyage from Lisbon to Mozambique. The troopship *Moçambique* was escorted by the *Adamastor*, which carried the governor-general designate, 36-year-old Álvaro Xavier de Castro. During the convoy's journey round the Cape, Álvaro de Castro impressed upon Moura Mendes, the importance of rapid military action in order to invest and occupy the Kionga Triangle. Moura Mendes was yet another makeshift leader, chosen with the usual hasty improvisation. He manifestly lacked the requisite experience of soldiering in Africa and furthermore, he was of an irritable disposition and considered unsuited for command. The Portuguese troop transports finally dropped anchor at Pôrto Amélia on Pemba Bay on 7 November. 3 Battalion, 21 Infantry Regiment, formerly based in Penamacor in Portugal, had rapidly formed the main element of the expeditionary force and was accompanied by artillery and cavalry elements. The expeditionary force totalled 41 officers and 1,502 troops. The effects of the voyage in cramped, insanitary conditions, allied to the drenching rains and sweltering heat of the coastal lowlands, began to take its toll. Within days of disembarkation, 545 soldiers were declared medically unfit for active service. Many of the medical and surgical supplies transported from Lisbon had been damaged; inferior quality stores had been dispatched incomplete.

Once again, the government had miserably failed its soldiers. The appalling administration in Lisbon, the substandard medical services, the corruption in the supply of medicines and other stores which were damaged, was exacerbated daily by the absolute neglect of sanitary precautions among the soldiers, many of whom were completely illiterate. These factors had been and continued to be a feature of every expedition.

Chapter 34
Conflict in German South West Africa and Angola

Lieutenant Colonel Alves Roçadas' successor, 65-year-old General António Julio Costa Pereira de Eça, was in Portuguese Africa at the time of the Naulila debacle, and had assumed command in April 1915. Pereira de Eça had left Lisbon on the steamer *África* on 5 March, and landed at Luanda sixteen days later. He was keen to get south as soon as possible, but did have time to review the Luanda garrison, and declared himself satisfied with what he had seen. But the general was less pleased with the state of the railway line from Mossâmedes and with the port itself. After inspecting the supply depot at Luanda, he came to the conclusion that much more matériel would be required from Lisbon. He then took ship for Mossâmedes aboard the *Luanda* arriving there on 7 April.

General Pereira de Eça, now commanded over 11,000 men, and had 7,000 mounts, pack-mules, camels and oxen. The organisation required to support and supply those enormous numbers was formidable. Simultaneously maintaining 5,000 troops in permanent battle readiness, and securing 1,200 kilometres of communication lines, was almost beyond the competence of Lisbon and its makeshift colonial administration. Pereira de Eça was appalled to discover that the port had almost no facilities for unloading supplies, having only one jetty and two ancient cranes. The warehousing for food supplies and matériel was almost non-existent. Tinned food, clothing and equipment were piled willy-nilly on the dockside in the open air, exposed to the weather, and to the depredations of vermin. The general discovered that military supplies were finding their way into the hands of corrupt civilian traders, to be resold to the army at vast profit. He ordered the port captain to build a second pier and to requisition all available boats to help with the disembarkation of supplies. As to the lack of warehousing, he ordered his sapper units to construct an enormous storehouse, but was unable to secure building materials from Cape Town, due to South Africa's involvement in German South-West Africa. Eventually Angola's naval authorities managed to supply the governor with his needs.

A more pressing problem was the quartering of his troops. There were two infantry battalions, four artillery battalions, cavalry and machine gun units, all with no accommodation. Every possible billet in the port city and tentage in the nearby sandy bush was occupied; it was a mammoth task.

General Pereira de Eça had chosen Humbe as his operational base, from where he could communicate easily with Mossâmedes, and with the Evale, Kwanyama, Kwamato, and Dongoena regions. 14 Infantry Battalion was based at Capelongo, Cahama and Gambos. 16 Infantry Battalion was at Lubango with

17 Infantry and a machine gun battery at Chibia. The Marine Battalion and a light field gun battery were stationed at Forno de Cal. 9 Cavalry was garrisoned at Tchiepépe with 11 Cavalry at Humpata, and a further machine gun battery was at Huíla, with the Boer auxiliaries at Otchinjau.

In spite of the chaos of Mossâmedes, General Pereira de Eça, pushed through the improvement of the rail line, from the Atlantic port to the foothills of the Chela Mountains and beyond; Artur de Paiva's dream had become a reality.

The first hostile movement the Expeditionary Force had to deal with, began in May 1915, and was directed against the mission at Tchipelongo. Naval Lieutenant Afonso de Cerqueira, commanded a force, made up of a Marine Battalion, and a company of 15 Native Infantry of Mozambique, holding a forward position at Chicuna. The gritty 43-year-old Portuguese officer was a tall, spare, bearded man, instantly recognisable on his grey mount. Sergeant Moreira quickly pointed him out to a dust-caked, French priest, who hurriedly informed him that the mission at Tchipelongo, and its priests and workers were momentarily under threat from marauding Kwanyama warriors, and in grave danger of being massacred. Though Cerqueira had received no official orders, he advanced to the mission on his own initiative. On reaching Tchipelongo, Cerqueira deployed his force around the whitewashed buildings and under the groves of fig trees.

The Portuguese had not been dug in long before Kwanyama horsemen were observed riding out from a defile and advancing on the Tchipelongo Mission. The buildings were located on steeply rising ground, and the riders met with unexpectedly stiff volley fire from the well dug-in defenders. The sustained and accurate Portuguese rifle and cannon fire decimated the Kwanyama horsemen, who were forced to withdraw up the narrow defile, followed by snorting, riderless mounts.

Meanwhile, the 17 Native Infantry Battalion, and a machine gun battery, were tasked to advance on the Gambos. 11 Cavalry squadron at Humpata deployed to Tchicusse where it was reinforced with the Marine Battalion and a company of 15 Native Infantry, prior to the reoccupation of Humbe. The Humbe force was to be commanded by Colonel António Veríssimo de Sousa, with Captain José Esteves de Mascarenhas, as second-in-command. A second detachment, made up of two squadrons of 9 and 11 cavalry and Boer auxiliaries, under overall command of Major Vieira da Rocha, left Gambos to advance on Humbe, following the Otchinjau and Dongoena route, to establish direct communications between Gambos and Mulondo. The two columns reached and occupied Humbe on 7 July, after overcoming enormous difficulties on the trek, caused by a grave shortage of water; all the *cacimbas* along the Kakulovar

River were found to be dry. At Humbe, the fort, adjacent barracks, and traders' stores, were reduced to smoke-blackened ruins having been destroyed after the Portuguese army's rapid withdrawal from the region. The only people remaining at Humbe were emaciated old women and children; the men had fled over the Kunene to the lands of the Kwamato and Kwanyama.

On 9 July, Pereira de Eça and his headquarters, made a detailed reconnaissance of the Kunene River close to *Forte Roçadas*. While the general was still at *Forte Roçadas*, he received a signal from Lubango, informing him that enemy forces in German South-West Africa had surrendered to General Botha. On 11 February 1915, Germany's 8,000 *schutztruppe* had been put under heavy pressure by General Louis Botha's troops, from their base at Walvis Bay, in the north, while Jan Christian Smuts, had made Lüderitzbuch on the Atlantic coast, his firm base from April of that year. The Germans were soon beaten back and retreated towards Windhoek, which General Botha entered on 12 May. Having driven a wedge across the territory from west to east, Union Forces then began mopping up operations. On 9 July 1915, north of Otavi, Dr Seitz, Governor of German South West Africa and Colonel Franke, commanding German Forces, which amounted to 204 officers and 3,166 other ranks, signed the surrender document in the presence of General Botha, who had earlier played his part in Boer successes against the British at Colenso, Spion Kop and Val Krantz in the South African War. The German threat had been removed from Portuguese Angola thanks to the sacrifices of the Union Forces. Upwards of 40,000 Union troops had taken part in the campaign in German South West Africa; 269 soldiers had been killed in action with a further 263 wounded. Now General Pereira de Eça was free to prosecute his campaign against the Kwanyama in Portuguese Ovamboland.

Chapter 35
Paramount Chief Mandume

Four months after the German surrender, General Pereira de Eça received intelligence from Portuguese and Boer traders and hunters in the region, that 482 kilometres from Mossâmedes, a hostile force numbering thousands of warriors from the Kwanyama, Kwamato and Evale regions was on the move. The rebel impis were under the leadership of Chief Mandume. Mandume's reputation had gone before him; prisoners must be put to death was his cry. Mandume's executioners would step forward and drag their terrified prisoners out to strangle them, those that he did not kill instantly, were made to roast meat on their hands, held over hot coals; others were scalped and thereafter given their own scalps to roast. Sometimes, he would shoot at Kwanyama women carrying calabashes of water on their heads, as they entered his kraal. Mandume's warriors captured a hunting party of a rival, Chief Ipumbu, whose men had crossed into Mandume's lands, after he had warned them to keep out. Mandume had their ears sliced off and a stick put through them, which was then sent back to Chief Ipumbu. The mutilated messengers carried a graphic warning from Mandume; as their chief appeared to be deaf, he was sending him something to improve his hearing.

Mandume had been educated at a German mission station in Eque in Angola, and consequently, was considered by the Portuguese to be pro-German. Many of Mandume's battle chiefs had received basic military instruction from German officers and *schuzttruppe* NCOs on the empty borderlands between the two countries. The missionary, Father Keiling, attended an *indaba* with Mandume in 1914 at the paramount chief's royal kraal at N'giva. Mandume was described as being a tall and pleasant looking man with a small scar over his left eye and was always dressed in European clothes. Mandume's kingdom was composed of 330 *indunas* who in wartime acted as his trusted battle chiefs. The *indunas* oversaw the 250 *mukunda* – there were no villages in Ovamboland, only stockaded kraals. Each *mukunda* had between 30 and 40 – *kubata* – timber and straw huts, housing between four to twenty people. It was estimated that the smallest *mukunda* would contain 120, giving Mandume's Kwanyamaland kingdom a total of at least 30,000 subjects. Mandume retained 30 *indunas* as part of his entourage. He had twenty rifles of his own, of different calibre and manufacture. His personal bodyguard was made up of 100 handpicked, young warriors. Each member of his bodyguard was armed with a Kropatschek rifle, a stabbing spear and a shield. The 30 *indunas* carried either Martini-Henry or Mauser rifles. Madume had ordered that no Kwanyama was to leave his hut unarmed. Mandume required 200 boy and 100 girl servants and attendants. His personal wealth extended to seventeen horses and over 8,000 oxen. Under

Mandume's iron-hard command were thousands of seasoned veterans of southern Angolan wars against Portuguese domination. Mandume's blooded impis combined disciplined weapon handling with expert horsemanship and skilful use of tactics. The chieftains like their king, were also on horseback. The main unit of the Kwanyama was the *etanga* composed of 100 warriors. Six *etangas* together made a *guerra* commanded by a *lenga* – military chieftain. A number of *guerras* constituted an *ohita* or army. Each had its own travelling *ondiai* – spirit medium. This vast Kwanyama fiefdom encompassed all of Kunene: Humbe, Gambos, Jau, Chela, Mulongo and Capelongo.

General Pereira de Eça held a detailed briefing in which he set out his orders for the occupation of Lower Kunene. His plan was to occupy the region using Humbe as a firm base while simultaneously deploying columns to Naulila, Kwamato, Kwanyama and Evale. The Naulila Column, under command of Lieutenant Vasconcelos, was to descend the right bank of the Kunene River, cross Calueque Drift, and from there, move to Naulila, and from Naulila to *Forte Cuamato* to link up with the Kwamato Column. The Kwamato Column, under command of infantry Colonel Veríssimo de Sousa, was to cross the Kunene River close to *Forte Roçadas*, and move to *Forte Cuamato* in order to reoccupy the Kwamato region. The Kwanyama Column, under command of Lieutenant Colonel Manuel José Pereira Caldas, was to cross the Kunene at Muespa Drift, and move to N'giva kraal in order to subdue Mandume's impis and occupy the Kwanyama region. The Evale Column, under command of infantry Captain João Carlos Pires Ferreira Chaves, was to occupy Kiteve, cross the Kunene, move against Evale kraal on the left bank of the Cuvelai River, and arrest Chief Mastilefo, who had been responsible for the murder of the Portuguese commander at *Forte Cafima*.

The force was to operate on a vast, sun-scorched, thorn bush plain. Some *omaramba* would be found but they would most certainly be dried up. In the Kwanyama region, the going would be more open but with thicker camel-thorn bush, in belts up to two-kilometres deep. Water might be found near the stockaded *mukunda* but the column was ordered neither to drink it, nor let the animals drink it, as it might have been poisoned. The Evale region would be heavily wooded with numerous water holes, but further south it would be dryer with less vegetation, and from Evale to Mongwa, the going would be very hard for both men and animals as the ground was sandy underfoot.

Just after dawn on 12 August, the Kwanyama Column reached the arid banks of the Kunene River at Chimbua Drift 22 kilometres from Humbe. The column was composed of 2,600 officers and men, made up of artillery, cavalry, marines and infantry, with 13,000 animals and 234 wagons. The fording of the Kunene presented great problems due to its deep, sand covered bed. Men and animals floundered and sank up to their shoulders in a river of sand; it took the column more than three hours to cross, under a pitilessly hot sun.

General Pereira de Eça was well aware of the Kwanyama's formidable reputation, and feared a swift three-pronged attack against his ungainly and largely inexperienced force. He was relieved to receive a report from Colonel Pereira Caldas, that the Kunene River had been crossed without mishap. Vedettes from 15 Mozambique Regiment, reported the tell-tale signs of Kwanyama hoof marks. Orders from General Pereira de Eça were sent to Colonel Reis e Silva's 640-man Evale Column, to break in that direction. The word was passed down to Colonel Veríssimo de Sousa's sweat-soaked column to continue due south. Watching Kwanyama scouts carried the news of the Portuguese order of battle to Chief Mandume. The chief, mounted on his grandest horse, and surrounded by his personal Mauser-armed bodyguard, ignored Pereira de Eça's feint, and instructed his *lengas* to hold their impi regiments in check. The Evale Column was sniped at by Kwanyama skirmishers but pushed its way through towards Evale. The military posts at Kiteve, Cafu and Evale were in a relatively good state of repair, however; the living accommodation had been completely destroyed. When the Portuguese entered Evale, they found Chief Chimbobolo's people on the right bank of the Cuvelai River, busy at work in the fields surrounding it; they felt they had done nothing to antagonise the Portuguese. Chief Mastilefo on the other hand, was reported to have fled with his people to Kwanyama or, according to others, to Kuriamanya, eighteen kilometres north-east of Evale. The column was relieved to find *cacimbas* close to the riverbank, which provided enough water for both men and beasts. Unfortunately, the drovers were unable to stop a number of oxen drowning in their frenzy to reach water. In a gesture of friendship, chief Chimbobolo arrived at the Portuguese laager, with gifts of bullock and fowl. A garrison of 11 Company, 16 Infantry was left to occupy Evale and the rest of the force, including the naval contingent, was dispatched under command of Lieutenant-Commander Caroliano da Costa, to rejoin the main body of the column.

Meanwhile, Colonel Veríssimo de Sousa's column came into contact with Mandume's impis. A sharp battle ensued around the water holes at Inyoka, but the column's combined firepower; rifles, machine guns and field guns, overwhelmed the ferocious impis. With the Kwanyama in disarray, the road to Kwamato lay open, and by the early afternoon on 15 August, the green and red Portuguese flag was raised over the kraal at Kwamato.

Colonel Pereira Caldas' Kwanyama Column, whose final objective was the reduction and occupation of N'giva, seat of Mandume's royal kraal, reached the arid, bolder strewn, Mongwa plain on 16 August, and deployed as two echelons around a cluster of eight water holes in square order. As the African day was swiftly drawing to a close and there had been no sightings of the enemy, Pereira Caldas ordered the two squares to reform as one, and await in strength the next day's inevitable attack.

Possession of the small *cacimbas* at Mongwa; a valuable source of water in a pitiless region, was as crucial to the Kwanyama as to the expeditionary force. On the following day, the Kwanyama warriors, commanded by Chief Kalola, attacked the Portuguese square, but were driven off after fifteen minutes, by artillery fire and by a cavalry sortie. The column had used much of its artillery ammunition and needed to resupply, but discovered that communications had been cut between it and the other columns. Just after 8:30 on the morning of 18 August, the fidgeting Portuguese square stood to. As the cold and weary soldiers rubbed the night's sleep and caked sand from their squinting eyes, they saw clouds of red dust swirling into the sharp morning air, and heard the chilling cries and chants which presaged a massed assault by Mandume's impis. Soldiers began to fall, as Kwanyama sharpshooters, taking cover behind ant heaps, accurately picked off the front ranks of the Portuguese square. Colonel Pereira Caldas and his staff remained on horseback in the centre of the square. Chief of Staff, Henriques Pires Monteiro, was one of the first officers to be hit. He provided an excellent mark, but at the same time, his example gave heart to the officers and troops under his command.

The attack lasted two and a half hours, and in an attempt to lessen the pressure on the square, troopers of 4 and 11 cavalry squadrons, commanded by Viera da Rocha, made a daring but foolhardy sortie, and under withering fire, charged the powerful and well-armed impis. The charge was in vain and cavalry losses were extremely heavy. But shouts of encouragement came from the machine gun battery covering the front of the Portuguese square, and from 17 Infantry, as it moved forward as one, to provide covering fire to the badly mauled cavalrymen. Elements of 17 Infantry defending the square, stopped shooting, stood up and began to sing *A Portuguesa* - the Portuguese national anthem. The words echoed around the beleaguered square and for a moment there was silence from Mandume's surging impis. Then, following the Portuguese example, they began to intone the resonantly deep, war chant, in praise of their all-powerful king - *bayete inkose!* The impis then began to withdraw, but marksmen still hiding behind iron-hard ant heaps, continued to snipe at the exhausted and thirst-racked Portuguese square.

Long before volunteers moved forward of the square, to collect rifles and bandoleers from the bloody mounds of Kwanyama and Portuguese dead, the vultures and kites had been steadily at work on their bounty of flesh. Pereira de Eça's force had lost sixteen dead. Thirty Portuguese had been wounded, including Major José Afonso Pala, and Captain António Carlos Cortes. At nightfall, the sharpshooters withdrew, and the Portuguese square incurred no further losses that day. But the night was bitterly cold and the troops' morale at rock bottom.

At first light on 19 August, Mandume's impis appeared through clouds of dust to the rattle of spears on oxhide shields, to throw themselves against the Portuguese, but by midday they were forced to call off the attack. The Portuguese square had suffered a further fifteen dead and eighteen wounded. But now the troops were faced with yet another adversary – thirst. Indiscipline, apprehension and fatigue had caused many soldiers to drain their water bottles, and the water supply situation had become critical. As the water holes around the square had been drunk dry during the day and a half's fighting under a merciless sun, Pereira de Eça was left with no alternative, other than to move forward to another larger cluster, some two kilometres distant.

Cavalry vedettes from 3 Squadron, 4 Cavalry, were ordered out to reconnoitre the *cacimbas*, which had been abandoned by Mandume's forward impis. As they advanced, vultures rose up and noisily flapped on to nearby kiaat trees, the bodies of ten dead warriors were lying together in a heap. They had been hit by Portuguese artillery. Even closer to the water holes, behind an ant heap, the scouts located the body of Second Lieutenant Damião Dias of 11 Cavalry; his eyes had been gouged out, his nose cut off and his genitals removed.

The column slowly moved towards the *cacimbas*; the stitching on shoddily made boots had quickly disintegrated; many soldiers were hobbling over burning hot granite chippings, with bloody bandages wrapped clumsily around their blistered and broken feet. There were thick clouds of black, buzzing flies everywhere. The field ambulance and commissary wagons were unable to deal with the mounting numbers of wretched, limping soldiers. Tempers were fraying; the commissary officer had to draw his revolver and threaten to shoot any soldier who attempted to climb on to his wagon in order to escape the trek to the water holes. The two-kilometre advance took the straggling column more than two hours to accomplish.

The Portuguese began to dig in, but the new position sited on a small hill in a clearing, was surrounded by thick bush, which would make its defence very difficult. However, the column now occupied the only water holes in the area. There were constant minor alarms; edgy and exhausted sentries fired off rounds into the blackness at shadows of jackals and hyenas. Then, except for the seriously wounded and medical personnel, everyone stood to, and waited, peering into the night until the alarum passed without further incident. The Portuguese had fortified their position with rocks, sandbags and wagons, and awaited the enemy from behind their makeshift defences with 75mm field guns, machine guns and rifles. A Kwamato warrior, who had taken part in the attack on 19 August, approached the camp and surrendered. Through an interpreter, he told Pereira de Eça, that Mandume himself with 50,000 well-armed warriors from Kwanyama, Kwamato, Evale and Humbe, would launch an attack early the next morning. The Kwanyama had suffered hideously heavy casualties during the previous day's fighting, but Mandume's faithful spirit mediums had foretold a glorious victory over the Portuguese intruders, and so his warriors were poised for a final assault on the enemy square.

The massed impi attack began just after 7:00 on 20 August. The Kwanyama warriors showed reckless bravery, charging to within 120 metres of the Portuguese defences. The impis began to falter; shrapnel and machine gun bullets had begun to sow destruction among the Kwanyama ranks. The Portuguese square's superior firepower was gradually beating back the attackers. A thrusting sally by blue jackets of the naval battalion, and sections of 17 Infantry, under Colonel João Pais Veigas, and 15 Mozambique Native Infantry, commanded by the intrepid Afonso de Cerqueira, routed the ragged impis with the bayonet. By sundown, Portuguese artillerymen had fired off no less than 2,000 rounds from their 75mm field guns.

The Portuguese lost seventeen officers and men, including 47-year-old Captain João Francisco Passos Sousa, commanding 11 Company 3 Battalion 17 Infantry. He had taken part in the naval battalion's surprise thrust, and had been seriously wounded on 19 August, but could not be evacuated, and died within the square. Thirteen officers and 54 men were wounded; some of the wounded were in a very serious condition. General Pereira de Eça estimated that 4,500 Kwanyama warriors had fallen in front of the Portuguese square. Because of the ferocity of the final battle, no prisoners were taken. Later, the fly-covered Kwanyama dead, lying outside the Portuguese position, were dragged over to hastily dug trenches, drenched with petrol and set alight. However, the troops' privations were not yet over. The difficulties of their arduous marches and constant skirmishes with the Kwanyama had forced the column to abandon many of its supply wagons; provisions had been left to rot or were carried away by jackals, wild dogs and kites. Only four horses were left, as over 80 had been wounded, and some 25 had bolted into the bush; the Kwanyama chief knew that without mounts the Portuguese would be incapable of decisive movement. To attempt withdrawal now would be to embolden Chief Mandume, and jeopardise the security of the column, and the success of the whole campaign. So the column, with its thirst-maddened wounded, stood fast among the now dried up *cacimbas*, well within sight of the still burning funeral pyre, and the ever-watchful vultures, to await the Kwamato relief column.

On 21 August, Pereira de Eca's was forced to reduce the column's rations, and in response to the grave situation, sent out a small marine reconnaissance detachment. As the marines failed to return, on 22 August, Lieutenant Roma was ordered to search for the relief column. By nightfall, no relief had come to the hard-pressed defenders at Mongwa. Pereira de Eça held a meeting with his senior officers to discuss the situation, and all agreed that to move the column would be a disastrous mistake in the circumstances; they would have to go on waiting. At midnight on 23 August, a runner brought a message to Pereira de Eça, informing him that Colonel Veríssimo de Sousa's Kwamato Column, plus supply wagons, was fifteen kilometres from Mongwa, and would reach them by mid afternoon on 24 August. Veríssimo de Sousa's column had been about to march directly on N'giva as previously ordered, but when he learned that communications with the Kwanyama Column had been cut, moved back towards Humbe, where the column was re-supplied, and then made a forced march in order to cover the 130 kilometres between Humbe and Mongwa. On 24 August, the relief column received a rapturous welcome from General Pereira de Eça and the exhausted defenders of the water holes at Mongwa.

Chapter 36
Major Pritchard, Chief Mandume and General Pereira de Eça

On 30 August 1915, Stanley Archibald Markham Pritchard, formerly of the Cape Mounted Rifles and the Basutoland Mounted Police, was in Ovamboland as Controller of Native Affairs, in the rank of major in the Union of South Africa Army. A runner, from 23-year-old Headman Martin Nambala of the Ndongas, told him, that Chief Mandume had crossed the border into Ovamboland that morning. After hearing the news of Mandume's crushing defeat at the hands of the Portuguese, and fearing that he could be the target of a hostile invasion, Headman Martin had hurried to Pritchard's laager at Namakunde in order to inform the officer of the potentially dangerous situation. Martin's fears were unfounded; Mandume had already sought the South African's whereabouts and was directed south to Namakunde.

Major Pritchard was laagered with a small detachment including Captain Liefeldt and Lieutenant Moroney, when Chief Mandume and his mounted escort approached their camp. Chief Mandume rode forward while his fifteen-strong bodyguard held back. He was mounted on a spindly-legged grey and was dressed completely in khaki and wore a large, battered, wide-brimmed bush hat. The South Africans were keenly aware of the danger, and kept a watchful eye on the Mauser rifle Mandume carried crooked in his right arm, and on the Browning service revolver hanging from a black leather holster round his waist. Pritchard was the first to note Mandume's empty bandolier and his sagging shoulders, and wondered if this apparition could really be the scourge of Lisbon. Mandume dismounted and still carrying his Mauser rifle, addressed the major. Major Pritchard noted that he looked to be in his early twenties and had a somewhat cruel and forbidding appearance. He begged Pritchard to help him and his people, telling the Protectorate officer that the Kwanyama had suffered enormous losses and that most of his battle chiefs had been slain. Mandume explained that they had known the Portuguese for many years, and that the Portuguese had brought rifles, ammunition and alcohol in exchange for ivory and cattle. Mandume explained that in his opinion, the Portuguese had never made any attempt to annex their ancestral lands. Mandume told Pritchard, that one day, he had been on a hunting expedition and had sent two of his men to the Portuguese post at Kafima, to obtain liquor and supplies; one man had been killed and the other locked up by the Portuguese. As Mandume's expedition had peacefully made its way back to his royal kraal at N'giva, it was suddenly and without warning, fired on by mounted Portuguese soldiers intent upon capturing Mandume and the supply wagon. The Kwanyama chief then admitted that after that incident, he had told his people that they could take what they liked from the Portuguese. Shortly after, the Kwanyama captured two weapons presumably from a Portuguese patrol but the wily chief did not elaborate further. However, the chief assured Pritchard that there had been no further hostilities between his people and the Portuguese. Mandume desperately hoped that Pritchard's Protectorate force, and the Kwanyama clans south of the Angolan border, would rally to his aid against the Portuguese. Failing this Mandume proposed an *indaba* with General Pereira de Eça, to discuss through a mediator, the conditions of peace between himself and the general. Major Pritchard told him that it was Mandume's lawless acts, which had caused the present situation, then retired to his tent and hastily composed a letter addressed to General Pereira de Eça at Mongwa, which Mandume eagerly promised to deliver by messenger under a white flag. In the letter Major Pritchard proposed an *indaba* between himself and the Portuguese general. Chief Mandume quickly remounted and followed by his escort, headed northward over the border to his kraal at N'giva.

On 3 September, Major Pritchard received a hand written note from the Reverend August Wulfhorst, at the Rheinish mission station at Omupanda. Mandume had sent him a message to say that the Portuguese were advancing on N'giva in strength and that he would burn his *mukunda* to the ground and seek refuge at Namakunde. Wulfhorst took the Kwanyama chief at his word, as he had known Mandume since the time he had first arrived in the German colony in 1890, and crossed over into Portuguese territory, to establish a mission station at N'giva in September 1891.

Pritchard ordered Captain Liefeldt and Lieutenant Thomas Moroney, to ride over the border to Omupanda and bring the missionary to the British laager at Namakunde. Upon his return to Major Pritchard's laager that same evening, a disconsolate Chief Mandume told him, that before the Portuguese had had time to reach his Royal Kraal at N'giva, he had set it ablaze and then had transported all his belongings and valuables over the border into Ovamboland. Mandume, with tears streaking his haggard face, appealed to the major to give sanctuary to his people. In answer Mandume was told to put his request down on paper.

Mandume was extremely agitated and kept looking over his shoulder in the direction of the Angolan border. He wanted Pritchard to show him exactly where the border was, as he believed that the Portuguese were fully prepared to snatch him and take him back to Pereira de Eca's camp. He told Pritchard that they would not be satisfied until he and his people were totally crushed. In order to pacify Mandume, the major told him that he would ride across the border into Angola, and speak to the Portuguese, in order to get a firm understanding as to the southern limits of the Portuguese colony. He then told the paramount chief that once the agreement was made, he would be expected to remain on the British side of the border, and not cross over into Angola under any circumstances.

Captain Liefeldt and Lieutenant Moroney turned in early, as they were to saddle up at first light on 4 September for Ondonga and inform Headman Martin of Mandume's latest whereabouts. The two officers returned to Namakunde early in the evening and reported that Headman Martin had been greatly relieved to hear of Major Pritchard's instructions to Mandume, and that all was quiet in his district.

Early on the morning of 5 September, the camp was awoken by the sound of nearby rifle fire, coming from a south-westerly direction. A runner told Major Pritchard, that Chief Mandume had sent some of his warriors out to protect his recently widowed mother against a suitor whom she had fallen out with. During the exchange of fire, the suitor had been captured, and his raiding party killed by Mandume's men. An angry Pritchard, ordered the runner to bring the recalcitrant Mandume to his camp, where he would deal with him. Mandume appeared with two of his *indunas* and was interrogated by Pritchard. When asked why he had taken the law into his own hands, Mandume answered that at least he had not killed his mother's suitor, and that normally, depending on his frame of mind, he would probably have beaten him to death with a knobkerrie or would have shot him. Pritchard told him it was known that he had often killed on the pretext of witchcraft, and sometimes for the most trivial offences, but that from now on, he would have to obey the laws of British Ovamboland, and ordered him to free his captor.

General Pereira de Eça was resting in his tent at Mongwa when his attention was drawn to Major Pritchard's letter, sent to him from Namakunde, and dated 30 August 1915:

'Sir, it has been with regret that, while on an official visit to Ovamboland I have heard of the outbreak of hostilities between the Portuguese forces in Angola and the Ovakuanyama Tribe of the Ovambo Nation. I have the honour, in this connection to inform you that Mandume – Chief of the Ovakuanyama – hearing of my presence in this country, has appealed to me for advice and assistance in enabling him to bring about a cessation of hostilities between himself, and the forces under your command. You are doubtless aware that the boundary line between Angola and the British protectorate of South West Africa passes through the country occupied by the Ovakuanyama, a very large proportion – at least one half of that tribe being resident south of that boundary and within British territory. I am led to understand that many of these natives have already been called by Mandume to his assistance, have crossed into Angola and become engaged in the hostilities now proceeding.

It is this latter fact, together with a very earnest desire to render all possible assistance in securing at the earliest moment a termination of hostilities and the avoidance of further bloodshed that impels me to place my services at the disposal of both yourself and Mandume for this purpose. Should you, in these circumstances, be willing to accept this proposal I shall be glad, to meet you wherever it may be convenient in order that matters may be discussed between us. I am camped at Namakunde and will here await your reply which, I have the honour to request, may be sent to me as soon as possible.'

General Pereira de Eça wasted little time in penning an answer to Major Pritchard. In his courteous but firm letter, he pointing out the erroneous information on which the note was based; it did not deal with warfare between two sovereign nations, rather, with the fact that Portuguese forces crossing unquestionably Portuguese territory had been attacked by an impi led by Mandume, therefore, it constituted a rebellion on Portuguese soil and as such was dealt with by the Portuguese - on Portuguese territory.

On 5 September, as Pereira de Eça's column warily approached the still smouldering ruins of Kwanyama power, at Mandume's royal kraal at N'giva, they saw human skulls and bones strewn over a large area; Mandume had exacted retribution on his failed battle chiefs and their numerous families. Kwanyama tradition dictated, that anyone killed by the chief's own hand, would remain unburied as meat for the scavengers of the veld. On 7 September, Pereira de Eça left N'giva moving north to Lubango. Prior to his departure, the general had briefed his staff officers that it was his intention to inform Luanda of the creation of a new administrative district – the Military Protectorate of Lower Kunene – over which he would personally assume command. As a consequence of Mandume's flight across the border into the former German colony, Pereira de Eça took the opportunity to order the construction of a chain of fourteen military posts, stretching from Roçadas to Anyoka; Angola's southern border would finally be secure.

Two years later in 1917, Natal born Major C.N. Manning, was posted as Intelligence Officer to an expedition designed to curtail Mandume's depredations in the South West African Protectorate. Mandume had given an undertaking that he would not again enter into conflict with the Portuguese. He was asked to surrender to British forces but refused. He sent a characteristic message to Major Manning, telling him that if the English wanted him, then they would have to come and get him, as he was a man not a woman, and would resist to his last bullet. The expeditionary force led by Carl Hugo 'Cocky' Hahn and Colonel M. J. de Jager, moved up into Ovamboland in February 1917. Soon soldiers began to go down with malaria, and horses sickened, but the column carried on. Chief Mandume was forced to flee and sought refuge in the village of Oihole on the border. He then fled from Oihole, which was captured and destroyed by the South Africans on 6 February. Whilst standing under the shade of an ancient tree, the paramount chief had his last *indaba* with his three most trusted *sekulos*. Taking up his weapon, he shot two of them, and then turned the carbine on himself. The remaining *sekulo* was left to spread the news of Mandume's death among the proud yet demoralised Kwanyama warriors.

Chapter 37
Germany Declares War on Portugal

On 28 August 1914, the 3,548-tonne German steamer, the *Sophie Richmerz* had steamed into the Tegus and anchored in the roadstead off Sodré Quay. The ship was in ballast, having discharged its cargo of Ruhr coal at Oporto. On 4 March 1916 Richard Beerfelde, the wireless operator, had given Hamburg born Captain Gerhard Noske a message; he and First Mate Albrecht Weisser, had been ordered to present themselves at once, at the offices of their agents, the *Lisbon Insular Steamship Company*. Since war had been declared between Britain and Germany, the Royal Navy's blockade had forced 75 German and Austro-Hungarian registered ships to remain within the safety of Portuguese harbours: the *Sophie Richmerz* was one of them.

It was a blustery day and the small rowing boat wallowed through the swell towards the steps at Sodró Quay. The two men rapidly climbed the rough stones, crossed the tram tracks and entered the shabby-looking, second floor offices of their Portuguese shipping agents. Noske was surprised to see so many German skippers on the quayside. The two men were discussing the harbour tax payable to the Lisbon Port Authority, when a Portuguese naval lieutenant, brandishing a revolver and a closely typed document, pushed the door open. Without looking at the startled Germans, the naval lieutenant read the document out loud. Noske and Weisser did not catch a word. In spite of being stranded in the Tagus for sixteen months, neither of them understood any Portuguese; it was translated and explained to them by the German wife of an employee of the steamship company.

The Germans were informed that as the ship had been afforded protection for more than a year, the Portuguese government, in accordance with the internationally accepted principle of *eminent domain*, was requisitioning his ship and all other German and Austro-Hungarian vessels in home waters and in the islands of Madeira, the Azores and the colonies.

Captain Noske and Weisser were led out of the office under armed guard, and were left to stand helplessly by the quayside, to glumly watch, as sailors from a Portuguese motor launch clambered aboard the *Sophie Richmerz*, and after lowering the German ensign, rapidly replaced it with the green and red of Portugal.

After heated exchanges between Germany and Portugal, Berlin's minister to Lisbon, the oriental scholar, Dr Friedrich Rosen, announced on 9 March 1916, that a state of war existed between the two countries in Europe and in Africa.

Dr Rosen rightly believed it had been a British instigated action, and it was in fact carried out in the name of the Anglo-Portuguese Alliance.

On 10 March, the Portuguese government confirmed the German declaration of war and on 12 March, Sir Lancelot Carnegie informed Lisbon that Britain would be at Portugal's side against Germany and that in accordance with the Anglo-Portuguese Alliance, would furnish all aid possible and necessary.

On 15 March, the Austro-Hungarian ambassador to Lisbon broke off diplomatic relations with Portugal and left the country for the Viennese capital.

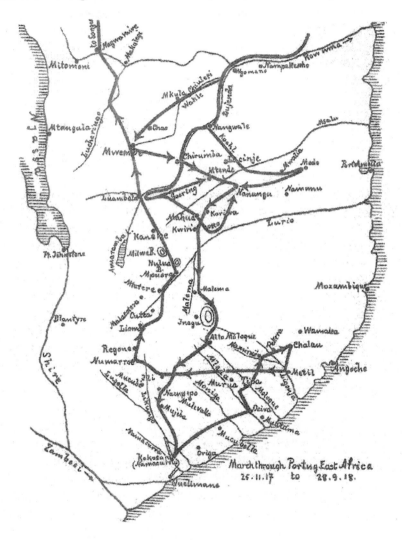

German Route through Mozambique 1917-18
(Hurst & Blackett)

Chapter 38
Operations in Mozambique after Germany's Declaration of War

As a state of war existed between Germany and Portugal, the strategic impetus had changed, now the operational plan was for Portuguese forces to invade and occupy German East Africa up to the River Rufiji line, in concert with British forces operating against the Germans in the region.

After a period of inactivity, Álvaro de Castro telegraphed Lisbon that on 10 April 1916, a Portuguese column, had accomplished the peaceful occupation of Kionga village, part of the contentious Kionga Triangle. The governor-general's drive and enthusiasm had prevailed over Moura Mendes more cautious approach.

Having returned to Lourenço Marques, Álvaro de Castro initiated the mobilisation of a mixed infantry and Republican Guard cavalry force, comprising Portuguese and Mozambican troops. On 21 May, he embarked with them on the *Adamastor* and was present at the attempt to force the Rovuma River, in order to attack the German posts on its far bank. Due to a combination of inferior quality ordnance, and the intense fire directed against the Portuguese gunboat *Chaimite* and the aged *Adamastor*, the attempt was temporarily abandoned. By 28 May the Portuguese infantry had evacuated the newly occupied positions on the German bank of the Rovuma River.

In July 1916, 3 Expeditionary Force set sail for Africa with General Ferreira Gil in overall command. Yet another officer lacking colonial experience, General José César Ferreira Gil, had gained a reputation for being an uncompromising disciplinarian. The 3 Expeditionary Force was composed of three infantry battalions, two artillery batteries, three machine gun batteries, two sapper battalions, plus troops from the 2 Expeditionary Force. The force totalled 128 officers and 4,356 men. Two companies of 21 Infantry stationed at Mafra in Portugal, were hastily incorporated into 3 Expeditionary Force; they had mutinied, when told of their planned deployment to the Western Front as part of the Portuguese Expeditionary Force. The mutinous soldiers were hastily embarked; they had received almost no training for colonial warfare, and many of them had not even been issued with tropical kit. Between May and July, the expeditionary troops left Lisbon on the *Portugal, Moçambique, Zaire, Machico* and *Amarante*. The military authorities acknowledged the troops' lack of preparedness and their potential lack of resistance to the African climate; ten local infantry companies were hastily formed, but their four months' basic training hardly prepared them for the rigours of war against the Germans.

Lisbon ordered the ill-prepared force to mount a rapid offensive, rather than risk the soon expected end of the war.

Two years earlier on 31 July 1914, Captain Max Looff had taken the 3,400 tonne light cruiser *Königsberg* out of harbour at Dar es Salaam, and steamed north up the Indian Ocean to the Gulf of Aden, where on the outbreak of war, he had sunk the merchantman, the *City of Winchester*. On the return journey he sent *H.M.S. Pegasus* to the bottom in Zanzibar harbour. A Royal Navy force was dispatched to East Africa with orders to search and destroy the *Königsberg*. In the hope of escaping the British cruisers, Captain Looff took his ship up the Rufiji River delta. In July 1915, the *Königsberg's* hiding place was discovered, and the British monitors *H.M.S. Mersey* and *H.M.S. Severn* eventually sank the German cruiser. However, Captain Looff and his blue jackets had managed to salvage the *Königsberg's* large 105mm guns, which were to play a decisive rôle in the future plans of the German commander, Lieutenant Colonel Paul von Lettow Vorbeck.

A strong Portuguese force composed of three columns, had bridged the Rovuma River into German East Africa on 19 September 1916. Contact was established with the British forces that were occupying Mikindani, and the Portuguese set up telegraph lines running south to Nichichira on the Rovuma River. The effort to occupy the Rovuma valley, and advance 220 kilometres northward to Liwale, had begun with a measure of success. The columns' first objective was the heavily defended German post on the heights at Nevala in the Makonde Highlands, 140 kilometres to the north.

The first contact took place on 4 October 1916, at Mahuta, on the Lurio River, two kilometres east of Nevala. As the Portuguese expeditionary troops had been sent south to Nangadi by motor ambulance, the defence of Mahuta was left to 200 soldiers of 21 and 24 Mozambican Infantry. A small Portuguese led patrol was ambushed, suffering a number of casualties, including its commanding officer, Captain Liberato Pinto; the patrol withdrew to its defensive line and then turned south to make for the post at Nichichira.

On 22 October, five kilometres south of Nevala, the Portuguese under command of Major Azambuja Martins, came up with a German platoon entrenched around a group of water wells. The Portuguese advanced unseen through the jungle, and launched a surprise attack, driving the German *askaris* from the wells, but not before they had lost two expeditionary soldiers. Fourteen Mozambican soldiers were wounded. The Portuguese pushed on and dug in within sight of the German post to await reinforcements. Three Portuguese columns had now concentrated before Nevala, and after a short artillery duel, the Germans abandoned their position.

Once Nevala had been occupied on 26 October, the Portuguese sent out a reconnaissance patrol towards Massassi, which was ambushed by the Germans and withdrew to Nevala. On 8 November, German and Portuguese forces clashed at the battle of Kivamba; the Portuguese patrol retreated on Nevala carrying their mortally wounded commanding officer, Major Leopoldo Silva, with them. The Portuguese force which numbered less than 450 men, had little alternative other than to defend Nevala, rather than suffer further casualties on the northward trek to Liwale.

Meanwhile, on 2 November, on the Lugenda River, Lieutenant Kempner commanding the advance guard of 11 *Askari* Company, came up with the Portuguese post at Nangwale. The post lay on a bare hill with a wide field of fire; it would be a hard nut to crack. Kempner deployed his men along the edge of the bush and, due to the lack of cover, began the attack by advancing over open ground. Kempner and his African subaltern quickly got into the Portuguese entrenchments and the startled Portuguese surrendered at once. Little had the defenders realised that the rest of the *askaris* were still struggling up the steep hill, loaded down with full kit, ammunition and rations.

At Mpotora, Lieutenant von Boemken's two *askari* companies were dug in and awaiting instructions. On 12 November, Rufiji's Principal Postmaster Rothe received a telegraph message releasing him from his civil post and ordering him to Mpotora. The first intimation von Boemken had of Rothe's arrival was when his forward sentries appeared escorting a German officer pushing a bicycle. Rothe had cycled from Niakisiku, and as a reserve officer in the rank of captain, informed the lieutenant that had been given temporary command of his two *askari* companies and the detachment's 105 mm gun. After briefing his NCOs, he set off towards Nevala. Meanwhile, Captain Looff, who was en route from Lindi, was to rendezvous with Captain Rothe and assume overall command of the force.

The Germans began their advance on the Nevala position and on 22 November, recaptured the vitally important water wells at Ribeira do Nevala, and began the siege of the Portuguese force at the Nevala redoubt. Since the onset of the siege, officers, and NCOs had tried to ignore the weak cries from the trenches, as African soldiers begged for *maji* – water. But by the seventh day, the defenders' morale was beginning to give way. Many lay at the bottom of their trenches, too exhausted to man the fort's entrenchments. Having given up the slightest hope of rescue, and tormented by hunger and thirst, the African soldiers were forced to eat the only remaining rations, salty, tinned tuna. Those who still had sufficient energy drank the last drops of water from the bottom of the storage tanks; it was stinking and filthy, but was fought over by more than

100 men. As the Mozambican troops died of thirst in their trenches, their bodies were dragged out and piled up inside the fort. Desertions began to increase, especially at dawn, when soldiers slipped away into the bush to lick the drops of overnight dew, and having done so, make off into the jungle heading south towards the Rovuma.

At midday on 28 November, Looff's powerful guns came into action and laid down an incessant, ear-splitting bombardment. The soldiers were eating up what was left of their tinned rations when, with a screaming howl, a heavy shell rushed over their heads, and exploded in a plume of smoke, causing panic among the Portuguese and their African soldiers. Captain Francisco Pedro Curado in command of 21 Infantry Company, took out his pistol and fired it into the air in a desperate and futile attempt to halt the panic, but to no avail. Curado and his officers were left to man the defences with NCOs and the few soldiers who had dared to brave the barrage. Fortunately for the Portuguese, many of the German shells fell short and exploded among the thick bush in front of the Nevala position setting fire to the trees and affording them some temporary respite.

In heavy rain, on the night of 28 November, the bedraggled and starving Portuguese defenders of Nevala began the slow retreat towards the Rovuma River carrying their machine guns with them. After a nightmare journey, at times sinking up to their waists in the morass-like 'black cotton soil' and hacking their way through the almost impenetrable bush, constantly harassed by German patrols, Captain Curado's rearguard finally recrossed the Rovuma two days later; however, they had been forced to spike and abandon seven of their precious machine guns.

At the silent, rain-swept post, the Germans seized four mountain guns, rifles, ammunition and transports. Sharp-eyed *askaris* also discovered caches of ammunition that had been hastily buried by the Portuguese.

The Portuguese-led troops arrived at Nichichira hotly pursued by the enemy. To the utter amazement of the Portuguese officers, the communications post came under artillery fire. The Germans' bearers, numbering 110 men, had manfully pulled one of Looff's 10cm cannon, mounted on an improvised limber of ropes, through the thick jungle. Three shots landed on the camp, one of them was a direct hit on the telegraph hut. As the post could not be defended, the officers set fire to it, after destroying the remaining signals equipment. The Portuguese crossed the Rovuma under fire and made for Nangadi eight kilometres south of the river.

In the early afternoon, the disorganised force reached Nangadi, where the men collapsed on to their ground sheets. Suddenly, artillery rounds rushed overhead, tearing up the tall palm trees on the hill to the rear of the post; the Germans were already at Nichichira. On 1 December, the Portuguese, believing the Germans were on the Mozambique side of the river, blew up the post's ammunition dump, and with Captain Curado in command, withdrew towards the Alto Serra position. The defenders at Alto Serra welcomed the arrival of the eccentric, pipe smoking, Captain Curado. Curado was a very experienced officer having served in the 1895 campaigns in Mozambique. It was well known to the men that he had fought against Gungunyana's impis at the decisive battle of Coolela Flats and had taken part in the storming of Gungunyana's kraal with Mousinho de Albuquerque.

The Alto Serra camp was a staging post on the communications line to Nevala and was the terminus of the motor lorry road from Palma on the coast. It was strategically sited on the very top of a high hill, partially hidden by tall trees. Its main disadvantage was that constant patrolling was needed to defend it, but it had the advantage of being virtually unobservable by the enemy. Curado and his men were resupplied with food and ammunition and told to remain at Alto Serra and await further orders.

Governor-general Álvaro Xavier de Castro, had taken over interim-command of Portuguese forces, as Ferreira Gil had been recalled to Lisbon. On 12 September 1917, he handed over to Colonel Tomás de Sousa Rosa, in command of the final 4 Expeditionary Force to Mozambique, which had arrived that day at Mocimboa da Praia. It was a makeshift force, which was to pay a costly price. Colonel Sousa Rosa had mounted a parliamentary campaign - a relatively easy undertaking, when compared with the military variety - defending the need for a Portuguese offensive. Between 5 January and 2 July the troopships *Portugal*, *Moçambique* and *Moçâmedes* transported 5,267 officers and men of Infantry Regiments 21, 29, 30, 31, plus artillery and engineers from Portugal to Mozambique. An NCO cadre was tasked with the training up of 20 native companies to be deployed alongside the soldiers from Portugal.

Sousa Rosa's force was confronted by a series of disasters. At Negomano, the Germans, led by Lettow-Vorbeck and von Wahle, had outmanoeuvred the Portuguese. They had been ordered to dig in on the Lugenda River, a kilometre from its confluence with the Rovuma, facing north towards German territory. On 25 November 1917, German forward platoons had waded across the Rovuma under the gaze of the defenders at Negomano, followed by the main force, composed of nine companies. On clambering up the south bank, they came under fire, and while the Portuguese were fully occupied, three companies led by Captain Goering crossed over further up river, and using a belt of thick bush to cover their movements, encircled the Portuguese position and with Captain Koehl in the lead, attacked it from the rear. The manoeuvre was a complete success. Major Teixeira Pinto whose tactical knowledge of soldiering in Angola and Portuguese Guinea, was peerless, had been given command of the newly arrived troops tasked to defend the Negomano position. *Kurika*, who had survived so many pitched battles in Africa, was killed early on during the German assault on his position.

The Germans buried 200 dead and took 150 Portuguese and 200 African soldiers prisoner. The Germans also captured valuable medical supplies plus Maxim machine guns, 256 brand-new Mauser rifles, thousands of rounds of ammunition and 2,000 kilos of supplies.

In *Niassa Chartered Company* lands, two Portuguese columns had been organised with the intention of driving the Germans out of the Lugenda Valley. The columns met up at the Nanguar post in October under Major Quaresma. Second-in-command, Captain Curado had earlier been tasked to make a reconnaissance of the area and chose Puxa-Puxa on the Chilueze River between the Lugenda River and the M'kula Mountains. The columns marched out of Nanguar for Puxa-Puxa with ammunition and supplies, leaving a small force to defend Nanguar.

The Portuguese fortified the Puxa-Puxa position turning it into an almost impregnable fortress; it was ideally situated on a hill, and had the advantage of easy access to fresh water. Yet a signal had arrived at the post, ordering a column of troops under Major Quaresma, to reinforce Captain Teixeira Pinto's redoubt at Negomano. The majority of the remaining troops were sent to garrison the isolated posts strung out along the frontier at Oisulo and Mokolo. Captain Curado had voiced his opposition to the pull out, but as Major Quaresma was already on his way to Negomano, he had little alternative other than to assume command of the small force. The Germans were astounded that the Portuguese could abandon Puxa-Puxa as their reconnaissance patrols had reported that it was the best-defended position in the region. The order was countermanded but by then it was too late.

The German forces were now moving up the Lugenda in two columns; the first column on the right bank under Lettow-Vorbeck, was marching toward Nanguar while the second, commanded by General von Wahle and the German colony's governor-general, Dr Heinrich Schnee, followed the left bank towards Puxa-Puxa. Von Wahle had been in German East Africa on a private visit when war broke out, and had agreed to serve under Lettow-Vorbeck, a junior officer, for the duration of hostilities.

At Nanguar Second Lieutenant Salgado was told by his Mozambican soldiers that a German patrol had been sighted some two kilometres distant. Salgado, had been given specific instructions by Captain Curado, that if the Germans attacked the weakly defended post, he was to destroy the ammunition and food supplies, in order to deny them to the enemy. However, Salgado and his men wasted no time, and in their hurried withdrawal from the Nanguar post, left their valuable supplies to the Germans.

On hearing of von Wahle's approach, Curado dug in on a rocky 800-metre high hill at M'kula to await the German onslaught. He ordered captains Pimenta and Paulo Rêgo to supervise the setting up of bivouacs. The 283-strong Portuguese force was equipped with rifles, and a machine gun battery of five machine guns, under command of Lieutenant Viriato de Lacerda.

Curado then set up an advanced post hidden amongst the rocks. During the night of 2 December, shadowy figures were seen moving through the bush. The sentries reported seeing what looked like Portuguese soldiers, when challenged, they rapidly made off. The *askaris* had been dressed in Portuguese uniforms, which they had taken at Negomano. One of them was later captured wearing Teixeira Pinto's own bloodstained uniform. In the early morning, as the thick mist cleared from the mountain, the NCO-commanded post opened up on the Germans, giving Curado time to prepare for the main German assault.

Between 3 and 7 December, Captain Curado's position repeatedly came under heavy attack. The powerful German force comprised eight infantry companies, ten machine guns plus artillery and reserves. The Portuguese were isolated, as allied forces were some three days' march away. The German attack was repulsed, but once the two German columns had joined forces, M'kula rapidly became indefensible. On the night of 7 December, Lieutenant Lacerda and his machine gun battery groped its way up through the slippery rocks in an attempt to enfilade the German positions. Two machine guns were already in position and began to fire on the Germans, when they in turn were raked by enemy fire from the heights above them. The situation for the Portuguese was now critical and Curado ordered the destruction of food supplies and equipment that could be useful to the enemy. At that moment, German field guns opened up on the Portuguese with shrapnel, causing many casualties among the defenders of the rock-strewn redoubt. Further down the hill, a kilometre away, the Germans had been involved in a daylong battle with soldiers of the Niassa Company before gaining control of the water wells; the end of the siege was in sight. On the 8 December, a heavily camouflaged German detachment began to infiltrate the dead ground directly in front of the Portuguese forward trenches held by Lacerda and his machine guns. After two hours of intense fighting, Lacerda was hit in the head by rifle fire, and the machine gun battery was overrun.

After the Portuguese surrender, von Wahle entered the trenches and called out for M'kula's commanding officer, he was surprised to be confronted by the pipe-smoking Curado. The Germans demanded word of honour from the Portuguese that as a condition of liberty they would not again take up arms against Germany, the demand was refused. As the Portuguese officers had refused to give their word of parole they had to be sent back to Portuguese lines under guard, as von Wahle had insufficient supplies to feed enemy prisoners of war.

The Portuguese lost one officer and thirteen Mozambican troops, 59 men were taken prisoner; seven of them seriously wounded. The Germans force lost only one soldier, with nineteen wounded. On 9 December, the Germans took part, with full military honours, in the funeral of Lieutenant Viriato Sertório da Rocha Portugal de Lacerda of 21 Infantry. Dr Schnee conducted the service. Lacerda had been carried back unconscious to the German field ambulance, where Doctor Albert Müller gave him first aid, but a bullet had lodged in his brain and he died shortly after. The Germans, who had been running seriously short of food, were now able to divide up the captured supplies.

On 10 December in heavy rain and poor visibility, the Portuguese, escorted by a German platoon, left M'kula and began their long trek to Negomano, but the escort became confused by the muddy tracks and the blinding rain, and led them through Unde and Macochero before reaching Negomano. After resting at Negomano, they continued on to Mocimboa do Rovuma where the escort set them free. The Portuguese and their escorts had trekked over 450 kilometres in thirteen days in appalling weather conditions and with very little food.

Meanwhile, after studying the captured maps at the M'kula post, which appeared to show that Alto Molocue was only defended in company strength, and was the site of a large ammunition dump, von Wahle and his officers, had set off towards the Portuguese position. Scouts were sent out ahead of the main column and reported back that Alto Molocue was visible in the distance. With the aid of his binoculars, von Wahle could make out a cluster of European-style houses on a heavily wooded hill. The Germans, sensing a trap, sent a section of men forward to draw enemy fire from the Portuguese held position. The section was surprised not to meet with any resistance, and on entering the settlement discovered that apart from women and children, it was deserted as its defenders had already withdrawn. Almost on the outskirts of Alto Molucue was a finely built mansion where the Germans came up with a small number of unarmed Portuguese officers drinking coffee on its verandah. The unsuspecting officers were taken prisoner but refused to answer the Germans' questions. However, some welcome food supplies had been located, but the ammunition dump had been destroyed, consequently, the Germans decided to push on further south in order to resupply.

Late June 1918, found Captain Müller in charge of a German force following the railway line making for Nyamacurra some 40 kilometres north of Quelimane. The sizeable town of Nyamacurra was held by a Portuguese force of three infantry companies with one and a half companies of 2 Battalion, 3 King's African Rifles, under overall command of twenty-eight-year-old Major Eric Gore-Brown. The allied defenders were dug in on the northern outskirts of the town; to the south was the Nyamacurra River. On reaching the outskirts Captain Müller was met by intense fire from the Anglo-Portuguese force, and as it was fast getting dark, he withdrew into the bush. On the following morning, the 3 July, the Germans began an accurate bombardment of the forward trenches. The Anglo-Portuguese defenders were unnerved by its intensity and began to waver, just at that moment, Müller and his *askaris* went on to the attack, roaring war cries and charging with the bayonet. After a limited resistance, the trenches were abandoned, and were quickly occupied by the Germans. Panic ensued among the allied force and Major Gore-Brown ordered a general withdrawal through the town towards the nearby Nyamacurra River. As no crossing point could be found, the panic-stricken soldiers threw themselves into the river, in a hopeless attempt to escape; most were drowned, including Gore-Brown. The total allied casualties at Nyamacurra were 46 killed and 56 wounded. The Germans were able to supply themselves from the sugar refinery and its store-houses and unexpectedly, from supplies landed the previous day from a motor launch skippered by army Captain Lionel Cohen, British liaison officer with Portuguese headquarters at Quelimane, which had steamed up the Nyamacurra River to resupply the King's African Rifles with 300 boxes of ammunition and 350 rifles. When the battle was over, Müller was directed to a storeroom where he discovered an ample cache of Portuguese wine. While he and his officers proceeded to celebrate, the *askaris* sought different pleasures – when the Germans pulled out of Nyamacurra, the *askaris* newly-found women companions happily followed them and served with their menfolk as cooks and porters.

Following the Nyamacurra debacle, Colonel de Sousa Rosa, returned to Portugal on 7 July 1918, and was replaced by General Gomes da Costa.

On 28 September 1918, German forces, under Lettow-Vorbeck, had crossed the Mozambique border due south of Songea, and then headed towards Northern Rhodesia, where they came up with the frontier post at Fife. The German force suffered a number of casualties, only to be caught in open country by the King's African Rifles. The bruised column had begun to head further into Northern Rhodesia when news reached Lettow-Vorbeck of the German armistice.

Portugal's colonial borders were once again secure, yet some forty years later Portugal would be faced with a bitter and bloody anti-colonial war encompassing Angola, Mozambique and Portuguese Guinea, which would lead to Portugal's final ignominious withdrawal from her African colonies.

***

Bibliography

Almeida, F. de. (ed.) *História de Portugal* vol. X. *1816-1910* Coimbra: 1929

Almeida, José de. *Dezoito Anos em África* Lisbon: Adolfo Mendonça 1898

Ameal, João. *História de Portugal* Oporto: Tavares Martins 1968

Andrade, Freire de. *Relatório do Capitão Freire de Andrade* Arquivo Histórico Militar Lisbon

Anonymous, in *Anais do Club Militar Naval No. 9* Lisbon: 1937

Archer, Maria. *Sertanejos* Cadernos Coloniais Lisbon: Cosmos

Arnot, Frederick, S. *Bihé and Garenganze – Four Years' Further Work and Travel in Central Africa* London: Hawkins 1916

Arnot, Frederick, S. *Missionary Travels in Central Africa* London: Alfred Holness 1914

Baker, Ernest. *The Life and Explorations of Frederick Stanley Arnot* New York: Dutton 1920

Baptista, Jacinto. *O Cinco de Outubro* Lisbon: Arcádia 1964

Batalha Reis, Jaime. *Os Portugueses na Região do Nyassa* Lisbon: Imprensa Nacional 1889

Becker, Peter. *Inland Tribes of Southern Africa* London: Granada 1979

Blennerhassett, Rose & Sleeman, Lucy. *Adventures in Mashonaland* London: Macmillan 1893

Bley, Helmut. *South-West Africa Under German Rule 1894-1914* London: Heinnemann 1971

British South Africa Company Historical Catalogue & Souvenir of Rhodesia Johannesburg: 1936-37

Brown, William, H. *On the South African Frontier* New York: Charles Scribner 1899

Bureau of Intelligence and Research, *International Boundary Study No. 39* Washington: Department of State 1964

Cabral, Augusto. *Raças, Usos e Costumes dos Indígenas do Distrito de Inhambane* Lourenço Marques: Imprensa Nacional 1910

Cabral de Moncada, Francisco. *A Campanha do Bailundo em 1902* Luanda: Imprensa Nacional 1903

Caetano, Marcello. *Portugal e a Internacionalização dos problemas Áfricanos* Lisbon: Ática 1971

Caldas Xavier, Alfredo, Augusto. *Reconhecimento do Limpopo: Os Territórios ao Sul do Save e os Vátuas* Lisbon: Imprensa Nacional 1894

Campos Júnior, António. *Victórias de África: A Defesa de Lourenço Marques e As Campanhas do Vale do Incomati e do País de Gaza: 1894-1895* Lisbon: 1897

Capelo, Guilherme, Augusto, Brito de. *As Campanhas de 1895 em Moçambique* in Boletim da Agência Geral das Colónias 1933

Castro, Velloso. *A Campanha do Cuamato em 1907* Luanda: Imprensa Nacional 1908

Catálogo da Exposição Histórica da Ocupação Lisbon: Agência Geral das Colonias, 1937

Chagas, João. *Cartas Políticas* Lisbon: Bayard 1908

Cidade, Hernâni. in *História de Portugal, Edição Monumental,* vol. VII. Barcelos: Portucalense Editora 1928

Clifford, Hugh. *The Gold Coast Regiment in the East African Campaign* London: Murray 1920

Coelho, Trindade. *Manual Político do Cidadão Português* Oporto: Empresa Literária 1908

Colquhoun, Archibald, R. *Dan to Beersheba* London: Heinnemann 1908

Colquhoun, Archibald, R. *The Africander Land* London: Julian Murray 1906

Conferência de Mousinho de Albuquerque – Porto 19/1/1898 in Boletim Geral das Colónias 1936

Cordeiro, Luciano. *Silva Porto* Lisbon: Comércio 1891

Corpechot, Lucien. *Memories of Queen Amelie of Portugal* London: Nash 1915

Costa, Mário. *Como Fizeram os Portugueses em Moçambique* Lisbon: Rodrigues 1928

Costa Mário. *Voluntários de Lourenço Marques* Lourenço Marques: Imprensa Nacional 1928

Costa Oliveira, Eduardo. *Viagem á Guiné Portuguesa* Lisbon: Imprensa Nacional 1890

Couceiro, Henrique Mitchell de Paiva. *Relatório de Viagem entre Bailundo e as Terras do Mucusso* Lisbon: Imprensa Nacional 1892

Crosthwaite, Sir Charles. *The Pacification of Burma* London: Edward Arnold 1912

Cunha, Pedro, José da. *A Companhia de Moçambique e a sua Obra* in Boletim da Agência Geral das Colónias Lisbon: 1925

Darter, Adrian. *The Pioneers of Mashonaland 'One Of Them'* Bulawayo: Books of Rhodesia 1977

De Wall, D. C. *With Rhodes in Mashonaland* London: Juta 1896

Dias, Gastão, Sousa. *Jornadas Heróicas de Artur de Paiva* Lisbon: Agência Geral das Colónias 1949

Dias, Gastão, Sousa. *Os Auxiliares na Ocupação do Sul de Angola* Lisbon: Agência Geral das Colónias 1943

Dias, Gastão, Sousa. *Os Portugueses em Angola* Agência Geral do Ultramar Lisbon: 1959

Eça, António, Julio da Costa Pereira. *Relatório da Campanha em Angola 1915* Lisbon: Lusitania 1922

Edwards, Adrian, C. *The Ovimbundo Under Two Sovereignties* London: OUP 1962

Ennes, António. *A Guerra de África em 1895* Lisbon: Edições Gama 1945

Ennes, António. *Relatório Moçambique* Lisbon: Divisão de Publicações e Biblioteca, Agência Geral das Colónias 1966

Fernandes das Neves, Diocleciano. *Itenerário de Uma Viagem Caça dos Elefantes* Lisbon: Universal 1878

Fernandes de Oliveira, Manuel & Mendes de Couto, Carlos. *Angolana – Documentação sobre Angola* Lisbon: Centro de Estudos Históricos do Ultramar 1968

Ferreira, Manuel. *Viriato de Lacerda* Lisbon: Cosmos 1939

Ferreira Martins, Luís, Augusto. *Portugal Na Grande Guerra*, vol. 1. Lisbon: Ática 1934

Freire, João, Paulo. *Lisboa do Meu Tempo e do Passado* vol. 2. Lisbon: 1932

Goodwin Green, Elsa. *Raiders and Rebels in South Africa* Bulawayo: Books of Rhodesia 1976

Green, Lawrence. *Lords of the Last Frontier* Cape Town: Timmins 1952

Guimarães, Luís, Augusto, de Pina. *Campanha Do Humbe 1897-98* Lisbon: Ática 1938

Hambly, Wilfred, D. *The Ovimbundu of Angola* Chicago: Field Museum Press 1934

Hansard Vol 161.House of Commons Debate 19 March 1923 vol. 161

Hennig, Richard. *Deutsch-Südwest im Weltkriege* Berlin: Susserott 1920

Hickman, A. S. *Men Who Made Rhodesia* Salisbury: British South Africa Company 1960

Howard, A.G. L. *How We Made Rhodesia* Bulawayo: Books of Rhodesia 1973

Johnson, James. *Reality versus Romance in South Central Africa* New York: Fleming H. Revell 1895

Júnior, Manuel, Francisco, Contreiras. *O Massacre do Cunene* Cadernos Coloniais Lisbon: Cosmos

Junod, Henri. *Usos e Costumes dos Bantos: A Vida de uma Tribo Sul Africana* Lourenço Marques: Imprensa Nacional 1939

Keiling, Luís. *Cuanhama* in Boletim da Agência Geral das Colónias 1926

Keiling, Luís. *Cuanhama* in Boletim da Agência Geral das Colónias 1927

Leite de Magalhães, *A Guine através da História* Cadernos Coloniais Lisbon: Cosmos

Lettow-Vorbeck, Paul von. *My Reminiscences of East Africa* London: Hurst & Blackett 1922

Leonard, Arthur, G. *How We Made Rhodesia* London: Keegan Paul 1896

Lichnowsky, Karl, Max. *Heading For The Abyss* London: Constable 1928

Lima, David, Martins de. *A Campanha dos Cuamatos* Lisbon: Ferreira 1908

Lima, Maria, Helena, Figueiredo. *Paisagens e Figuras Típicas do Cuanhama* Lisbon: 1969

Lopo, Júlio de Castro. *Paiva Couceiro – Uma Grande Figura de Angola* Lisbon: Agência Geral do Ultramar 1957

Loureiro, António da Silva. *Tributo de Sangue – Monografia das Campanhas Militares para a Ocupação da Guiné* Lisbon: 1934 1a Exposição Colonial Portuguesa

Lyons McLeod. *Travels in East Africa: With the Narrative of a Residence in Mozambique* London: Hurst & Blackett 1860

Machado, Carlos, Roma. *A Região Cuamato-Cuanhama celeiro do planalto* in Boletim Geral das Colónias 1927

Matoso, António, G. *História de Portugal* vol. 2. Lisbon: Livraria Sá da Costa 1939

Millais, John, G. *The Life of Frederick Courtney Selous DSO* New York: Longmans 1919

Möller, Peter, A. *Journey in Africa through Angola, Ovampoland & Damaraland 1895-1896* Cape Town: Struik 1974

Morse, Henry. *Portugal* London : Unwin 1891

Muller, C. F. J. (edt.) *Five Hundred Years - A History of South Africa* Pretoria: Academica 1981

Noronha, Eduardo de. *A Rebelião dos Indígenas em Lourenço Marques* Lisbon: O Dia 1894

Nowell, Charles, E. *A History of Portugal* Princeton: Van Nostrand 1962

Nunes, António, Pires. *Mouzinho de Albuquerque* Lisboa: Prefácio 2003

Oliveira Martins, J. P. *Portugal em África* Oporto: Lugan & Genelloux 1891

Omer-Cooper, J. D. *The Zulu Aftermath* Longmans: London 1966

Ornelas, Aires de. *Cartas de África: Campanha do Gungunhana em 1895* Lisbon: São José 1930

Padrel, Justiniano. *Expedição ao Humbe* in Boletim da Sociedade de Geografia de Lisboa. Lisbon: 1892

Padres Missionários do Espírito Santo. *Diccionário Português-Olunyaneka* Huíla: 1896

Paiva de Andrada, Joaquim. *Relatório de uma Viagem ás Terras dos Landins* Lisbon: Imprensa Nacional 1885

Paiva de Andrada, Joaquim. *Relatório de uma Viagem ás Terras do Changamira* Lisbon: Imprensa Nacional 1886

Paiva, Artur de. *Artur de Paiva* vols. 1 & 2. Lisbon: Agência Geral das Colónias 1938

Phiri, Desmond, Dudwa. *History of Malawi from Earliest Times to the Year 1915* Blantyre: Claim 2004

Pinto, João, Teixeira. *A Ocupação Militar da Guiné* Lisbon: Agência Geral das Colónias 1936

Pritchard, Stanley, A. M. *Report on a Tour to Ovamboland by Major S.M. Pritchard, Officer-in-Charge of Native Affairs* (U.6 38-15) Union of South Africa Government: 1915

Pritchard, Stanley, A. M. in *Report on the Natives of South-West Africa – Their Treatment by Germany* London: HMSO, 1918

Rankin, Daniel, J. *The Zambesi Basin and Nyassaland* Edinburgh: Blackwood 1893

Resende, Manuel. *Ocupação dos Dembos 1615-1913*: *Subsídios para a História de Angola* Cadernos Coloniais. Lisbon: Cosmos 1939

Roçadas, Álves, José *Conferência Sobre o Sul de Angola* Lisbon: Imprensa Nacional 1908

Santos, Manuel, Martins dos. *A História de Angola através dos seus personagens principais* Lisbon: Agência Geral do Ultramar 1967

Scheepers Strydom, C. J. *Afrikaners In Die Vreemde* Cape Town: 1976

Selous, F. C. *Travel and Adventures in South-East Africa* London: Ward 1893

Serpa Pinto, Alexandre, A. da Rocha. *Como eu atravessei a África* vol. 1. London: Sampson Lowe 1881

Silva, Fernando, Augusto da. & Meneses, Carlos, Azevedo. *Elucidário Madeirense* vol. 1. Funchal: Esperança 1921

Silva, Joaquim, Duarte. *General Padrel* Cadernos Coloniais Lisbon: Cosmos 1939

Sociedade de Geografia de Lisboa. *75 Anos de Actividades a Serviço de Ciência e da Nação – 1875-1950* Lisbon: 1950

Sociedade de Geografia de Lisboa. *Expedição ao Humbe do Major Justiniano Padrel*

Sousa, João, Francisco de. *Infanteria 17 em África* Lisbon: Cosmos

Southern, Paul. *German Border Incursions into Portuguese Angola prior to the First World War* in *Portuguese Journal of Social Science* vol. 6. Bristol: Intellect Journal 2007

Teixeira, Alberto de Almeida. *Naulila* Lisbon: Agência Geral das Colónias 1935

Teixeira Mota, A. *A Guiné Portuguesa* in Boletim Cultural da Guiné Portuguesa, Número Especial do V Centenário da Descoberta da Guiné Lisbon: 1947

The Mandalay Herald 22 January 1889

The New York Times 19 January 1892

The Times 23 November 1890

The Times 27 May 1891

The Times 29 May 1891

The Times 5 June 1891

The Times 10 June 1891

The Times 11 June 1891

The Times 16 June 1891

The Times 11 November 1938

The Times 10 February 1943

Torres, Ruy de Abreu. *Cultura Portuguesa* vol. 15. Lisbon: Empresa Nacional de Publicidade 1975

Torres do Vale, Ernesto. *Dicionário Shironga-Português* Lourenço Marques: Imprensa Nacional 1906

Union Government of South Africa *Report of the Authority of South West Africa for the Year 1922* (U.G.21-23)

Van der Walt, A. J. *Noordwaarts* Cape Town: 1929

Vasconscelos, A. Leite de. *A Guiné* in Boletim da Agência-Geral das Colónias Lisbon: 1929

Vedder, Heinrich. *South West Africa in Early Times* London: Frank Cass 1966

Vilhena, Maria da Conceição. *Gungunhana – Grandeza e Decadência de um Império Africano* Lisbon: Colibri 1999

Walker, Eric, A. (ed.) *Cambridge History of the British Empire* vol. 8. Cambridge: CUP 1963

Warhurst, Philip, R. *Anglo-Portuguese Relations in South-Central Africa* London: Longman 1962

Wienholt, Arnold. *The Story of a Lion Hunt with Some of the Hunter's Military Adventures During the War* London: Andrew Melrose 1922

Wills, W. A. and Collingridge, L.T. *The Downfall of Lobengula* Bulawayo: Rhodesian Reprints 1971

Worsfold, W. Basil. *Portuguese Nyassaland* London: Sampson Low, Marston 1899

Paul Southern ©

Index

A

A Portuguesa, 13, 36, 214
Abreu e Sousa, de, Gen., 36
Ábuto, 172
African Lakes Company, 34
Aguiar, João Maria de, Capt., 129-133
Aires de Ornelas de Vasconcelos, Capt., 44, 60-61, 70-71
Aires de Saldanha, govnr., 32
Alecrim Street, 31-32
Alentejo,125
Alfá Mamadu Leilu, 176-177
Almeida, António José de, 36
Almeida, Filemon, Ensign, 129
Almeida, José de, politician, 61-63
Almeida, João de, Capt.,145-148, 193
Almeida, Miguel Duarte de, Lt., 80
Almeida, Manuel Tomás de, 2/Lt., 72
Almeida, Simpliciano de, 2/Lt., 84-85, 89, 95
Alto Molocue, 234
Alto Serra, 231
Amado, 2/Lt., 85
Ambriz, 32
Ambrósio, Pte., 113-114
Ambuila, 145
American Protestant Mission, 94
Andrade de Corvo, govnr, 38
Alberts, Andries, farmer, 135
Alberts, Gert, farmer, 79
Alemão Coimbra, José da Costa, Capt., 76
Amaral, Francisco Maria do, Dr., 69
Anglo-German Accord, 181-182
Anglo-Portuguese Alliance, 30, 181, 185, 187-188, 226
Angoche, 70
Angola Bund, 182
Angra Castle, 69
Anguane, 44
Antas, Artur de Sampaio, Lt, 156
António, servant, 113, 115
Antule, 173, 175, 177
Antunes e Duparquet, José Maria, priest, 79
Anyoka, 222
Atlantic Ocean, 32, 35, 87, 125, 150, 154, 182, 189, 208-209
Aucongo, 138
Augusta Vitoria, 152
Aragão, António José de, Col., 43
Aragão, Francisco Xavier da Cunha, Lt., 197-198, 200
Arnot, Frederick, Dr, missionary, 89, 94
Austro-Hungary, 66, 225-226
Azevedo, Lt., 153
Azevedo, Constantino Pereira de, govnr., 33
Azevedo Coutinho, João de, Lt., 34, 70
Azores, 35-36, 214

B

Bailundo, 87-88, 90
Bailundo War, 203
Balanta, 154-155, 157-159, 163-177
Baltic Medal, 35
Baluchistan, 15
Bambi, 148, 158, 165
Banda, 90
Bandim, 153-154, 176
Baptista, Pedro João, trader, 33
Barata Feio, Júlio César, Lt., 154
Barbosa du Bocage, José Vicente, politician, 33
Baron de Resende, João, 17, 22, 24,
Baron Quintela Square, 31
Baron von Water, Capt., 199
Barotseland, 57, 87-88, 92
Bartlett, Abraham Dee, 186
Basserel, 163-164, 171
Basutoland, 219
Basuto Wars, 25
Bay of Tigers, 183
Bechuanaland Border Police, 15
Bechuanaland Expedition, 23
Beerfelde, Richard, 225
Beira, 17, 19, 20, 22, 25-27, 29, 38-39
Belém, 151
Belgian Congo, 57
Belmonte, 57, 87-89, 93- 95
Bengo River, 145
Benguela, 73, 82-83, 90, 105, 182, 203
Bérá, 166
Bergdama, 97
Beit, Alfred, 15
Berlin, 11-12, 31, 34, 37, 80, 101, 126, 181, 182, 203, 225
Bettencourt, Augusto de, Capt., 26-30
Bettencourt, José, 2/Lt., 30
Bettencourt Furtado, Raul, Sub/Lt., 51
Bianga, 163
Bié, 57, 75, 87-92, 94, 95

Birmingham, 186
Bismarck, Otto von, 101
Bissau, 97, 153-154, 162, 168, 172, 175-179
Bissau Region, 153, 175-176
Bissoram, 155-156, 164, 166, 168-169
Bivar, Capt., 118
Black Horse Square, 149
Blantyre, 206
Boemken, von, Lt., 229
Boers, 37, 79, 80, 89-90, 92-93, 101-102
Bolama, 153-155, 164, 168, 175
Borges da Fonseca, Carlos, Alberto, Col., 9
Borrow, Lt., 16
Botelho, Cpl., 191
Botha, Jakobus Frederick, Magistrate, 79
Botha, Jaquemina, 79-80
Botha, Louis , Gen., 209
Bourqui, Charles, priest, 183
Bowden, Montague 'Monty', trooper, 24
Braia, 158
Brame Grande River, 166
Braunsdorf, Police Sgt., 189, 191, 192
Brazil, 33, 39, 87
British and Dominion Forces:
British South Africa Police, 16, 30
Cape Field Artillery, 25
Cape Mounted Rifles, 25, 219
Hampshire Regiment, 15
King's African Rifles, 235, 236
Inniskilling Dragoon Guards, 15
Royal Horse Guards, 15
British India, 15
British South Africa Company, 15, 17, 19, 23, 27, 29, 37, 186
Brito, Augusto César de Brito, 2/Lt., 25
Brito, Francisco Maria Correia de, Capt., 28-30
Brown, Edward, trader, 58
Bua River, 82
Bunja, 193
Bunyi, 169
Buramos, 162
Bushman, 84

C

Cabelo Drift, 199
Cabiri, 145-146
Cabo Delgado District, 203, 205-206
Cabo Verde, 95, 97, 153
Cacheu, 155, 161-162, 164, 166
Cacheu Column, 161, 163

Cafu, 107, 142, 213
Cafuntuka, 106, 108
Cahama, 97, 111, 119-120, 207
Calaputi, 71
Caldas Xavier, Alfredo Augusto, Maj., 26-28, 49, 50-53, 55, 59, 60
Calequisse River, 164
Calueque Drift, 190-192, 196-199, 212
Calvet de Sousa Magalhães, Vasco, govnr., 156, 158-159
Cambela, 148
Camões, Luís Vaz de, 35
Campo Santo Ovidio, 36
Canja, 72
Cape Coloured, 74
Cape of Good Hope, 15
Cape Town, 24-25, 38, 53, 195, 207
Cape Town Mail, 58
Capelo, Carlos de Brito, explorer, 33
Capelongo, 135, 207, 212
Caprivi de Caprera de Montecuccoli, Georg Leo von, politician, 101
Carmo Azevedo, Joaquim António do, Capt., 153
Castro, Álvaro Xavier de, gov-gen., 206-227, 231
Cardoso, António Maria, explorer, 34
Cerqueira, Afonso de, Lt., 208, 216
Carmo Square, 151
Carnegie, Sir Lancelot, 187, 226
Caroliano da Costa, Lt/Comm., 213
Casal, 147-148
Cassai River, 33
Cassinga, 33, 82, 84, 182-183
Catigi, 164
Catumbela Falls, 57
Cauas-Okava, 189
Cayó, 164
Cazembe, 33
Cazuangongo, 147-148
Cerveira de Albuquerque, Joaquim, Gen., 205
Chagas, João, politician, 36, 125
Chaimite, 45, 69
Chamba, 204
Chamusca, 2/Lt., 71
Channel Squadron (British), 35
Chão, 176
Chartered Company, British, 16-17, 22, 28
Chartered Company, Portuguese, 40, 204, 232
Chela Highlands, 57, 76, 79, 86, 95, 123, 137, 208, 212

Chibia, 79, 97, 101, 117-118, 120, 208
Chicomo River, 45, 59, 63, 65
Chicuna, 208
Chief Aliburi, 177
Chief Amule, 38, 43
Chief Ananga, 192
Chief Bonga, 23
Chief Braime Dan, 168, 178
Chief Cabeça Grande, 76-77
Chief Chikarapira, 82, 84
Chief Chimbobolo, 213
Chief Chietakelo, 133, 138
Chief Dingiswayo, 44
Chief Dunduma, 87-88, 91-95, 97
Chief Dungula, 135-136
Chief Ganda, 20
Chief Guenjere, 20
Chief Gungunyana/Mondugaz, 12, 21, 22,
24, 25, 45-47, 59-63, 65-66, 69, 71, 185-
187, 231
Chief Iluero, 98
Chief Ipumbu, 196, 211
Chief Jamba, 88-89
Chief Jugudul, 172
Chief Kakulo Kahenda, 148
Chief Kalola, 214
Chief Kaoko, 95
Chief Khama, 16
Chief Kitokulo, 81-83
Chief Lhambeze, 84-85
Chief Lobengula, 16, 25, 35, 186
Chief Mahazuli, 43-44, 47
Chief Mamadu Sissé, 156, 166, 168, 171,
176-177
Chief Mandume, 211-216, 219-223
Chief Manikuse, 44-46
Chief Marave, 71
Chief Mastilefo, 212-213
Chief Matibejana, 43, 51, 54, 61
Chief Matulo, 71
Chief Modiadi, 168
Chief (*Muene*) Dekango, 112
Chief (*Muene*) Dilungo, 85, 121
Chief Mugundwana,
Chief Mutasa, 17, 21-25, 28
Chief Mzilikazi, 44
Chief Nambonga, 116
Chief Namhadi, 73-74, 79
Chief of Basserel, 164
Chief of Bor, 179
Chief Pazmane, 64
Chief Samba-Ly, 159
Chief Shinako, Luís, 82- 86

Chief T'hope, 65
Chief Zwide, 44
Chilomo, 34, 72
Chilueze River, 232
Chimbemba, 118
Chimbua Drift, 212
Chaves, Pedro Augusto, Capt., 76-77
Chimoio, 20, 27, 29-30
China Sea, 59
Chinde Concession, 205
Chinde Estuary, 34, 38, 205-206
Chitado, 79
Chitanda River, 73, 82
Chua Hills, 25, 28
City of Winchester, steamer 228
Clarke, Joseph, trader, 58
Cobonche, 169
Coelho, Guilherme Gomes, govnr., 76
Coelho, Manuel Maria, Lt., 36, 182
Cohen, Lionel, Capt., 235
Coimbra, 25, 35, 187
Colenso, 209
Colquhoun, Archibald Ross, 15-17, 19, 22-
25, 29, 30
Conference of Berlin, 31, 37, 80
Contumo, 154
Convention of 12 May 1886, 155
Coolela Flats, 66, 231
Cordeiro, Luciano, explorer, 31
Correia, Francisco, Sgt., 121
Correia de Brito, Francisco Maria, Capt., 28,
30
Correia de Sá, Salvador, govnr, 32
Cortes, António Carlos, Capt., 215
Cossine, 60- 64
Costa, Raul da, Capt., 66
Costa de Baixo, 162-164
Costa e Silva, Lt., 66
Crisóstomo, João, govnr, 37
Council of Foreign Bondholders, 126
Count Almoster, Capt., 105, 108-115
Countess of Carnaervon, steamer, 187
Couto, José da Costa, Lt., 69
Craveiro, Sgt., 65
Crown Prince Luís Filipe, 146, 149
Cuboi, 167
Cuhor, 156
Cuju, 177
Cumeré, 175-176
Cunha, Álvaro Herculano da, Sub/Lt., 153
Cunha, Aristides, Capt., 197, 200
Curado, Francisco Pedro, Capt., 230-234
Cussano, 167-168

Custódia Borja, Capt., 129
Cutáto, 89
Cuvelai River, 212-213

D

Dacoit, 15
Damara, 84-85, 89, 90, 93,
Damaraland, 189
Damequer, 138
Damião Dias, 2/Lt., 215
Dande River, 145-146
Dar es Salaam, 228
Delagoa Bay, 38, 53, 59
Delpuech, Isidore, priest, 75
Dembos Campaign, 145, 148
Doyle, Dennis , interpreter, 185-186
Dias Ferreira, José, politician, 126
Difaqane, 44
Diogo de Sá, Francisco, Lt., 105
Dirico, 193
Djimba, 123
Domingos, Cpl., 52
Dom Carlos I, 35-37, 69, 126,149
Dom Luís I, 46, 83
Dom Manuel II, 149-152
Dom Pedro II, 32
Dom Pedro IV Square, 36
Dombeafungwe, 98-99
Dona Amélia, 149, 152
Dongo, 81, 83-84
Dongoena, 98, 137, 196-198, 201, 207-208
Duarte de Almeida, Miguel, Lt., 80, 83
Duke and Duchess of Fife, 185
Duke of Béja, 150
Duke of Braganza, 135, 149
Duke of Palmela, 35
Duplessis, Jan, farmer, 199
Durban, 57-58, 61
Durham Castle, steamer, 203-204

E

East Africa Squadron British), 35
Echeia, 166-168, 171
Edinburgh, 186
Ediva, 120, 197
Marques, Eduardo, Capt., 135, 142-143
Egypt, 23
Ekovongo, 87, 92-93
Eminent domain, 225
Encoche, 158
Encoge, 145

Endasse, 171
English Brethren Mission, 89
Enkonde, 118
Ennes, António, 37-41, 43-44, 47, 49, 50-53, 55, 57, 59-63, 65-66, 69
Eque, 211
Eriksson, Axel, trader, 85, 89, 105
Esteves, Capt., 197
Etosha Pan, 189
Evale, 74, 135, 207, 211-213, 216
Evale Column, 212-213
Evora, 204
Eyre Crowe, Alexander, politician, 187

F

Faria, João Rodrigues, Sgt., 163, 166, 170
Farim River, 154
Fauqué, 166
Felix, José, Lt., 109, 116
Fiennes, Eustace, Lt., 23
Ferreira da Costa, Eduardo, Maj., 60, 145-146
Ferreira do Amaral, Francisco Joaquim, govnr., 76, 87
Ferreira Chaves, João Carlos Pires, Capt., 211
Ferreira Durão, Joaquim,Lt., 192
Ferreira Gil, José César, Gen. 227, 231
Ferreira, Jaime, Maj., 27
Fernandes, Lt., 197
Figueiredo, Amadeu de, 2/Lt., 199
Fisher, Dr., missionary, 89
Finis Patriae, 36
Fonseca, Carlos, Lt., 129
Fonseca, Jaime, 2/Lt., 173
Forbes, Patrick, Maj., 23-24
Forjaz, Manuel Pereira de, govnr., 32
Forno de Cal, 129, 208
Fort Salisbury, 16-17, 23-24
Forte Artur de Paiva, 95
Forte Bissau, 154, 173, 175
Forte Cafima, 212
Forte Cuanavale, 193
Forte Cuangar, 192-193
Forte Eduardo Marques., 139
Forte Humbe, 75-77, 97-99, 105-112, 114, 116-117, 119-120, 123, 130, 136, 141, 199
Forte Humpata, 57
Forte João de Almeida, 148
Forte Maria Pia, 83-84
Forte Maziua, 203

Forte Muchelia, 71
Forte Mulondo, 136
Forte Princesa Amélia, 83- 85, 92
Forte Roçadas, 137-138, 196, 209, 212
Forte Tchicusse, 120
Francisco, José, 2/Lt., 28
Franco-Prussian War, 19
François, Curt Carl Bruno von, Capt., 101,
Franke, Erich Victor Carl August, Maj., 198-199, 201, 209
Freire de Andrade, Alfredo Augusto, Capt., 44
Freire de Andrade, António, Captain, 60-62
Fulwell Park, 152
Funchal, 80
Fulani, 156, 159, 161, 168-169, 176

G

Gaika and Galeka Wars, 25
Galangue, 182
Gambos, 73, 75-77, 97, 109, 117-119, 129, 136, 182, 201, 207-208, 212
Gambos, João of, 135
Garanganja, 33
Gazaland, 21-22, 26, 43-46, 49, 53, 58, 61-62, 67, 69, 72, 146, 186, 187
Geba River, 154-158, 165-166, 172
Gendum, 159
General, steamer, 61
German Army
11 Askari Company, 229
2 Infantry Regiment, 199
Schutztruppe, 209
Survey Company North, 189
German East Africa, 72, 203, 205-206, 227-228, 232
German South West Africa, 57, 73-74, 101, 105, 117, 181-183, 189, 191-193, 195, 199, 207, 209
Gibraltar, 150, 152
Gimbo Alúquem, 147
Glasgow, 186
Godinho de Melo, Capt., 75
Goering, Capt., 231
Gombe, 147
Gombe Amukyana, 147
Gombe do Sasse, 148
Gomes Pereira, Maj., 60, 63-64
Gore-Brown, Eric, Maj., 235
Gorongosa Mountains, 21-23, 29
Gould, Albert, trader, 58

Greater Kwamato, 98, 131, 137, 139, 141-143
Graham, James, Lt., 23-25
Green, Frederick, trader, 89
Grey, Albert MP, 185-186
Grey, Sir Edward, 181, 187
Grobler's Drift, 16
Grootfontein, 74, 182, 189
Grumete, 158, 175-179
Guadiana River, 149
Guavá kraal, 50
Guerra Junqueiro, 36,
Guimarães, Capt., 120, 122
Gulongo Alto, 146
Guy Fawkes Night, 23

H

Hahn, Carl Hugo 'Cocky', Capt., 222
H.M.S. Enchantress, 35
H.M.S. Severn, monitor, 220
H.M.S. Mersey, monitor, 228
H.M.S. Pegasus, 228
Hamburg, 225
Harrison, secretary, 16-17
Heany, Maurice, Capt., 16
Heydebreck, Joachim von, Capt., 101
Heyman, Melville, Capt., 25, 27-30
Hickey, Sgt/Maj. 28
Herero, 89, 199
Homem Ribeiro, Captain, 200
Honkombe, 119
Honorato da Costa, Francisco, Col., 33
Hoornkrans, 101
Hotel Criterion, 58
Hotel Métropole, 30
Hottentot, 102-103, 105-106
House of Braganza, 36
House of Deputies, 187
Huambo, 91, 182
Huíla, 75, 79, 80, 84, 86, 95, 97, 109-110, 118, 135, 195, 208
Huíla Highlands, 32, 77, 101, 196
Huluhulu, 185
Humbe, 73, 75-77, 79, 97, 98, 105-109, 114, 117, 120, 123, 130, 132-133, 136-137, 189, 190-191, 196-197, 201, 207-209, 112, 216-217
Humbe Column, 5
Humpata, 76, 79-80, 83, 89-90, 101-103, 108-110, 115, 117, 135, 208

I

Ibo, 40
Ibo Island, 39
Ibraimo, 71
Imbundo, 147
Impernal River, 166, 173, 175, 177
Inkoluwane, 63-65
India, 33
Indian Ocean, 29, 32, 34-35, 45, 205, 228
Injai, Abdul, Lt., 156-159, 161-163, 166-168, 170, 173, 175-178
Intenté, 166
Intim, 153, 176-177
Inyambane, 20, 22, 26- 28, 39-40, 46, 59-60, 205
Inyango, 22
Inyoka, 138-139, 213
Iraouaddy, steamer, 44
Irrawaddy River, 15
Ivanhoe, 57
Ivens, Roberto, explorer, 33

J

Jaal, 178
Jager, M. J. de, Col., 222
Jambacamufate, 105, 112, 114, 117, 121-123
Jameson, Leander Star, Dr, 16, 186
Jau, 212
Jensen, Carl, interpreter/trader, 189-191
Jetá, 162, 164
Jordan, William Worthington, trader, 74
Júnior, José Ribeiro, Maj., 49
Junod, Henri, missionary, 47

K

Kafima, 219
Kakolongongo, 129
Kakulovar River, 80, 97-98, 105, 110, 112, 117-121, 138, 208
Kalibulala, 138, 141-144
Kamba, 116-117
Kaokoveld, 103, 199
Karuvapa, 90
Katekero, 110-111, 115, 117, 123
Katunga 34
Kauva, 74
Kempner, Lt., 229

Keto, induna, 69
Kichona, 147
Keiling, Luis, priest, 211
Kimberley, 15
Kimberley Club, 15
Kimbungo, 148
Kimmel, Georg, vol, 189
King George V, 152
King Nande, 183
Kionga Bay, 205
Kionga Triangle, 37, 205-206, 227
Kipungo, 84
Kiteve, 19-22, 106-107, 109, 116, 136, 212-213
Kivamba, 229
Kivolane, 69
Koehl, Capt., 232
Komondongo, 94
Königsberg, warship, 228
Königsburg University, 192
Kotoko, 83
Krusse Gomes, Lt., 62, 64
Kubango, 32, 57, 73, 80-86, 88-89, 92, 129, 192-193
Kubangui, 81, 83
Kukema River, 92-93
Kumbana, 59
Kunene, 32-33, 73-74, 79, 81-85, 88-90, 97-99, 103, 105, 123, 129-130, 133, 135-138, 141-142, 182, 189, 195-197, 199, 201, 209, 212-213, 222
Kurika, 180, 232
Kuring-Kuru, 192
Kwamato Column, 212, 217
Kwambi, 196
Kwanjululu, 89
Kwanyama, 73-75, 79, 80, 83, 117, 135, 163, 170, 175, 183, 190, 199, 207-209, 211-214, 216-217, 219-220, 222
Kwanyamaland, 73-74, 183, 211
Kwanza River, 33, 82

L

Lacerda e Almeida, Francisco José de, Dr, 33
Lacerda, Viriato de, Lt., 233
Lake Amaramba, 72
Lake Moero, 33
Lake Nyasa, 32, 34, 72, 205
Lake Shirwa, 205
Leball, William, trader, 75-76
Lecomte, Ernest, priest, 80, 82-85, 90

Lehmann, Wilhelm, Police Sgt., 192
Leiria, 79
Leitõo, Pedro, Lt., 62
Leitão, Amaral, Capt., 36,
Leite de Sepúlvedra, Victor, Sub/Lt., 43
Lemos, Emilio de, Lt., 54
Lesser Kwamato, 129, 131, 137-139, 141
Lettow-Vorbeck, Paul von, Lt/Col., 228, 231-232, 235-236
Liberato Pinto, Capt., 228
Libonta, 87
Lichnowsky, Prince Karl Max, 181-182
Liefeldt, Capt., 219-221
Ligonya River, 69
Lima, Augusto de, Lt., 153, 156
Limpopo Column, 59
Limpopo River, 26, 34, 44, 59, 67, 71, 186-187
Lindobe River, 90
Lisbon, 19, 21, 23, 25, 34-36, 40-41, 44-46, 57, 60, 80, 81, 87, 101, 127, 135, 149, 152, 154, 181, 185-187, 190, 195, 200-201, 204-207, 227-228
Lisbon Coliseum, 46
Lisbon Geography Society, 31-32, 84
Lisbon Insular Steamship Company, 225
Lisbon Port Authority, 225
Lisbon Zoo, 36
Liverpool, 186
Liwale, 228-229
Liz River, 79
Loch, Sir Henry, govnr., 24
London, 15, 30, 34-35, 82, 126, 181, 185-187,205
London Zoological Gardens, 186
Looff, Max, Captain, 228-230
Lopes, José António, trader, 99, 105, 110-111, 113-115, 117-118, 129, 142, 146
Lord Salisbury, 30, 34, 186
Lourenço Marques, 25-26, 30, 35, 37-41, 43-45, 47, 49, 50, 53, 55, 58-61, 69-71, 187, 204-206, 227
Losch, Alexander, Capt., 189, 191
Lower Kubango, 92, 192
Luamba Luambeze, 72
Luanda, São Paulo de, 33, 57, 76, 79, 87, 101, 117, 137, 145-148, 203, 207, 222
Luanda Observatory, 31
Luango, 148
Lubango, 31, 79, 105, 129, 137, 189, 193, 195, 209, 222
Luceke, 81, 83, 90
Lukin, Henry 'Harry' Brig/Gen, 195

Luchilingo, 72
Lugenda, 72, 229, 231-232
Luna de Carvalho, Joaquim, Capt., 98, 142-144
Lurio River, 69, 228
Lyons McLeod, 37

M

M'gogo, 142
M'kula Mountains, 232-234
M'shamene, 66
Macao, 59
MacDonell, Sir Hugh, politician, 126
Macloutsie, 15
Maceia, 34
Machado, Joaquim José, Col., 26
Machado, Bernardino, politician, 185, 187, 188, 205
Machado, Carlos Roma, Capt., 28, 182
Macochero, 234
Macontene, 71
Madame Tussaud, 185
Madeira, 15, 125, 150, 195, 225
Madureiro, Bandeira de Melo, 32
Mafamama, bro. Gungunyana, 45
Mafamba-Basuko, 17
Mafeking, 15
Mafra, 152, 227
Magaia, 43, 61, 63
Magude, 60, 62
Magul Plain, 63
Mahuta, 228
Maia Magalhães, Capt., 198
Makololo, 34-35
Makonde, 204
Makonde Highlands, 228
Makosi, 67
Makuve, 138
Malange, 116
Manchester, 186
Mandalay, 15,
Mandalay Herald, 15
Mandanjiva, 27
Mandele, 148
Mandingo, 153-154, 156, 165
Mangwato, 16
Manhlagazi, 45, 61, 65-67
Manica, 17, 19, 26
Manicaland, 17, 19, 21-25, 45
Manjako, 163-164, 171
Manning, C.N. Maj., 222

Mansoa, 155, 157-159, 164-167,169-172, 178
Manuel, António, 2/Lt., 52
Manyissa, 60-62
Manyune, 69
Maota, 43
Mapandas, 20
Mapulangwene, 71
Maravila, 147-148
Maria Pia of Savoy, 83
Marie Woermann, troopship, 101
Marques, Carlos, Lt., 200
Marracuene, 44, 49, 51, 60-61
Marracuene Column, 53-54
Marseilles, 44
Martins, Azambuja, Maj., 228
Martins, Francisco, Sgt., 165
Mascarenhas, José Esteves de, Capt., 208
Mashonaland, 15-16, 24-25, 38
Mashonas, 28
Massablano, João, 71
Massano de Amorim, Pedro, govnr., 203-205
Magne, Charles Pierre, 155, 157
Massassi, 229
Massi-Kessi, 17, 23-25, 27-30
Massinga, 46,
Massinga Heights, 50, 54
Massingire, 34
Massurissi, 21
Matabele, 16, 21
Matabeleland, 15-16, 44
Matadama, 72
Matola, 44-45, 54-55
Mebeze, 34
Melo Ramalho, Paulo Amado, Cornet, 89, 91
Melo Vieira, Lt., 145
Mendes dos Reis, Captain, 197
Middleton, Frederick Dobson, Gen., 23
Mikindani, 228
Minyome, 169
Matias, 2/Lt., 198
Miranda, Eduardo, Lt., 65
Moamba, 44, 54-55, 71
Moçambique Island, 40
Mocambo Bay, 71
Mocimboa, 204, 231, 234
Modus vivendi, 27, 29, 36
Mões, António Ribeiro, Sgt., 175-176
Mokolo, 232
Möller, Peter, explorer, 77
Mondongo, 123

Monteiro, Delfim, Lt., 62
Monterroso, Dr., 65-66
Morais, Augusto de Sá, Sgt., 165, 208
Moreira da Fonseca, Pedro, Lt/Col., 153
Moreira, Professor, 179
Morier, Lt., 27-28
Moroney, Lt., 219, 220, 221
Mossâmedes, 33, 57, 76-77, 79-80, 82, 86, 95,105, 117, 129, 137, 154, 195-196, 201, 207-208, 211
Mossumba do Muatianvua, 33
Mossuril, 70
Mount Hampden, 16
Mount Tongo-Tongo, 129
Moura Mendes, José Luís, Maj., 206, 227
Mousinho de Albuquerque, Joaquim, Capt., 60-61, 69-72, 203, 231
Mozambique, 19, 21, 26, 32-33, 37,39-41, 43-44, 59-60, 69-70, 72, 117, 126, 132, 185, 187, 196, 203-206, 227, 231, 235-236
Mozambique Channel, 60-61, 69-72, 203, 231
Mozambique Company, 17, 21-22, 24, 26-27
Mozambique Expeditionary Force, 203-204
Mpotora, 229
Muando, 148
Mubango, 45
Muchuwakae, 118
Mucusso, 193
Muiza, 33
Mujenga, 70
Mukankalas, 120
Mukohimo, 130, 132
Mukongo Drift, 137
Mukumbi, 148
Mulondo, 116-117, 135-136, 208
Mulongo, 212
Müller, Albert, Dr, 234
Mundell, Marmaduke, Lt., 24
Munongolo, 97
Munssul, 172
Munyade, 121
Mussorongo, 203
Mutukwa, 110, 119, 121
Muzila, 45-46
Mwawe, 45

N

N'giva, 211-213, 217, 219-220, 222
Nabuangongo, 145
Naga, 169

Nagate, 169, 171
Naguema, 70
Nagwe, 173
Naloeke, 139, 141-143
Namakunde, 183, 219-222
Namarral, 69-71
Nambala, Martin, Headman, 219, 221
Nangadi, 228, 230-231
Nanguar, 232-233
Nangula Drift, 199
Nangwale, 229
Nano War, 75
Natal, 44, 58, 222
Natal Mercury, 58
Natule, 70
Naulila, 190-192, 196-200, 207, 212
Naulila Column, 212
Ndongas, 219
Necessidades Royal Palace, 150-151
Negomano, 231-234
Neuparth, Augusto Eduardo, Admiral, 205
Neutel, Martins Simões de Abreu, Capt., 204
Nevala, 228-231
Neves Ferreira, 26
Nganguelas, 80, 81, 83, 94
Niakisiku, 229
Niassa Chartered Company, 40, 204, 232
Niassa Province, 34
Nichichira, 228, 230, 231
Nkomati River, 44-45, 49, 51, 53-54, 59-60, 62-63
Nkumbi, 98, 105-106, 112-119, 121-123
Nogueira, José, 2/Lt., 117
Nondwene, 51, 53
Noronha, Fernando António de, govnr, 33
Northern Column, 60-61, 65
Norton de Matos, govnr., 182
Noske, Gerhard, Capt., 225
Nossa Senhora do Humbe, 76
Nugent, Lt., 15
Nunes da Mata, Sebastião, Col., 80
Nunes, Felipe, Lt., 44
Nyakra, 154
Nyamacurra, 235
Nyasaland, 34, 72, 205-206
Nyengue, 167
Nyoca, 118

O

Oihole, 223
Oisulo, 232

Okavango, 89
Oko, 173
Old Tom Bechuana, 89
Oliveira, José Inácio de, 2/Lt., 146
Oliveira Leitão, João Rogado de, Lt., 76
Oliveira Muzanty, govnr., 156
Oliveira, Lopes de, Col., 32
Ompaba, 168-169
Omupanda, 220
Ondalo River, 177
Ongo, 122
Onkankwa, 197-199
Onofre de Andrade, govnr., 45
Ophir Company, 19
Oporto, 36, 87, 152, 204, 225
Order of the Bath, 35
Orleans, Duke of., 152
O Século, 191
Os Lusíadas, 35
Ostermann, Oswald, Police Sgt., 192-193
Otavi, 209
Otchinjau, 196, 208
Otokero, 112, 190
O Ultimato, 36
Outjo, 189, 199
Ova-kua-nyama, 73
Ovambo, 189, 221
Ovamboland, 89, 138, 199, 209, 211, 219, 220-222
Oxford Street, 185
Oyo, 154-155, 157-180

P

Pacheco, Roberto, Lt., 129
Padrel, Justiniano, Maj., 97-99
Pahlke, Volunteer, 189
Pais Veigas, João, Col., 216
Paiva, Artur de, Col., 7, 79, 80-95, 101, 103, 108-109, 117-123, 208
Paiva Couceiro, Henrique Mitchell de, Capt., 44, 49-50, 53, 57-58, 60-65, 88-89, 92, 146, 151, 152, 183, 186
Paiva de Andrada, Joaquim Carlos, Maj., 19-24
Pala, José Afonso, Maj., 215
Palermo de Oliveira, António, Lt., 97, 99
Palma, 231
Palule, 71
Pango-Alúquem, 147
Paris, 19, 36, 125
Park Lane, 185
Passene, 60

Passos Sousa, João Francisco, Capt., 216
Paula Cid, Francisco de, Capt., 90
Paxe, 166-167
Pecixe, 162
Pedro, Police Const., 71
Pedro, Maunel Augusto, Lt., 163, 165-171
Pellagra, 125
Pelundo, 161-163, 179
Pemba Bay, 204, 206
Pembe Drift, 98, 129, 135, 137, 141
Penamacor, 206
Pennefather, Edward Graham, Lt/Col, 15, 23
Pepel, 153-154, 159, 162, 165, 172-173, 175-179
Pequito, Rodrigo Afonso, 31
Petrie, Sir George, 34-35
Pereira, 2/Lt., 85
Pereira, António, Sgt., 116, 165
Pereira, Zacarias, Capt., 136
Pereira de Azevedo, Constantino, govnr., 33
Pereira de Eça, António Julio Costa, Gen., 204-209, 211-217, 219-222
Pereira do Nascimento, José, Dr, 97
Pimenta, 2/Lt., 156-157
Pinto, 2/Lt., 52
Pernambuco, 33
Pimenta de Castro, Gen., 205
Pinheiro Baião, Francisco António, Capt., 31-32
Pinto Basto, Alberto Celestino Ferreira, Capt., 175
Pinto de Almeida, Capt., 129, 132-133
Pinto Furtado, Manuel, trader, 145-146
Pio, Sgt., 113, 115
Pires Monteiro, Henriques, Major, 214
Pita, Sgt., 64
Port Gole, 158
Port Herald, 206
Port Mansoa, 155, 158, 163, 165-166, 170-172, 175
Pôrto Amélia, 206
Portugal, 9, 11, 12-14, 17, 22, 25, 28, 31-41, 45, 54, 58-59, 62, 69, 76, 84, 95, 97, 103, 125-127, 143, 150, 152-154, 156, 179, 181-183, 187-188, 190, 195, 200-201, 203-206, 225-227, 231, 234-236
Portuguese Africa, 9, 11, 31-32, 37, 76, 125, 207
Portuguese Army:
14 Infantry Regiment, 195, 197, 199-200, 207
15 Infantry Regiment, 203-204

16 Infantry Regiment, 151, 207, 213
17 Infantry Regiment, 208, 214, 216
18 Infantry Regiment, 201
19 Infantry Regiment, 36
21 Infantry Regiment, 206, 227, 230, 234
Light Infantry:
2 Light Infantry Regiment, 49, 52, 97
3 Light Infantry Regiment of Angola, 44, 49, 66,
Light Infantry Regiment of Mozambique, 30
3 Light Infantry Regiment, (Portugal), 36
4 Light Infantry Regiment, 79
5 Light Infantry Regiment, 84
16 Mozambique Light Infantry Regiment,, 254
West African Light Infantry Regiment, 71
Cavalry:
1 Cavalry Regiment, 60, 190
3 Cavalry Regiment, 190
4 Cavalry Regiment, 215
6 Cavalry Regiment, 36
11 Cavalry Regiment, 208, 214, 215
Police Cavalry, 52
Republican Guard Cavalry, 227
Lourenço Marques Mounted Police, 23, 49, 219
Angolan Dragoon Regiment, 138
1 Dragoon Regiment, 197
Artillery:
1 Artillery Regiment, 151, 201
2 Artillery Regiment, 59, 201
4 Artillery Regiment, 60-61
7 Artillery Regiment, 201
Portuguese Navy:
Naval Artillery, 129
Naval Battalion, 216
Naval Contingent, 43, 213
Naval Detachment, 70, 132
Naval Division, 40
Adamastor, cruiser, 150-151, 206, 227
Almirante Reis, cruiser, 203
Afonso de Albuquerque, sloop, 44, 49
África, troopship, 227
Amarante, troopship, 227
Ambaca, troopship, 60-61
Auxiliar, gunboat, 41
Bacamarte, gunboat 50, 53-54, 62
Búfalo, gunboat, 41
Carabina, gunboat, 62
Chaimite, gunboat, 227
Cunene, gunboat 137
Dom Carlos I/Almirante Reis, cruiser, 150-151, 203

Flecha, gunboat, 153, 157-158, 164, 166, 168, 171-172, 175-179
Lacerda, gunboat, 64
Liberal, gunboat, 38-39
Luanda, steamer, 207
Machico, troopship 227
Marechal Mac-Mahon, gunboat, 41
Mindelo, gunboat, 153
Moçambique, troopship, 195, 206, 227, 231
Moçâmedes, troopship, 231
Neves Ferreira, gunboat, 41, 50- 51, 54, 60
Quanza, gunboat, 43
Rainha de Portugal, corvette, 43, 49
República, cruiser, 163, 175
República, motor launch 163, 175
Rio Ave, gunboat, 154
Sabre, gunboat, 62
São Gabriel, cruiser, 175
São Rafael, cruiser, 151
São Tomé, steamer, 57, 97
Vega, steamer, 61
Xefina, gunboat, 50-51
Zagaia, gunboat, 153, 158, 166, 168, 171
Zaire, gunboat, 38, 76
Zaire, troopship, 227
Portuguese and Brazilian Review, 31
Portuguese East Africa, 19, 32-33, 37-39, 57, 126, 204-205
Portuguese-German Commission, 182
Portuguese Goa, 135
Portuguese Guinea, 11, 14, 97, 146, 153-154, 156-157, 163, 169, 180, 232, 236
Portuguese India, 135
Portuguese Royal Maritime, Military and Geography Society, 33
Portuguese Royal Military College, 31
Posto X, 61-63
Praia de Cabo Verde, 97
Pretoria, 9, 54, 135
Prieto Valadim, Eduardo, Capt., 72
Prinsloo, Barend, farmer, 99
Pritchard, Stanley Archibald Markham, Maj., 219-221
Pungwe River, 19-20, 27, 38-39
Puxa-Puxa, 232

Q

Quaresma, Maj., 232
Queen Victoria, 35, 186
Queimado de Sousa, Sub/Lt., 157, 164
Quelimane, 19, 34, 40, 235
Queré, 171

Quibaxi, 145
Quihita, 118
Quipuengo, 145

R

Ramalho, Cornet, 97
Rankin, Daniel, Dr, 34
Rêgo, Paulo, Capt., 233
Rei Island, 175
Reichstag, 101
República Portuguesa, 36
Reis, Artur José dos, Lt., 154
Reis, Clarim Augusto dos, Lt., 200-201
Resende, Francisco, Capt., 132
Reuben Point, 49, 59, 63
Révuè River, 29
Rheinish Mission Station, 220
Rhodes, Cecil, 15-17, 19, 28, 34, 38, 187
Rhodesia, 37, 57, 236
Ribeiro, Alberto, Major, 52
Ribeiro, Dionísio António, gvnr., 38
Ribeira do Nevala, 229
Riel Rebellion, 23
Rikatla, 47
Rinderpest, 105, 109
Rio de Janeiro, 69
Rios de Sena, 33
Roach, Jack, Capt., 16
Robbertse, Jan Harm, farmer 102-103
Roby, João, Lt., 132
Rocene, 172
Roder, Kurt, vol., 189, 191
Rodolfo Malheiro, Cornet, 36
Rodrigues, Sgt., 175
Rodrigues Braga, António, Dr, 44, 65
Rodrigues da Costa, Matias, Capt., 81
Rodrigues da Fonseca, Hermes, politician, 151
Rodrigues Galhardo, Eduardo Augusto, Col., 59
Rodrigues Sepúlveda, Capt., 197
Roque, António Bernardino, Dr, 105-106, 109-110
Roque de Aguiar, Francisco, Capt., 52
Rosa, José da, Capt., 32
Rose-Coloured Map, 5, 31-32
Rosen, Friedrich, Dr, 225-226
Roslin Castle, steamer, 185
Rothan, Lucius, priest, 75
Rothe, Capt., 229
Rotunda Square, 151
Rovuma, mail ship, 26

Rovuma River, 34, 37, 72, 203-204, 227-228, 230-231
Royal Colonial Institute, 30
Royal Navy, 35, 189, 225, 228
Ruco, 34
Rugby School, 23
Ruhr, 225
Rume, 166
Rural Police, 155, 165, 168

S

Sabi River, 28, 45, 60, 67
Saca, 177
Sá e Simas, José Augusto de, Gvnr., 38
Sagaing District, 15
Saleie, 72
Salgado, Alberto, Maj., 196-198, 233
Sambio, 193
Sambo, 90-91
Samfim, 153, 178
Samuel, 7, 144
Sana, 158-159
Sanches de Miranda, 59
Sanders, missionary, 94
Sandhurst, 23
Santo António do Zaire, 203
Santo António Street, 36
Santos Pedro, António Raimundo da Costa, Lt., 157
Santos, Filipe dos, Lt., 153
Santos e Silva, Capt., 28
São Januário de Humpata, 79, 103
São Paulo, Brazilian warship, 150
São Sebastiao, 46
São Tomé, 57, 97
Sarmento, 20, 26-27, 29
Sasse, 145-146, 148
Schaaps, Constable, 189
Schubert, Dr, 182, 193
Schultz, Dr, 186
Schultze-Jena, Dr, 189-192
Seitz, Theodor von, govnr., 189, 209
Sereno, Manuel Antunes, Lt., 190-191, 200
Serpa Pinto, Alexandre Alberto da Rocha, explorer, 33-34, 36, 241
Schnee, Heinrich, Dr, 232, 234
Scott, Sir Walter, 57
Scramble for Africa, 11-12, 31, 37
Selous, Frederick Courtney, 15-16, 22, 240-241
Selous Road, 24
Sena, 22, 33

Serpa Pimental, António de, politician 36
Shaka, 44
Shangane Estuary, 59, 67
Shangani, 44
Shardi, 47
Shawlo, 131, 141, 144
Shibuto, 71
Shinavane River, 26, 60, 62, 64
Shire, 35, 72, 205
Shire Highlands, 34, 20
Silva, Carlos Augusto da, Cornet, 105
Silva, Fernando Augusto da, Cornet., 105, 110, 241
Silva, José Eugenio da, Capt., 105-106, 108-111, 113, 114, 117, 120
Silva Guardado, Aristides da, Lt., 105-111, 114-115
Silva, Leopoldo, Maj., 229
Silveira, Manuel João da, Dr, 132
Silva Porto, trader, 5, 87-89, 94-95, 238
Silveira, Tomás Maj., 76
Simão, interpreter, 163
Smuts, Jan Christian, Gen., 209
Soares Poças, Fernando, Dr, 27
Sodré Quay, 225
Sofala, 39, 45
Soller Trading Company, 155, 157
Songea, 235
Sophie Richmerz, steamer, 225
Soshangane, 44
Sousa, Augusto de, Capt., 80
Sousa, João de, Lt., 131, 216, 241
Sousa Lage, Zacarias de, Capt., 154
Sousa, Manuel António de, (Gouveia), Reserve Col., 17, 22-25
Sousa Machado, Manuel de, 72
Sousa Machado, António Júlio de, Maj., 67
Sousa Miranda, Aníbal Augusto Sanches de, Lt., 69
Sousa Guerra, Henrique Alberto de, Lt., 175-176, 178, 179
Sousa Rosa, Tomás de, Col., 231, 235
South Africa, 9, 13-14, 24, 27, 74, 126, 185, 195, 207, 219, 223
South African War, 126, 209
South West African Protectorate, 222
Southampton, 15
Southern Column, 7, 59-63
Southwark, 37
Soveral, Luís, politician, 126
Spion Kop, 209
Spiritan, 79-80
SS Mexican, steamer, 15

Stewardson, James, trader, 99
Stokolo, 60-62
Streitfontein Farm, 182
Sud-Express, 44
Sultan Karropo-Memo, 72
Sultan Mataka, 72
Sultan of Zanzibar, 37
Swakop River, 89
Swakopmund, 101
Swartboois Drift, 79, 196
Swiss Reformed Church, 47

T

Tabua, 102
Tagus, 31, 35, 39, 150-152, 225
Tamanke, 196
Tamegão, Lt., 129
Tampé, 166
Tandane, 40
Tavares Leote, Lt., 63, 237
Tchicusse, 105, 110-111, 113, 119-121, 208
Tchiepépe 208
Tchifito, 122
Tchiongo, 118
Tchipelongo, 98, 110, 196, 208
Teixeira da Silva, Justino, Capt., 57, 87-88, 93
Teixeira de Barros, José Xavier, Maj., 175
Teixeira Gomes, politician, 187
Teixeira Pinto, João, Capt., 7-8 146, 154-156, 159, 161-179, 232
Terreiro do Paço Square, 149-150
Tete, 19
Thames, 37, 44
The Times, 15, 241
Thirstland, 14, 79, 102
Tomar, 204
Torre e Espada 14, 69, 192, 203
Trainer, Georg, Capt., 201
Transvaal, 38, 60, 135, 195
Transvaal Republic, 71, 126
Triple Alliance, 187
Tswana, 89
Tuandiva, 110
Tugela River, 44
Twickenham, 152

U

Uatiner, 169
Ugab, 189

Ultimatum, 30, 35-37, 57, 88, 150, 185
Umba, 37
Umfeti, 185-186
Umtali, 17, 28-30
Unche, 166-167
Unde, 234
Unfaré Jungle, 170-171
Upper Burma, 15

V

Vageler, Paul, Dr, 191-192, 199
Vahle, 2/Lt., 199
Valbom, Carlos, politician, 30
Val Krantz, 209
Vale de Andrade, 2/Lt., 197
Van der Kellen, Pete, trader, 97, 99
Van der Merve, P. J., farmer, 79
Van der Wat, Piet, farmer, 99
Varela, Lt., 200
Vasco da Gama, 11, 35
Vasconcelos e Sá, govnr., 154
Vasconcelos, Lt., 44, 212
Venter, Stephanus, farmer, 99
Venter, Willem, farmer, 79, 101-102, 103, 135-136, 146
Ventura, Lt., 129
Veiga, Alves de, Dr, 36
Veríssimo de Sousa, António, Col., 208, 212-213, 217
Victor Emmanuel, 83
Viera da Rocha, Filipe Trajano, Capt., 214
Vienna, 226
Vigo, 35
Vilaça, Sergeant, 167
Vila da Ponte, 182
Vila Gouveia, 23
Vila Pereira de Eça, 182
Vila Viçosa, 149
Viljoen,Kobus, 122
Virginia, 16
Viseu, 204
Vita Tom Oorlog, 89, 93

W

Wahle, von, Gen., 231-234
Walvis Bay, 101, 209
Warren, Sir Charles, Gen., 23
Weisser, Albrecht, seaman, 225
Wejulu, 73-74, 79, 83, 199
Westminster, 181, 185
Westminster Abbey, 185

Whitehall Rooms, 30
Willoughby, Sir John, 15
Windhoek, 9, 189, 209
Windsor Accord, 126
Witbooi Namas, 101
Wulfhorst, August, priest, 220
Wurnenburger, Carl, priest, 76
Wolof, 156

X

Xalé, 167-168
Xangué, 166, 173
Xinge River, 148
Xugué, 172
Xuro, 162
Xuroenque, 161
Xurubrique, 162

Y

Yoba, 118

Z

Zambezi, 32, 34-35, 40, 45, 83, 126, 205
Zambézia, 19, 22, 39, 41, 57, 205-206
Zanzibar, 37, 205, 228
Zenza River, 146
Ziegler, Heinrich, 182-183
Zishasha, 43, 51-52, 54-55, 65
Zomba, 9, 205
Zongue, 148
Zululand, 23
Zunguze, 46